EVERYTHING AND THE KITCHEN SINK

EVERYTHING AND THE KITCHEN SINK

UK FILM, MUSIC AND TV BEFORE THE BEATLES

SIMON MATTHEWS

Oldcastle Books

First published in 2025 by
Oldcastle Books Ltd,
Harpenden,
Herts, UK

oldcastlebooks.co.uk
@OldcastleBooks

Editor: Michael O'Connell
© Simon Matthews, 2025

A CIP catalogue record for this book is available from the British Library.

ISBN
978-0-85730-596-1 (Paperback)
978-0-85730-597-8 (eBook)

2 4 6 8 10 9 7 5 3 1

Typeset in 11.75 on 14.6pt Goudy Old Style
by Avocet Typeset, Bideford, Devon, EX39 2BP
Printed and bound in Great Britain by
CPI Group (UK) Ltd, Croydon CR0 4YY

FSC
www.fsc.org

MIX
Paper | Supporting
responsible forestry
FSC® C013604

The manufacturer's authorised representative in the EU for
product safety is Easy Access System Europe, Mustamäe tee 50, 10621
Tallinn, Estonia
gpsr.requests@easproject.com

CONTENTS

FOREWORD

I was discovered while I was still at drama school. I was a scholarship boy, one of the beneficiaries of the 1944 Education Act. Caspar Wrede saw me at RADA and cast me in a TV play, *Private Potter* that was later made into a film.

I was never an angry young man... I was frightened to death most of the time. I wasn't at war with middle-class or upper-class people but I was very much aware that I was working-class.

The Loneliness of the Long-Distance Runner was of its time. People are still interested in it now, because the last part of it remains very powerful. The shot at the end of the race happened by accident with Tony Richardson calling out 'don't smile!' But I already had and it's in the film. That's why people are still interested in it now. I was knackered during the filming because I had to do *Billy Liar* on stage in the evening. Looking back, I think Tony Richardson was very clever. He knew my limitations because of my inexperience and used to tell me to say what I liked, to improvise. I met the author Alan Sillitoe when he gave me a lift in his Austin A40. I asked him how long it took to get a driving licence to drive it and he said 'I don't have a driving licence!' He was a bit of a rebel.

I was less keen on filming *Billy Liar*, because of how much I'd done it on stage. I was in awe of Albert Finney, though we became best friends years later after *The Dresser*. I would have liked to do *Waiting for Godot* with him, but he didn't like it. I miss him.

Things were different in the 60s, but I was very young then. My favourite film was *One Day in the Life of Ivan Denisovich*. I was very close to the director, Caspar Wrede, who was my guru. But it didn't get a fair crack of the whip in the US and Solzhenitsyn thought I was too young!

I retreated from being so famous and turned down a lot of work in the 60s. It cost me millions. Later I turned down a part that someone else got an Oscar for, but I couldn't see myself as an American. In the end I went back to the theatre in Manchester.

The best advice I ever had was from Dirk Bogarde, making *King and Country*, about a young lad in the war who is shot for deserting. He said, 'Preserve your acting energy.' I'd been playing football with some of the extras that morning, so when it came to the scene we were filming that day I wasn't that sharp. He was right!

Everything is of its time.

Sir Tom Courtenay, August 2024

ACKNOWLEDGEMENTS

This book attempts to catalogue the films, novels, plays and television programmes that the UK produced as it moved away from the period of post-war austerity toward the more liberal and colourful years of the 60s. These are often referred to as emanating from the 'Kitchen Sink' or 'angry young man' era and these rough and ready (and in both cases not particularly accurate) terms are used throughout the text, subject to the caveat that they are merely a shorthand method for identifying what is being discussed.

Rather than provide a simple chronological study, it groups the material that appeared during these years into specific categories, within which there are some distinctive sub-genres of their own. It is not a study of everything written, staged or filmed then. Nor is it an exhaustive account of each book, play or film, radio and TV production. Instead, it provides an overview of as much as possible, within a single volume.

Much of this can be viewed on DVD, YouTube or specialist TV channels and some still occasionally get shown in repertory cinemas. Sadly, many of the TV plays have vanished (though some readers may have memories of them) and accounts of these have been culled, wherever possible, from reference books and reliable internet sources. Happily, the books and plays that constitute their sources can still be purchased – one way or another – from shops, or online platforms.

It is hoped that the narrative informs and entertains.

I am grateful for having had the opportunity to speak with Sir Tom Courtenay, and Ken Loach about this period and with Boff

Whalley of Chumbawamba about the degree of inspiration his band drew from it.

Thanks are due to Ion Mills and his team at Oldcastle Books in commissioning this and taking it forward to publication, and to Michael O'Connell, Robin Ramsay and Margaret Cooney for their many helpful suggestions in preparing the text.

Simon Matthews

INTRODUCTION

They lived in another world, an England clogged with coal smoke. Rising undisturbed in the still air from countless factories, yards and depots amidst perfect geometric rows of tiny houses. The setting could be Leicester, Leeds, Stoke, Nottingham or possibly Bradford, Bolton, Halifax and Wakefield. Sometimes overt, sometimes disguised, these were dense, tangled old towns astride polluted rivers and canals. Their main streets were lined with gin palaces that glittered in the dark. Ornate civic buildings attesting to wealth and pride radiated like the threads of a spider's web to sports grounds that were thronged with thousands on noisy Saturday afternoons.

Our character is male. Most likely called Joe, though Albert, Arthur, Jimmy, Billy, Harry and Vic are also popular. He might be as old as his mid-30s or as young as 11. Collectively they are like a multi-tiered range of brothers and cousins within an extended family. At the upper end they have memories of before the war: grim times when people were hungry and brutally unhealthy. If you were lucky then a minor clerical job was best, keeping you indoors with some sort of pension, and a chance of night school to better yourself. For the main part their fathers, brothers and friends toiled in industry, sometimes dying, worn out by disease at 50, looking 80. Usually, they remained at home. Occasionally they rented a room elsewhere.

Some had been in the war, but were never heroic. None were officers. They might have been prisoners of war. They shared a low opinion of their superior officers' abilities having observed them at close quarters. Later, many endured National Service. Sweltering in high temperatures but evading death or serious injury in pointless escapades in Malaya and Cyprus. They disliked militarism. Once demobilised, some returned to become school teachers or junior lecturers uncertain about being retained and feeling socially out of place; others became librarians, or just single men in minor positions wanting to move on and become independent. Most of the time they were bored, and some people were quick to make the assumption that they were incompetent. A few were university graduates with uncertain ambitions, drifting along and struggling to find a place in society.

He is white, about five feet nine inches tall and lean. As a child he was wiry and carried little body fat. His hair is short, brushed back and held in place by Brylcreem. His appearance is important to him and maintained by quiet rituals in cold sculleries where he shaves and washes. His complexion is pale and he avoids having a pre-war matinee idol style moustache. He smokes continuously. Clothing is dark, made of cotton, wool, serge and worsted. Grey, black, navy blue. Long overcoats (a few ex-naval duffle coats survive too) and scarves. Shirts are white, ironed and worn with a jacket and tie when going out, the tie the only drop of colour. Jumpers and tank tops suffice on cold days, with a scarf if required. No jewellery.

It is a time of full employment and he has the money to spare, so he also drinks. Beer, in copious amounts. His diet is plain: fried food, a lot of tea, bread, butter, jam, cheese, pickles, meat, fish, vegetables. An increasing amount comes from tins and some of the younger element drink coffee as well. None of them own a car, though they aspire to do so. Most have a bicycle or just accept walking about their home town and using the plentiful bus services, where they spread themselves out on the upper deck, smoking and arguing.

Disaffected, denunciatory, uncompromising: concerned about getting even, clashing with authority, amused by the ignorance of their contemporaries, deeply class conscious, jealous of their rivals, prone to envy, wanting the good things in life as often as possible and at as low a cost as possible, happy to embrace cheap materialism, no matter how farcical, they look on with bilious indifference as the affluent society destroys the older social structures that they had grown up amongst.

Sex looms large. In pubs, factory canteens and dance halls, young women are keenly observed. How to arrange beneficial encounters with them consumes a lot of his time. He dislikes courtship rituals. Going steady. Getting engaged; buying the ring. Privately he wishes he were elsewhere. There is adultery, and enjoyable casual sex with older women. Some get on by marrying the boss's daughter. Others don't: they marry and move in with the wife's mother. Life after marriage is dull and heavily circumscribed. Everything is straight. Sexual quirks hardly figure though a tiny number are privately fond of other men. The women who feature sometimes explore mixed race relationships and have affairs with older men who have yet to be divorced. Pregnancy, abandonment and abortion haunt the narrative. Both sexes have unsuccessful relationships.

Undecided, frustrated, one morning he packs a suitcase, and heads down to the station. On a long, slow train of blood-red corridor carriages hauled by a grimy black steam locomotive he departs for London. Once they would only have gone down for the Cup Final, with possibly time for a discreet visit to Soho. Now, on a journey that takes a whole day, with some savings and the address of a friend or relative, they strike out and pursue a new career.

It brings them initially to bedsit land where they live amongst an odd collection of fellow lodgers, crowded into an ill-kept tall thin house in a street scheduled for demolition. However dingy their surroundings, London is another country, with a floating population of young bohemians and even greater sexual opportunities. It provides music and entertainment late into the night. Others find themselves in soulless suburbs marked by petty rivalries, one-upmanship rituals and social conformism. Some settle in new towns or new housing estates.

Success brings money, extreme consumerism, and even more fraying of the social fabric. There is more adultery, alcoholism and failed marriages. They move on to other houses, other partners, new flats, new cars, new jobs. They don't think of the north any longer, although occasional returns are permitted. Lives can go seriously awry too, usually through mixing with delinquents. Once involved in criminality a minority of cases end in murder with the grim possibility of the death penalty looming large. In prison they mix with outsider communities: the predominance of Maltese, Italians and Irish means the atmosphere in this environment is pervaded with Catholicism and the unfamiliar concept of guilt. Some West Indian, African, Chinese and Indian characters also appear.

Whatever their fate, they couldn't have stayed in the north. If they had, their ambitions would have drained away and been replaced with either glum acceptance or despair.

As we shall see, many of these attributes had always existed. Those who read the novels and short stories set in the north of England before 1939 would not have been surprised by the emergence of a similar phenomenon after 1955. Social realism in drama and fiction, in either London or the 'provinces' had been around at least a century before Osborne, Braine, Amis and others became prominent.

Authors who wrote about the north, commenting on poverty and the circumstances faced by those who lived there had been available since Mrs Gaskell's *Mary Barton* (1848). Later there were well observed and realistically drawn humorous stories by the Grossmiths and Jerome K Jerome about characters from modest backgrounds. There were political plays and novels too, particularly from H G Wells and George Bernard Shaw. Both lampooned the English political and landed classes with their readers being clear that major changes were overdue in the order of society. And, following the path trod by Dickens, there were writers such as W W Jacobs who chronicled the fortunes of the London lower classes. Three authors, though, are of particular interest as precursors of the Kitchen Sink genre: George Gissing, Arnold Bennett and D H Lawrence, all of whom hailed from the north and were published prior to 1914.

Gissing, from Wakefield, was 20 when he arrived in London in 1877. In books like *Demos* (1886), *New Grub Street* (1891) and *The Odd Women* (1893) he tackled political change, lack of money and the day-to-day struggle experienced by most people. His novels tended to have unfortunate and miserable endings. The least well-known of the trio, he was much liked by George Orwell who described him in a 1948 essay as 'the chronicler of vulgarity, squalor and failure'.

In contrast Arnold Bennett, from Hanley, Staffordshire, enjoyed a lucrative and successful career. He caught the train to London in 1889 (at 21) and his key works in Kitchen Sink terms would be *Anna of the Five Towns* (1902) and the *Clayhanger* quartet (from 1910). Both have northern settings, and both deal with poverty, though in an arguably less dismal fashion than Gissing. Bennett also wrote *The Card* (1911) a picaresque account of the rise of a resourceful young man in his home town.

Like Bennett, Lawrence also left early for London, arriving there in 1908 at the age of 23. From Eastwood, Nottinghamshire, listed then as a 'colliery village' (actually, a small town) about halfway between Ilkeston and Kirkby-in-Ashfield, his experiences of growing up in this locale form the backdrop to his novels *Sons and Lovers* (1913), *The Rainbow* (1915), *Women in Love* (1920) and *Lady Chatterley's Lover* (1928). Inveighing against class, sexual and emotional repression and hypocrisy, Lawrence's attitude, and those of his most memorable characters – Paul Morel, Clara Dawes, Ursula Brangwen and Oliver Mellors – clearly form something of a template for the drama and fiction that emerged in the mid-50s. For years, though, obtaining his key books was difficult. With many of them banned, either by the law courts or local authority Library Committees, obtaining a well-thumbed pirated edition of, say, *Lady Chatterley's Lover* required care and planning by those wishing to explore its content.

After the great catharsis of the 1914-1918 war, others joined their ranks. Among the most notable were J B Priestley, A J Cronin and Walter Greenwood. From Bradford, Priestley produced a stream of plays, essays and novels, many of which were adapted for cinema

or TV. His work was thoughtful and entertaining, more akin to
Bennett than Gissing. Greenwood, from Salford, concentrated
closely on the poverty experienced during the depression years,
particularly in *Love on the Dole* (1933). Cronin, who like Priestley
sold in huge amounts, was noted for *The Stars Look Down* (1935) and
The Citadel (1937) both of which were set in mining communities,
in Northumberland and south Wales respectively.

The 30s also produced Howard Spring, originally a reporter with
The Manchester Guardian, who portrayed the rise of an ambitious
Labour politician in *Fame is the Spur* (1940). Filmed in 1947, its
screenplay was written by Nigel Balchin, author of *The Small Back
Room* (1943) with its flawed, alcoholic central character. Which
brings us, finally, to Graham Greene. Neither an angry young man,
or a 'northern' writer, he overlapped with both and the Kitchen Sink
generally, with his realistically drawn plots and characters, the use
of crime and shabby moral compromises as plot devices, penchant
for adultery and ambivalent view of authority. Published from 1929,
and with film adaptations from as early as 1934, works like *Brighton
Rock* (1938), *The Heart of the Matter* (1948), *The Third Man* (1949) and
The End of the Affair (1951) were tremendously successful studies of
sympathetically-drawn anti-heroes.

But it would be wrong to conclude that these held sway, or had
some sort of overwhelming dominance in the crowded field of
UK literature when peace came for a second time in 1945. They
were one strand of writing, important but competing with others.
Indeed, in many ways the key features of the 30s – detective novels,
romantic comedies with butlers and debutantes and the 'well-made'
West End play, as exemplified by Rattigan – continued, and were
in some ways even more prominent. A case can be made that the
overarching theme of the decade 1945-1955 was not social realism
but escapism. This was the time of the Ealing comedies with their
cosy assumptions about Englishness, war heroics and films like
Maytime in Mayfair, a musical comedy set in a *haute couture* fashion
house. Not only that, for those seeking to forget the travails of
austerity and the threat of atomic incineration, these were the years
of Mervyn Peake's *Titus Groan* and *Gormenghast*, William Golding's

Lord of the Flies, John Wyndham's *Day of the Triffids* as well as C S Lewis's *Narnia Chronicles* and Tolkien's *The Lord of the Rings*.

Social realism remained, but within constraints. Typically, it occurred within crime dramas, usually set in London, the best of which were *It Always Rains on Sunday* (from a novel by Arthur La Bern) and *The Blue Lamp*. In both the villain is caught and punished. Society's values prevail. As an example of how social realism was portrayed then it is interesting to consider the 1952 film adaptation of Bennett's *The Card* starring Alec Guinness, who makes a not wholly successful attempt at a regional accent. Partly filmed on location in Stoke-on-Trent, the town had changed so little since Bennett's time that there was no need to disguise background shots and it strikes the viewer as being rather more cheerful than its author would have intended.

Prefiguring some elements of the *Billy Liar* plot, *The Card* charts the rise of Denry Machin and focuses less on his character and motives than on his relations with three separate women: a Countess who is out of his reach, the older 'experienced' woman of uncertain background and the nice local girl that he ends up with, played by a 20-year-old Petula Clark. Then 38, Guinness played someone half his age for the film's first half-hour: by the end, he and Petula Clark are together and Machin has been elected the youngest ever Lord Mayor of the town.

This is slightly at odds with Machin's cynicism in the book: he might not be Joe Lampton whose exploits we will encounter later, but Machin knows how to cut corners and advance in provincial society. He runs a rent collecting business, evicting tenants if required, and knows that if he is to rise, he needs to do good by the local football club, and secure election to the council. People might like him enough to make him Mayor, but he is not afraid to stress 'I just want to make money...' Rather than emphasise this sardonic edge to Machin, the film instead plays rather like *Kind Hearts and Coronets*.

The Card was successful, nominated for an Academy Award and having Petula Clark's version of its jaunty main title theme released on a shellac 78 in May 1952. But it quickly appeared dated when *Look Back in Anger* and *Room at the Top* appeared a few years later. Both were northern/provincial and centred on a young man's view of the world with main characters – Jimmy Porter and Joe Lampton – enjoying far more beer and tobacco than Machin, Mellors and co could ever have dreamt of. Not only that, sex is much more available (or at least written about as if it is). Their materialism is more explicit. They do not defer and their attitude makes it clear that they can 'get on' should they need to, on terms they will set for themselves.

What caused this change in outlook? Quite simply, the Second World War. Following the trauma of the 30s, and its attendant hardships, it became the testing ground for the planned economy. The post-war Labour government brought the NHS and a commitment to full employment and though rationing continued until 1954, the consumer age was arriving and new outlooks took hold of the country.

Of course, the term 'kitchen sink', before Osborne and co were identified with it, was synonymous with the day-to-day drudgery that defined women's role in society. But women were also key beneficiaries of full employment, recruited in large numbers into industry, services and administrative positions. A good number of them were no longer tied to the home after the war and this contributed to changes in moral attitudes.

The war also had an impact on families. With most separated, often for years on end, and so many husbands and wives isolated (or bereaved), a great many people made arrangements of a type they wouldn't have entertained in 'normal' times, to give themselves some type of emotional succour. The cultural impact of large numbers of US armed forces being stationed in the UK after 1942 was significant, particularly the large cohort of black service personnel. They had money to spend, and they brought different attitudes with them. Although one cannot over-generalise on such matters, they were not imbued with the same deference and class consciousness as their British counterparts.

The massive reconstruction programmes that followed the war made their impact too, none more so than the huge house building programme. In the decade after 1945, 2.4 million new homes were built. The people who moved into these left behind them an abundance of older, less satisfactory rented accommodation in town centres. Whilst some of these were demolished many remained and attracted a shifting population of young people and immigrant families. Changes in education occurred at the same time. Whilst the numbers in universities remained low, those in further education and adult education institutes increased tenfold over the same period, with most of the students being supported by government grants.

The world of Osborne, Braine, Sillitoe, Waterhouse and others is thus qualitatively different to that of their forbears. There is a focus on younger characters and popular music starts to feature within plots, Waterhouse's Billy Fisher wants to be a songwriter, as well as write jokes for comedians. Rock 'n' roll offered riotous abandon, even if a satirical view is taken of it. The abject poverty that constrained their parents has gone, so straying from the straight and narrow is no longer disastrous. Avoiding unemployment is no longer the be-all and end-all. Characters are no longer doomed to remain where they were born. There is more social mobility: people move away to study in increasing numbers and can (and do) 'go down to London' to live and work in a different environment.

This is predominantly, but not exclusively, portrayed from the male point of view. This is hardly surprising given that around 80 per cent of the authors associated with the Kitchen Sink were men. We get a lot of shouty, opinionated twenty-something blokes in attic bedrooms or saloon bars. The women authors came along later, with Shelagh Delaney the first, and in many ways the most remarkable. Some who followed her were already in print, and adapted their style to fit kitchen sink themes. Others, like Lynne Reid Banks, Edna O'Brien and Nell Dunn became successful after Delaney's breakthrough with A Taste of Honey. From 1960 there were several books that tackled single parenthood, which was now presented as an option rather than a life-ending, shameful event. Importantly the narratives show young women living independently as part of a transient population, renting cheap, private bed-sitting rooms, and provide the reader with a feminine point of view on topics like adultery.

Unlike Denry Machin, who wants to ascend to local prominence and become wealthy, the central characters of the post-1955 era are far more questioning. Whole institutions are challenged: successful business leaders, local bureaucrats, the police, the British army officer class, minor officials, politicians, trade union leaders and organised religion. Literary form also plays a role here. Conventional narratives presented in books, plays and short stories are no longer the sole mechanism used to convey events. Street theatre, notably from Joan Littlewood, makes an appearance as does satire, absurdism and surreal observational comedy, extracted from peculiar situations.

Echoing Gissing 75 years earlier, the ability of London to corrupt is also a feature. There is more crime and violence. Delinquency and teenage gangs, never really features of the earlier writers, are common. There is even murder, leading to condemned cell dramas and their dreadful theatre revolving around the use of the death penalty, the validity of which is questioned.

Occasionally the writing of the 50s and 60s authors revisits places last trodden by Oscar Wilde. Eventually there will be tales of sexual transgression, sexual failure, studies of failed relationships, inappropriate relationships, homosexuality and lesbianism. We should note that the play which immediately preceded *Look Back in Anger* into the Royal Court Theatre was *The Mulberry Bush* by Angus Wilson, now embraced as one of England's first openly gay writers. Kenneth Haigh and Alan Bates appeared in both productions.

This generation of writers were also reappraising the UK's place in the world, which was certainly not something that would have occurred to their predecessors. This meant taking race, immigration and religion into consideration, providing more black characters in their narratives and, when needed, pointing up the anti-immigrant views of the white working-class.

Despite the updating of key aspects, the new world that was being portrayed here remained resolutely northern and working-class. Importantly, it did not reject outright the legacy it inherited. It even reclaimed some authors: the 1962 *Times* obituary of Richard Aldington, known best for his 1929 anti-war novel *Death of a Hero* defined him as 'an angry young man of the generation before they became fashionable'. Fresh adaptations of the most outstanding material from the earlier writers were made including a 1959 BBC production of Bennett's *Hilda Lessways* starring Judi Dench, and as late as 1976 a 26-part ITV serialisation of *Clayhanger* with Peter McEnery and Janet Suzman. Walter Greenwood's *Love on the Dole* was presented twice, in 1960 as a BBC *Sunday Night Play* with Billie Whitelaw, Tom Bell and Avis Bunnage, and again as an ITV *Play of the Week* in 1967 with Malcolm Tierney. The work of inter-war women authors like Storm Jameson and Phyllis Bentley was also re-appraised. Jameson, from Whitby, saw her novels *The Commonplace Heart* and *The Face of Treason* dramatized on TV in 1953 and 1959 respectively, whilst Bentley, from Halifax, had her 1932 trilogy *Inheritance* (in its day the most successful piece of regional fiction since Hardy) screened by Granada TV in 1967 with James Bolam and John Thaw.

Lawrence remained the final frontier; the great taboo. UK producers tip-toed around him. A short story, *The Rocking Horse Winner*, was filmed in 1949. Another, *You Touched Me*, which Tennessee Williams had adapted for Broadway, with Montgomery Clift in 1945, turned up as a BBC *Sunday Night Theatre* production in 1956, with a third, *Samson and Deliah*, following in 1959. His major novels though remained firmly embargoed. Although *Sons and Lovers* reached cinema screens in 1960 – and was astonishingly successful – the 1955 French version of *Lady Chatterley's Lover* with Danielle Darieux remained banned, and it would be the unlocking of public access to this book, after a semi-farcical obscenity trial, that helped launch the liberal climate of the 60s.

The scope of the post-war social realist authors was also technically broader than their forbears. Bennett, Lawrence et al were restricted to the written word. Osborne, Amis, Delaney and others could reach audiences through cinema, radio and television as well. The latter would be an important factor, with BBC and

ITV offering many hours of original drama per week by the late 50s. The significance of series like *Coronation Street* and *Z-Cars*, both firmly located out of London and, in the case of the former, often written and directed by women, was immense.

Which raises an important question. Which of these platforms – the written word, theatre, cinema, radio, television – can be looked on as the one most likely to have brought a particular work to prominence? Taking *Look Back in Anger* as an example, it ran on the London stage for seven months in 1956, during which, allowing for the size of the Royal Court Theatre auditorium, it would have been seen by about 100,000 people, possibly less. After a slow start it drew praise from critics (famously, Kenneth Tynan) and commentary in broadsheet papers and cultural magazines. A version, minus most of the leading members of its cast, was screened as an ITV *Play of the Week* in November 1956. It isn't clear how many people viewed this, but at the time only about a third of UK households had a TV licence. Nor would this have been deemed 'popular' viewing (it was screened on a Wednesday night). Thereafter the production played provincial theatres, normally for a week or two at most, through to March 1958 when it closed at the Citizens Theatre, Glasgow, where Fulton Mackay played Jimmy Porter.

In contrast, the September 1959 film adaptation with Richard Burton was surely seen by far more people. Although in decline, thanks mainly to the steady growth of television, UK cinema admissions in 1959 still totalled 580 million, roughly 11 million a week. To which could be added international audiences, an important factor with the film released globally through 1960 and 1961. In terms of 'impact' that would have been how most people, even domestically, saw Osborne's play. Indeed, even allowing for the small number of novels which sold in significant quantities (say, a million plus) it seems fair when writing about Kitchen Sink to concentrate at least as much on the cinematic versions as the book or play from which they were adapted, and to include in the account films made from original screenplays that are clearly part of the same genre. Which is what this narrative seeks to do as it wends its way through to that day in 1964 when the Beatles took the train from Liverpool to London in *A Hard Day's Night*.

One final point. The term Kitchen Sink – used to describe the books, plays and films that appeared between approximately 1955 and 1965 – was first used to describe a style of painting that briefly had prominence in the UK during the early 50s. It appeared in print in the December 1954 edition of *Encounter* when art critic David Sylvester, who wasn't overly impressed with what he was looking at, stated that this type of art was 'An inventory which includes every kind of food and drink, every utensil and implement, the usual plain furniture and even the babies' nappies on the line. Everything but the kitchen sink – the kitchen sink, too.'

He was referring to John Bratby, Derrick Greaves, Edward Middleditch and Jack Smith, whose work had been shown at the Beaux Arts Gallery in Bruton Place, London, curated by Helen Lessore, from 1951. It had also been championed by critic, novelist and painter John Berger who organised *Looking Forward: An Exhibition of Realist Pictures by Contemporary British Artists* at the Whitechapel Gallery in 1952 devoted to their work. The four were young (none were over 30, two were under 25) and still at art school when they came to critics' attention. Three of the quartet were also provincial (Greaves and Smith were from Sheffield, Middleditch from Nottingham), and they came to notice at a time when many art schools, further education colleges and adult education institutes were running evening and weekend classes in Fine Art. More working-class people were painting.

Their work often consisted of interior scenes, many in cold looking flats and houses, executed with a restricted use of colour. So, this was social realism, recording and celebrating ordinary day-to-day life. It also showed how much the UK of the 50s still looked like the UK of the 30s, or even earlier.

Seeming to skirt the avant-garde it seemed a million miles away from, for instance, abstract expressionism, the most talked-about art movement at the time. If anything, it resembled a continuation of the work of Walter Sickert and the Camden Town school, prominent between roughly 1900 and 1920. Which, when we consider Helen Lessore was the sister-in-law of Thérèse Lessore, Sickert's third wife, doesn't really come as a surprise. The circle is completed when we learn that Arnold Bennett and Sickert were friends. Thus Kitchen Sink was first applied (somewhat disapprovingly) to a group of young artists who were influenced by Sickert, a friend of Bennett.

They reached their apogee in June 1956 when they represented Britain at the Venice Biennale. Just two months later the Whitechapel Gallery would host another exhibition, *This Is Tomorrow*, which critic David Sylvester much preferred. A mixture of abstract art, graphic design, architecture, strip cartoons, interior design, furniture and interactive mobiles and robots, this would be the armoury that determined the course of art and design in the years to come. Thus, the artistic Kitchen Sink never really took off in Fine Art, even if, for a while, John Bratby seemed on the verge of becoming hugely successful. In 1957 he was commissioned to paint the pictures attributed to the fictional artist Gulley Jimson in the film adaptation of Joyce Cary's *The Horse's Mouth*. Alec Guinness, who played Jimson, even modelled his performance on Bratby by observing how he worked in his studio. Ultimately, although the Beaux Arts Quartet, as the four were named, continued to paint they never achieved the public recognition, fame or even notoriety of Bacon, Freud or the pop artists who dominated the 60s.

This study does not, therefore, focus on the connections between Fine Art and social-realist writing in the 50s. What it does instead is look at the books and plays, films and TV productions that constitute the Kitchen Sink corpus. Ranging from the well-known (*Saturday Night and Sunday Morning*, *A Taste of Honey* and so on) to the lesser known (*The Tinker*, *The Furnished Room* and many others) specific topics are explored in each chapter. These look at the emergence of provincial themes in fiction and drama, the part played by music, particularly the impact of rock 'n' roll, the role played by satire, comedy and the absurd, the sub-genre that swirls around London (and Soho in particular), the end of Empire and the impact this had on UK life and the accumulation of work exploring sexual, political and libertarian themes, before and after the *Lady Chatterley* trial. The rise of The Beatles is considered, as is a possible counter-factual about what might have happened to the Kitchen Sink had they not taken the world by storm in 1964.

Finally, the long-term impact of the material, particularly its visual imagery is considered. Is it still relevant and what can we learn from it today?

SCENES FROM PROVINCIAL LIFE

Before any of this took readers and audiences by storm, there were outliers that marked the course and prepared the way. If we agree the basic definition of the type – something set in the provinces, characterised by youth, aggression, disrespect for social convention, a freer attitude to sex and violence and embellished with more consumer goods – then one of the earliest sightings came in 1958 with the Rank Organisation's *Violent Playground*.

Much of this was filmed on location in Liverpool in the spring and summer of 1957, roughly when Paul McCartney and John Lennon were getting together in The Quarrymen. Why Liverpool? Rank had been much impressed by the phenomenal success of *Blackboard Jungle*, the American juvenile delinquent drama that made an immense impact when it appeared in the UK in September 1955. Teenage audiences rioted, tore up seats and danced in the aisles wherever it was screened, spurred on by the inclusion on the soundtrack of Bill Haley and the Comets' *Rock Around the Clock*. Only a minor hit when originally released in the UK in December 1954, on the back of the film's success this re-entered the charts in October 1955, reaching No 1, and was still in the Top 30 in February 1957.

Making a UK version of *Blackboard Jungle* – or something like it – meant looking at where juvenile delinquency was an issue, and commissioning a drama set in that location. It turned out Liverpool was an obvious place to start, as the police there had run a department specifically monitoring and dealing with young offenders since 1949. Rank signed up author James Kennaway, whose debut novel *Tunes of Glory* had been favourably reviewed, to produce a script and appointed Basil Dearden to direct. He was a reasonable choice, having explored a similar subject as early as 1952 in *I Believe in You*, with Laurence Harvey and Joan Collins playing troubled adolescents. The leading roles in *Violent Playground*, of Johnny Murphy and his sister Cathie, went to two Rank contract players, David McCallum, 24, whom the studio signed after seeing a photo-shoot in which he looked remarkably like James Dean, and Anne Heywood, 26. The policeman who gets involved in trying to sort out Murphy, and ends up much taken with his sister, is played by Stanley Baker, a huge UK star at that point and one of the few leading actors who combined contempt and aggression with a non-middle-class persona.

Whilst the credits roll, and underscoring its origins as a British take on *Blackboard Jungle*, the soundtrack bursts into life with a piece of early UK rock 'n' roll: *Play Rough* by Johnny Luck who sounds about 13, and still in short trousers. Attempts to trace him and assess any subsequent career have proved fruitless, and although the song was released by Fontana it was only available as a 78, which was going out of fashion by 1958. But it isn't a bad effort, and was written by a couple of Tin Pan Alley songsmiths, Philip Green and Paddy Roberts, Roberts being something of a satirist, a musical equivalent of Stephen Potter, and quite popular at the time.

We meet Johnny and Cathie Murphy, who live on an inter-war local authority housing estate in Liverpool. Johnny leads a gang, amongst whom can be spotted Sean Lynch, later associated with Joan Littlewood's Theatre Workshop, and a 14-year-old Freddie Starr, appearing as Freddie Fowell. They get their kicks from arson, as well as general delinquency. There is an anti-authoritarian theme running through much of the dialogue, strengthened by a Liverpool Irish, Roman Catholic, anti-English sub-plot that introduces Peter Cushing as a local priest who anxiously tries (and fails) to talk Johnny out of his activities.

As well as featuring many scenes filmed across Liverpool, the film contains a fair number of black and ethnic minority characters. Most have minor, uncredited roles, an exception being Tsai Chin, 12th in the cast as Primrose. (A year later she landed the starring role in the UK stage adaptation of *The World of Suzie Wong*, and through the 60s and 70s enjoyed a parallel career as a singer.) The acting is reasonable throughout, the plot rattles along and there is a lot of background detail to enjoy.

Eventually, Johnny runs amok with a machine gun and takes a class of school children hostage. Fortunately, his sister intervenes and delivers Johnny to the police, who take him away to be charged. Baker's character attempts to ingratiate himself with Cathie, but she declines him and proceeds instead to Cushing's church – the message here being that Catholicism (in Liverpool, and amongst the Irish) produces stronger loyalties than the state can impose.

Rank gave *Violent Playground* quite a push. It did reasonable business at home and played across Europe, but despite good reviews, it failed to make much impression in the US, where thrillers involving teenage tearaways had been common for years. For Basil Dearden it led to serious, socially conscious, and generally interesting films that included *Sapphire*, *Victim* and *The Mindbenders*, another James Kennaway adaptation. Looking at *Violent Playground* today, it is odd to think that Liverpool featured so early in the Kitchen Sink, whilst also being the location where, in 1964, it symbolically concluded with *A Hard Day's Night*.

Ironically, the success of The Beatles gave *Violent Playground* a profitable afterlife. After they took the US by storm, and all things related to Liverpool were in demand there, *Violent Playground* was re-released and, helped on by David McCallum's popularity playing Illya Kuryakin in the TV spy series *The Man from UNCLE*, did very well in America.

The second clear outlier was 1959's *Tiger Bay*, which Rank distributed. Set in Cardiff, another port with a multi-ethnic population, this also attempted to replicate the success of a foreign film, this time a French production. J Lee Thompson is best known for mainstream successes like *The Guns of Navarone* and *Cape Fear*, but, active since 1950, he had already introduced social realism into his work (e.g. *The Weak and the Wicked* in 1954) when he saw Louis Malle's *Asenseur Pour L'échafaud* in January 1958. Inspired by its artistic integrity he immediately pitched the idea of making something similar to sympathetic producers.

Malle's debut was an immensely accomplished piece of film noir set in a highly atmospheric Paris, with a plot centred on the moral ambiguity of its main characters. Adultery, murder and arms dealing all feature with a great cast led by Jeanne Moreau. One memorable scene has her walking alone through the nocturnal city, accompanied by music from Miles Davis. Stylistically, this made a huge impact and was much in advance of anything attempted in the UK at that time.

The source of *Asenseur Pour L'échafaud* was a 1956 novel by Noël Calef, and Thompson quickly came across a short story by the same author – *Rodolphe et le Revolver* – that he felt could be given similar treatment. About a boy with an unhealthy fascination for guns, it was reworked by crime novelist Shelley Smith, whose 1957 collection of short stories, *Rachel Weeping*, included 'An Idyll', in which a nine-year-old girl encounters a sympathetically portrayed psychopath.

The rewrite saw the child changed from a boy to a 12-year-old girl, and with the psychopath becoming a sympathetically portrayed Polish sailor, *Rodolphe et le Revolver* duly became *Tiger Bay*. Raising funding for a script based on an obscure French short story was still hard, however. Particularly when it was proposed that the key role, of the Polish sailor, would be played by Horst Buchholz, a young West German actor who might have appeared in screen adaptations of Tolstoy and Thomas Mann but had yet to make an English language movie. Eventually, Independent Artists, who mainly did second features, came on board, and shooting began.

The film begins with a ship arriving in Cardiff. Its crew are paid off at the end of their voyage. A Polish sailor makes his way into town to locate his girlfriend, but finds she has moved out and taken up with another man in his absence. A young girl, whom we meet as part of a street gang, helps him find her. The sailor and his ex-girlfriend argue and in a fit of anger he shoots her. The police, led by John Mills, get on the case, and as the net closes in on the sailor, a friendship develops between him and the girl, played, very strikingly, by Hayley Mills, daughter of John.

As in *Violent Playground*, much of the local street culture is shown, with the immigrant community clearly visible. The moral ambiguity of *Asensceur Pour L'échafaud* survives too, in this case in the relationship between Buchholz and the young girl. At a time when hanging remained in force in the UK Buchholz is not shown as an unpleasant character, but rather as someone flawed. The making of this point, together with the local footage, means the film remains of interest.

It's a worthy effort, if not as compelling as *Asensceur Pour L'échafaud*, which introduced Malle as a highly developed film *auteur* at the tender age of 24, though he was not necessarily part of the French New Wave. Whilst Mills, his daughter and Buchholz are fine, there isn't anyone who can match the haunted looks of Jeanne Moreau. More to the point, the soundtrack is by Laurie Johnson, who is no Miles Davis. Johnson worked on a lot of Thompson's films and tended toward a TV theme, big band approach (he later scored *The Avengers*). For *Tiger Bay* he went for a rather conventional, even jaunty sound. It didn't enjoy a vinyl release, whereas Davis's music for Malle was available on a 10" LP. One wonders why Thompson and Johnson didn't make some use of locally-born Shirley Bassey, getting her to do a bluesey number for the title sequences.

Halliwell in his pioneering *Film Guide* calls *Tiger Bay* a 'police chase melodrama' which seems about right. Released in March 1959, it did well at the UK box office, possibly because audiences were taken with the idea of seeing John Mills co-starring with his daughter. The critics liked it, too. Hayley Mills won a BAFTA and the film won the Silver Bear at the Berlin Film Festival.

Also paving the way – and another film confirming the centre of gravity was, at least for the moment, shifting away from London – was *Tread Softly Stranger*. This appeared in August 1958 and was notable for being filmed in and around Rotherham. It was adapted from a 1953 play, *Blind Date*, written by Jack Popplewell, a prolific Leeds-based author and songwriter, which was regularly performed in regional theatres. With audiences for repertory productions high in this pre-TV era, it was a popular work, and the film rights were quickly sold. Popplewell's forte was comedy and this was his attempt at a psychological drama with faint echoes of J B Priestley's *An Inspector Calls*.

The plot concerns two brothers. One (Johnny) returns from London to escape retribution from some gangsters. The other (Dave) is quiet, bookish and works in an office in a steel works. Both have financial obligations they are unable to meet, and both are involved with a nightclub singer, Calico. Motivated by greed, she inveigles them into carrying out a robbery. It goes wrong, an old man is killed and a witness to this keeps appearing and disappearing, leaving the characters, and audience, uncertain if this isn't a ploy by the police to force a confession out of the perpetrators.

Diana Dors, then the epitome of corrupting sexuality, stars as Calico. Just back from a none-too-successful foray in Hollywood, she was paid in cash (£10,000, equating to approximately £0.5m today) for her role. George Baker and Terence Morgan appear as the brothers and give solid enough performances. They all do what they can with the melodramatic script, even, on occasion, attempting to give it a weight it doesn't quite deserve. One of the problems – which also afflicts *Violent Playground* – is that despite being set in a northern manufacturing city, the accents used on the screen are not very authentic.

Where the film retains its interest, though, is in the background shots of the now-vanished industrial scenery and its murky, hazy surroundings. The photography by Douglas Slocombe, one of the British film industry's leading cinematographers, is rather good for a film so average. Which, sadly, is not the case with the music. Jim Dale does the main title theme, a guitar-strummed ballad drenched in reverb: Parlophone released it as a single, without success, in April 1958. The score was written by Tristram Cary, son of Joyce, and an early pioneer of electronic music. Sadly, his material here is very conventional.

It was against the backdrop of films like these that the big

Kitchen Sink literary adaptations hit the cinema screens. The first to appear was the film version of John Braine's novel *Room at the Top*. Braine was working as a librarian in Wakefield whilst he wrote the book, having originally started it five years earlier whilst recovering from tuberculosis contracted during an attempt to live as a struggling writer in north Kensington. It was a publishing sensation, eventually selling 159,000 copies in hardback and getting Braine an appearance on *Panorama* on 8th April 1957, where he was interviewed by former Labour MP Woodrow Wyatt, then between spells in Parliament.

This was seen by John Woolf, who ran Romulus Films with his brother James. He bought a copy of the book the next day, and quickly purchased the film rights. It went into production almost immediately. Romulus had a strong pedigree, with useful Hollywood connections having been involved with *The African Queen* and *Moulin Rouge*, both considerable successes. And this, at least initially, was how they approached *Room at the Top*. Neil Paterson, a Scottish novelist whose novel *Man on the Tightrope* had been filmed in the US a few years earlier, was hired to write a screenplay, and both Stewart Granger and Vivien Leigh were considered for the leading roles.

Stewart Granger and Vivien Leigh would have been seriously miscast: Granger, at 45, was already becoming too old to be a matinee idol and was definitely too old to play Joe Lampton, while Leigh's theatrical style suited famous roles in *Gone with the Wind* and *A Streetcar Named Desire* but not the downbeat story of Alice Aisgill – neither actor could be imagined in West Riding. But both might have been 'bankable' if your intention was to crash into the US market.

Instead of which, after due consideration, the Woolfs went for an arthouse approach. Laurence Harvey, later rumoured to be James Woolf's lover, and who'd been in several Romulus productions, as well as appearing with the Royal Shakespeare Company, was cast as Lampton. The key female parts went to Simone Signoret, as the older woman who fixes things for a younger man, and Heather Sears, as the younger woman – and boss's daughter – whom Lampton gets pregnant and marries. Sears was 23, under contract to Romulus, and had replaced Mary Ure in the stage production of *Look Back in Anger*. Signoret, though, was a real catch, widely known in European cinema for her roles in *La Ronde*, *Casque D'Or*, *Les Diaboliques*, *Death in the Garden* and *The Crucible*. She'd won a BAFTA for the latter, which came with a script by Jean-Paul Sartre. So, hiring her for a starring role in a UK film was clearly a pitch for the same market.

At 30 and 37 Harvey and Signoret were both appropriate ages for their characters. Harvey's acting style, undemonstrative, laconic, and the opposite of the 'Old Vic' approach still common at that time, suited his part perfectly. As did his neatly turned-out appearance. He plays Lampton as a working-class man determined to rise above his situation. Signoret's Alice Aisgill projects a mixture of eroticism, intellect and vulnerability that the producers correctly assessed was beyond the scope of any existing UK actress. Considering how iconic the film would become as portrayals of 'northern' English mores and social situations, it is striking that the two leading actors are both Jewish and from Lithuania (Harvey) and France (Signoret).

The Woolfs picked Jack Clayton to direct, after their 1956 production of his short film *The Bespoke Overcoat*, won an Academy Award. Filmed in Bradford and Halifax, *Room at the Top* closely follows the plot and mood of Braine's novel. Joe Lampton works his way to 'the top' from a lowly position at an accountancy firm in a Yorkshire market town. Despite his working-class background, he targets the beautiful daughter of a rich local businessman for marriage – while having a torrid affair with an older woman. Lampton is virtually amoral and the message conveyed is that personal freedom is paramount, and old societal constraints should be rejected. Lampton wants to be able to do whatever he wants, whenever he wants, which was pretty much what Braine thought after his novel achieved success: he quit his job in Wakefield and was quoted as saying 'What I want to do is drive through Bradford in a Rolls Royce with two naked women on either side of me covered in jewels.'

Released in January 1959, *Room at the Top* garnered good reviews, ending up the 4th most popular film released in the UK that year. Astonishingly – for a British film – it was nominated for six Academy Awards, winning two: Simone Signoret, Best Actress, and Neil Paterson, Best Screenplay. This was a triumph for Signoret, given she had never made a US film, and was thought to be a Communist 'fellow traveller'. But she swept the board that year, also picking up a BAFTA for Best Foreign Actress, and winning Best Actress at Cannes. A paperback edition of the novel followed the film release and doubled sales of the book.

The aspirational feelings exhibited by Lampton (and Braine) appeared radical in 1959 given this was the high watermark of the post-war consensus where equality was a driving force of the national economy, most heavily symbolised by the Welfare State. Today it is clear that Lampton is selfish and embraces rather than rejects capitalism.

In essence he is a proto-Thatcherite, something that gradually became clearer as Braine's career progressed. After his 1959 novel, *The Vodi* (set in a TB sanatorium) failed, he revived Lampton for *Life at the Top* (1962). This has the character and his wife both conducting adulterous affairs at opposite ends of the country, whilst Lampton enjoys being a successful businessman, something that requires near catastrophic levels of alcohol consumption, frequenting strip clubs and a lot of eating at expensive restaurants. It was filmed in 1965, with Harvey reprising the role, and Jean Simmons taking over from Heather Sears as his wife.

Braine moved to Woking a year later, and confirmed his rightward move politically by joining the Monday Club in 1968. They published his rejection of 'socialism' and he also endorsed US policy in Vietnam. He then returned to his bestseller for a second sequel, *Man at the Top*, in 1970. Written as a TV series, this has Lampton, now played by Kenneth Haigh, updated with a Zapata moustache and Aston Martin, working as a management consultant, and repeating the excesses portrayed in the *Life at the Top*. Audiences loved it, with individual episodes attracting up to 20 million viewers. In the final episode, *The Foreman's*

Job at Last, broadcast in September 1972, Lampton is standing for Parliament as an independent candidate. Had Braine been minded to write a third sequel, we might have been treated at some point in the late 70s or early 80s, to him vigorously 'sorting out' the country. Instead, after a 1973 film of the series, starring Haigh, the character was set aside. Both his popularity and political evolution reflected wider shifts in opinion during the journey the UK took from the end of the war to the beginning of the post-industrial era.

Room at the Top takes place in the early 50s, Lampton being a former prisoner of war. Like much of the genre the atmosphere of the grim post-war years clings to it. Other Kitchen Sink novels went even further back. William Cooper's *Scenes from Provincial Life* (1950) is set in 1939, with a hero, Joe Lunn, who is a grammar school teacher, and would-be writer. Self-interested, disaffected and undecided, he eventually takes the train from Leicester to London. Much admired by Braine, Kingsley Amis and others, neither film nor TV adaptations were forthcoming until a sequel, *Scenes from Married Life,* appeared in 1961. The two books were then amalgamated into *You Can't Win,* a 1966 ITV drama series with Ian McShane. John Wain's *Hurry on Down* (1953), considered by many to be a key work, and clearly predating rock 'n' roll, Suez and so on, got neither a film nor a TV adaptation, which suggests that its picaresque narrative may have been deemed too difficult to adapt. Wain had more luck with *The Contenders* (1958), broadcast as a Granada TV series in 1969, where the plot follows the rivalries of three young men from the Potteries from the 30s to the 50s.

The post-war austerity era also produced John Osborne, whose first play *The Devil Inside Him* (co-written with Stella Linden), was staged in provincial rep in Huddersfield in May 1950. A second, *Personal Enemy* (co-written with Anthony Creighton), appeared in Harrogate five years later. Neither enjoyed a lengthy run, but this was not surprising then for original drama staged in repertory theatres, where the programme usually changed weekly. For much of his time Osborne worked as a jobbing actor and it was while living in Derby and performing in Morecambe that he wrote, solo, *Look Back in Anger*.

This time fortune was kinder to him. In August 1955 he saw an advertisement in *The Stage*, seeking new plays for the English Stage Company, and sent them his script. They replied immediately, offering him £25 (about £1,500 today) for an option and requesting a meeting. Osborne duly met George Devine, a founder member of the company, and it was agreed that his play would be produced at the Royal Court Theatre and directed by Tony Richardson, who at that point was sharing Devine's house in London. Devine had been involved in the London stage scene since the 30s, directing Alec Guinness, Laurence Olivier and Vivien Leigh in various West End productions. He was well connected and would later describe the objectives of the English Stage Company as being to 'get writers, writers of serious pretensions, back into the theatre'.

Osborne's *Look Back in Anger* opened at the Royal Court in May 1956. It starred Kenneth Haigh as Jimmy Porter, Mary Ure as his long-suffering wife, Alan Bates as a friend who shares their one-room flat and Helena Hughes as the woman who briefly comes between Haigh and Ure. All of the cast were relative unknowns and audiences were not initially overwhelmed by the play. Angry young men were certainly known about, and Colin Wilson's polemic *The Outsider*, taken for a while as being the rallying flag of their cause, was in fact published the same month that Osborne's play started its run. The play had a downbeat set and a limited span of events in the drama but an awful lot of Porter shouting, much of it unpleasant and misogynistic. The latter point is often overlooked in explanations as to why the play was resistible to some, and had a slow build up to its eventual success.

Salvation came from two sources. Firstly, Kenneth Tynan gave it a strong review in *The Observer* noting the play's 'instinctive leftishness' something he subsequently explained as being because it 'represented the dismay of many young Britons... who came of age under a Socialist government, yet found, when they went out into the world, that the class system was still mysteriously intact'. In other words: the play is a plea on behalf of young people that the UK hasn't changed that much, and needs to change more. Secondly, and fortuitously, it was staged at exactly the point the Suez Crisis engulfed day-to-day life in the UK, dividing the country as it did so. The effect of this, whatever influence Tynan may have brought to bear on broadsheet readers, was critical. Put simply, when *Look Back in Anger* started its run in May 1956 the idea that there might be a war with Egypt, possibly as part of a nuclear conflict with the Soviet Union, would not have registered with the public. After President Nasser nationalised the Canal on 30th July 1956 (it had formerly been owned and operated by a UK-French consortium), and the talk in Parliament and the media was about taking military action to wrest back control, Porter's bitter monologues seemed to be hewn from the events of the day.

Osborne has him inveighing against the UK, making the point again and again that it is a small, deluded country, full of petty people, pointless restrictions and outdated social conventions. This kind of writing would never have been an easy sell, and together with the misogyny would have probably drawn its run to a conclusion within a month or so in 'normal' circumstances. Instead, it prospered, particularly after the UK, France and Israel commenced military action against Egypt on 29th October. Between then and 6th November, when the UK and its allies agreed to a UN-imposed ceasefire, events ran in parallel with the Soviet Union putting down an uprising in Hungary, hence the alarming possibility, however remote, for a few days, that a third, and potentially final, world war might break out.

And after the guns fell silent in Suez, arrangements were made for a TV screening of the play. The BBC declined to do this, and it was broadcast instead on ITV on 28th November. An estimated 5 million viewers tuned in to watch, with only Alan Bates of the original cast remaining in the line-up. (By then Haigh was filming, Hughes rehearsing a TV play and Ure appearing in the London premiere of Arthur Miller's *A View from the Bridge*: a bigger production at a bigger theatre.) Rank declined to fund a film adaptation so, wishing to retain control of the project,

Osborne and Richardson formed their own company, Woodfall Films, with Harry Saltzman.

Today the attitude of the BBC and Rank might seem puzzling. This is to forget that many, perhaps even most, people in the UK supported the attack on Egypt, and it was deemed a national humiliation when it was curtailed by international opprobrium, and the threat by the US to cause a disastrous run on the pound. Had either the BBC or Rank looked a little closer they would have seen that Osborne's key message was not anarchic at all but rather a complaint that contemporary life lacked noble causes. The clue is in the title. The best speech in the play – and film – is probably that given by Alison's father, a retired Indian Army officer about the day his regiment quit their base to return home for the last time. This chimes with one of the events in the build-up to Suez: the sacking of John Glubb, 'Glubb Pasha', the English commander of the Jordanian Arab Legion, under pressure from Egypt in March 1956.

Neither Kenneth Haigh nor Alan Bates appeared in the film, as Woodfall sought the widest possible distribution. Haigh, 25 in 1956 and the perfect age for Porter, was replaced by Richard Burton, who at 31 was too old, but had starred in 10 films in the previous 8 years and been twice nominated for Academy Awards. The omission of Bates was slightly puzzling, given that he was replaced by Gary Raymond, then with the Royal Shakespeare Company, but subsequently a much lesser-known actor. In the end, only Mary Ure (who by now was married to Osborne) remained from the original stage production, with Helena Hughes replaced by Claire Bloom, like Burton an established star.

Filming began in 1958, with much of it being shot in various rather down-at-heel areas of London, despite the action in the play clearly taking place in a provincial town. The opening sequence, in a jazz club, was filmed in Dalston and is memorable for including the Chris Barber Band, playing live at the height of their powers. With Osborne writing the script, assisted by Nigel Kneale, and Richardson directing, there are few alterations in the text and Burton's magnificent voice, full of spleen, is firmly centre stage.

Released in May 1959 with an X certificate, it was nominated for five BAFTAs. Importantly, it proved that a market existed for interesting and controversial material. It also established that something could be staged, filmed, pay back its costs and even make a bit of money despite being cold-shouldered by the cinematic and theatrical establishment. If this had just been a talk piece in a Derby bedsit about marital breakdown it would have gone nowhere. But Osborne gives Porter monologues – however indulgent and misogynistic they are – which take things to a completely different level. The message that the UK was now a diminished, dingy country with uncertain prospects still resonates today whilst the title, Look Back in Anger, has become a common phrase in the English language.

One of the people impressed by its visceral power was Laurence Olivier. He was nearly 50, had been nominated five times for Academy Awards (winning once for Hamlet in 1949) and was regarded as the greatest actor of his day. Bored with his career, he thought he was in a rut, and was looking for something that would keep him ahead of the curve. He asked Osborne what else he was working on. After being shown the opening act of The Entertainer, he asked to be cast in the leading role.

Osborne finished writing the play in early 1957 and, with Tony Richardson directing, it opened at the Royal Court in April. As with Look Back in Anger the action is set in the provinces, in this case a declining variety theatre in an English seaside town. Olivier plays Archie Rice, a middle-aged comedian, fronting a show that he hopes will provide him with a path back to more respectable bookings. Away from the stage, his character is a philandering undischarged bankrupt and semi-alcoholic. His family live and tour with him: the financial uncertainties of their life are stressed when his wife, whom he abuses verbally and continually betrays sexually, wails 'I don't want to end up in some awful place like Gateshead, or Hartlepool.'

Olivier had a strong supporting cast including Brenda de Banzie as his wife, George Relph as his elderly music hall veteran father, Dorothy Tutin as his daughter and Richard Pasco as his younger son. Tutin was replaced during the run by Joan Plowright, whilst the character of Rice's father was played by several different actors, amongst whom at one point was Albert Chevalier Jnr Given that Chevalier's father had been a legendary performer on 'the halls' as far back as the 1880s, this suggests that Osborne was keen to recreate the music hall atmosphere (the Faber edition of the play is dedicated 'To A C who remembers what it was like, and will not forget it').

The Entertainer is as much a state of the nation play as *Look Back in Anger*, with Archie Rice the embodiment of, as Tony Richardson commented, 'the ashes of old glory'. Much of the language is coarse, particularly toward the peoples of the Middle East, where, of course, the UK had recently sent troops. In many ways this explores the same psychological ground that Johnny Speight made famous with his character Alf Garnett in *Till Death us do Part*. Possibly the most political play of its time, it was brave of Olivier to do it, particularly as his part often required him to appear unaccompanied, giving surreal monologues of cringing comic patter. He is reminiscent of Chaplin's 'Tramp' character in his loneliness, but without the endearing traits – Archie Rice's faults are brutally exposed and evident to all.

But, with the Olivier name on the marquee, the play was a success, moving out of the Royal Court to a bigger venue and opening on Broadway in early 1958. Kenneth Tynan summed it up with 'Mr Osborne has had the big and brilliant notion of putting the whole of contemporary England onto one and the same stage... He chooses, as his national microcosm, a family of run-down vaudevillians. Grandad, stately and retired, represents Edwardian graciousness, for which Mr Osborne has a deeply submerged nostalgia. But the key figure is Dad, a fiftyish song-and-dance man reduced to appearing in twice-nightly nude revue.'

Richardson, Osborne and Nigel Kneale commenced work on a film version, Woodfall's second production, almost immediately. Filmed in Morecambe, Blackpool and Bradford to ensure maximum use of natural sound and light, this had the number of characters increased from 8 to 14 as the action is opened out.

Olivier, de Banzie and Joan Plowright remain from the stage production. Alan Bates replaced Pasco as the younger son with Roger Livesey, a much-underrated actor, as Rice's father. Extra parts were written for Albert Finney, as the elder son, referred to but not seen in the play, Shirley Anne Field as a beauty contest contestant seduced by Olivier, Thora Hird as her mother and Miriam Karlin as a soubrette. Finney makes a huge impact in his one scene, filmed at Liverpool Street Station, as he gets ready to embark for Egypt with his regiment.

The Entertainer is a finely executed piece and still works well as drama, being less of a polemic than the stage version, and not particularly stagey. John Addison's cod-variety/light comedy songs are effective, and, surprisingly for a film with so much music, there was no soundtrack album. Released in June 1960, the critics liked it, and Olivier was nominated for the sixth time for an Academy Award, but it was not a box office success.

Osborne wrote many more plays, the most notable of these being the historical studies *Luther* (1961, with Albert Finney) and *A Patriot for Me* (1965, with Maximilian Schell). In terms of works tackling contemporary issues his best was probably *Inadmissible Evidence* (1964, with Nicol Williamson), another study of failure. He later mixed writing with acting, doing a memorable turn as a villain in *Get Carter*. Today, his reputation rests largely on *Look Back in Anger* and *The Entertainer*, both of which are regularly revived.

For their third film, Woodfall adapted Alan Sillitoe's 1958 novel *Saturday Night and Sunday Morning*. Much of it had been written in Majorca where Sillitoe lived on a small RAF disability pension with Ruth Fainlight, a US poet and friend of Sylvia Plath. Whilst his best prose would remain densely poetic, he was persuaded by Robert Graves to aim for fiction.

The book was a success and ended up being voted best first novel of the year by the Authors' Club. Sillitoe memorably presents Arthur Seaton, possibly the finest angry young man of them all. A 22-year-old lathe operator in a Nottingham factory, he is awash with money, earning £14 a week with overtime and shiftwork (roughly £35,000 a year today). He is still living at home and, with money to spare, spends his evenings and weekends enjoying himself. Which means prodigious amounts of drinking, smoking, going to dances and getting involved in altercations with a range of people, some similar to him, others a bit more 'respectable'. Fighting and brawling, often whilst drunk, are a regular occurrence. He is also carrying on with the wife of a workmate who works different shifts, whilst seeing her sister on the side. Eventually he starts a third relationship with a younger girl, with whom he reluctantly settles down.

Tony Richardson stepped into the producer slot for this, with Karel Reisz, who had done several highly rated documentaries, directing. Albert Finney was cast as Seaton. A perfect match, he was 23, from Salford, and with just the kind of physical vigour required for the part. And the acting skills too: as well as making his screen debut in *The Entertainer*, he had replaced Olivier in *Coriolanus* at Stratford-upon-Avon and even done a stint in *Emergency Ward 10* on TV. Shirley Anne Field co-starred as Doreen, the younger girl, with Rachel Roberts as the married woman. (The character of Doreen's sister was dropped from the film, possibly because there was only so much adultery the censor would wear whilst still agreeing a release certificate.) Further down the cast were Norman Rossington and Colin Blakely, both of whom would be familiar players in many other Kitchen Sink productions. A significant amount of the film was shot on location in Nottingham, giving it an added authenticity.

The film repeats Sillitoe's message in the book, with Seaton rejecting the limitations of working-class life (even if he begrudgingly accepts them at the end), regarding consumerism as essentially pointless and he has nothing but sarcastic jibes for the aspirational values that his contemporaries see as essential for 'getting on'. Working-class life under capitalism is portrayed as brutal, nothing better than a lot of working, fighting, fornicating and drinking prior to settling down and conforming. It's a radical view, more so than that put across by either Braine or Osborne.

Throughout the action we hear jazzy incidental background music from Johnny Dankworth, including pianist Dudley Moore on a couple of tracks. Again, there was no soundtrack released, though Dankworth was an established artist at this time. Together with the mixture of black and white photography, social realism and location shooting, the end product clearly reminded some critics of the French 'nouvelle vague' with The Evening Standard declaring 'Here is a chance for our own new wave.'

Released with an X certificate in October 1960, it proved popular with UK audiences, many of whom felt they were finally being treated like adults. Characters like Seaton had always existed, with most people knowing of them (or being told about them), but up until then they were usually ignored in drama. Confirming this sense of identification, Sillitoe's text provided a treasury of cultural references, that would be repeated, modified, and pillaged for decades to come. Among those passing into the popular lexicon were the title, 'Saturday Night and Sunday Morning', together with 'Don't Let the Bastards Grind You Down', 'I Believe You, Thousands Wouldn't', and 'Whatever People Say I Am, That's What I'm Not'.

Famously banned by Warwickshire County Council (Shakespeare's homeland), it was a box-office success and one of the most popular UK films of 1960, eventually recording a profit of £145,000 (roughly £6.75m today). Finney, Roberts and Reisz all won BAFTAs and the film played on general release with Linda, a teenage drama with Alan Rothwell, from Coronation Street, Carol White, and music by Joe Meek. Seeing both on a big screen would surely have been a memorable experience.

By the time that happened, Finney was headlining in a stage adaptation of Keith Waterhouse's Billy Liar, directed by Lindsay Anderson. He relinquished the role to Tom Courtenay in June 1961. Towards the end of Billy Liar's stage run, Courtenay commenced filming Alan Sillitoe's The Loneliness of the Long-Distance Runner, the fifth Woodfall production. Based on a 1959 short story, the central character here, Colin Smith, was in many ways even more of a delinquent than Seaton. To start with he is younger, not holding down a steady job and living as part of a single parent family with his mother and siblings in a cramped 'pre-fab' housing unit in a dingy area of Nottingham. He prefers to commit burglaries and steal cars with his sidekick Mike. They enjoy themselves by taking a couple of teenage girls to Skegness for the weekend. Alas, one day, the police come knocking and he is shipped off to borstal.

He also has a massive chip on his shoulder and fully formed views about the class system. The borstal is run by a 'progressive' governor who enters his charges into a cross-country running race with the nearby public school. They are expected to 'play the game' and learn the benefits of good, sporting behaviour as they compete. Not Smith. Selected as the governor's star runner, he deliberately sabotages the competition, despite leading the field, heroically rejecting this attempt to make him conform. Unlike Seaton, he remains unconquered.

Directed by Tony Richardson, and adapted by Sillitoe, the drama unfolds mainly in flashbacks whilst Smith trains alone across a bleak landscape. Courtenay was cast in the leading role, and despite being 25 and therefore too old to play a borstal inmate, looks marvellous. Physically slight, and with a gaunt face, both surely the result of the UK's long spell of rationing, he effortlessly acts the part of a feral teenager. Michael Redgrave appears as the governor and there is memorable support from Avis Bunnage, a stalwart of Joan Littlewood's company, as Smith's put-upon mother and James Bolam as fellow delinquent Mike. The soundtrack boasts some nicely sketched out bits of jazz, performed by Pat Halcox and Dick Smith from the Chris Barber Band, assisted by guitarist Bill Bramwell and drummer Danny Craig. As with *Saturday Night and Sunday Morning*, the music remained unreleased, which seems something of an oversight.

The film appeared in September 1962. Well received by critics, it won Courtenay a BAFTA and made him a star for the rest of the decade. But the public were less certain. Though they went in reasonable numbers, and the title became part of English parlance, it was not a huge hit, for much the same reasons that affected *Look Back in Anger* and *The Entertainer*. It was too belligerent and anti-establishment. It was also rather downbeat, with an ironic use of *Jerusalem* over the end titles as the wretched borstal inmates dismantle WW2 gas masks.

Sillitoe followed it with *Key to the Door* (1961) a Seaton family prequel with a plot stretching from the 30s to Malaya in the 40s. Its anti-colonial theme was repeated in *The Death of William Posters* (1965), in which Frank Dawley, Sillitoe's central character, hates UK society so much that he abandons his job, and family, to fight in a third world guerilla movement. Neither were filmed. Instead, the Soviet Union embraced Sillitoe as the authentic voice of the west's frustrated and corrupted proletariat and invited him to explore their country, the results of which appeared in *Road to Volgograd* (1963), a fine travel book. The praise he attracted for his early works proved difficult to repeat, but he retained a considerable readership, with later adaptations including *The Ragman's Daughter* (1972, based on a 1964 short story) and *Pit Strike* (1977, an original script for a BBC play).

In between the two Sillitoe films, Woodfall took on another radical project: a film adaptation of Shelagh Delaney's play, *A Taste of Honey*. Staged at the Theatre Royal, Stratford by Joan Littlewood in May 1958, around the same time that *Saturday Night and Sunday Morning* appeared in print, the author was inspired by her instant reaction to seeing Terence Rattigan's *Variations on a Theme*. Believing Rattigan's treatment of homosexuality to be inadequate, she immediately put pen to paper and soon sent her script to Littlewood. Given that *Variations on a Theme* was performed in Manchester for a week (31st March to 5th April 1958) Littlewood must have decided to stage Delaney's piece almost immediately. Of course, Littlewood was an obvious person to approach: a former communist, she was once married to Ewan MacColl, hailed from Salford like Delaney, and was strongly influenced by Bertolt Brecht's Berliner Ensemble. Littlewood was committed to staging unusual plays with a strong social message, something that *A Taste of Honey*, with plot lines tackling race and sexuality, provided.

The play is a study of a fraught mother-daughter relationship: Helen is an alcoholic supported by several male friends; when her daughter Jo becomes pregnant after a flirtation with a young black man, their relationship is strained even further. It was most notable for having a sympathetically-portrayed gay character in the person of the sensitive young man who agrees to live with the daughter and act as father to her child.

Championed by Kenneth Tynan, it did well in London, where the two main roles were played by Avis Bunnage and Frances Cuka, and transferred to Broadway where the leads were Angela Lansbury and Joan Plowright respectively. For the film Dora Bryan was brought in as the mother, with Robert Stephens as her male admirer. Murray Melvin was retained as the sensitive young man and Paul Danquah, a black UK actor, at that point sharing a flat with painter Francis Bacon, played the sailor who gets the daughter pregnant. Rita Tushingham, from Garston, and like Delaney just 19, starred as Jo, the daughter. All of the cast gave outstanding performances.

Richardson directed, and with Delaney providing the script, the film was a fine version of the play. The tone was accurate and down to earth; melodrama was avoided. Much of it was shot around Salford and Manchester, with excellent photography from Walter Lassally. Indeed, the background detail, depicting a now vanished industrial, L S Lowry-type landscape, provided enough iconic images to fill out any number of galleries, with many of these being seen again on record sleeves in the 80s.

Released in September 1961, it was banned in several countries due to its content and had a lukewarm public reception. The public clearly took to the laddish adventures of Joe Lampton and Arthur Seaton, but had difficulty with the travails of Delaney's heroine. Tushingham explained in 2020: 'A lot of the reaction was "People like that don't exist" by which they meant homosexuals, single-mothers and people in mixed-race relationships. But they did.' Fortunately, A Taste of Honey was a critical hit. It won BAFTAs for best film, best screenplay, best actress (Dora Bryan) and best newcomer (Tushingham). Tushingham and Melvin also won best actress and best actor at the Cannes Film Festival.

Delaney's subsequent career would prove difficult. A follow-up play, The Lion in Love (1960) failed to make any kind of impact like *A Taste of Honey* had. Two films then appeared in 1967 based on Delaney screenplays. *The White Bus* was based on one of the short stories in her 1963 collection *Sweetly Sings the Donkey*, and was made into a short film by Lindsay Anderson. *Charlie Bubbles* had the unusual pairing of Albert Finney with Liza Minelli but neither film was popular with audiences, a sad fate for the latter which was exceptional. After that Delaney wrote mainly for TV, where the BBC twice remade *A Taste of Honey*, in 1971 with Diana Dors, and again in 1984. A final triumph came with *Dance with a Stranger* (1985), her screenplay based on the notorious Ruth Ellis murder case of three decades earlier. Perhaps the chief beneficiary of *A Taste of Honey* would be Tushingham, who was propelled to stardom becoming, with Finney and Courtenay, one of the great 'faces' of the 60s.

In keeping with custom and practice there was no soundtrack album. Rather curiously, though, John Addison's version of *The Big Ship Sails on the Alley-Alley-O*, by The Corona Kids, which can be heard in the film, managed to appear as a single on Philips. Addison claimed the songwriters' royalties, but in truth it was a traditional nursery rhyme, often sung by children in Salford due to its supposed connection with the Manchester Ship Canal. It didn't sell, unlike Bobby Scott and Ric Marlow's song *A Taste of Honey*, written for the Broadway production of the play. Although unconnected to the film, this became one of the great standards of the 60s, becoming part of The Beatles' set in Hamburg and a No 16 UK chart hit for Acker Bilk in 1963. Both songs have a child-like elegiac quality, which, for anyone who remembers it, is immediately reminiscent of that period.

The only other female author to make a significant impact with a style akin to that of the Kitchen Sink was Edna O'Brien, from County Clare in the west of Ireland. Whilst working as a pharmacist in Dublin she met a writer, Ernest Gébler, whose 1950 historical novel *The Plymouth Adventure* had sold 5 million copies and been made into a film starring Spencer Tracy. They began seeing each other, which ordinarily might have been considered an idyllic arrangement. Except that in Ireland then, a country in thrall to the mighty Archbishop McQuaid, it was deemed disgraceful for a young woman to be courting with a divorced Czech Jew. They duly left for the UK, where they married and set up home in Raynes Park, London.

It was here, in suburban surroundings, whilst bringing up children and working as a publisher's reader, that O'Brien wrote *The Country Girls*. It appeared in 1960, the first of a trilogy that would include *The Lonely Girl* (1962) and *Girls in Their Married Bliss* (1964). All were acclaimed and led to her working for TV. Her hour-long play, *The Wedding Dress*, was broadcast by Granada in late 1962, starring Cyril Cusack and Helena Hughes. With both Brendan Behan's *The Quare Fellow* and J P Donleavy's *The Ginger Man* becoming better known via film and TV adaptations around the same time, Woodfall optioned *The Lonely Girl* by their compatriot O'Brien. Renamed *Girl with Green Eyes*, it became their seventh production, after *Tom Jones* had become a box office sensation in the UK and US, winning Academy Awards for Finney, Richardson, Osborne, and Addison.

Desmond Davis, part of the crew on *A Taste of Honey* and *The Loneliness of the Long-Distance Runner*, made his debut as director with O'Brien writing the script. Taken from her heavily autobiographical novel, it follows Kate, a girl from Clare, as she leaves home, goes to Dublin, and shares a flat with her friend Baba. They drink, discuss men, and entertain themselves with the nightlife. Eventually she meets Eugene Gaillard, a middle-aged author. Rita Tushingham and Lynn Redgrave appear as Kate and Baba with Peter Finch as Gaillard (whose initials, EG, replicate those of O'Brien's husband). Peter Finch was a big star in UK cinema, having won five BAFTAs between 1956 and 1961 in fairly mainstream vehicles, and it's tempting to speculate that his involvement in a Kitchen Sink film was influenced by Richard Burton's swerve into the genre with *Look Back in Anger*.

Filmed on location in Ireland amongst Dublin's faded Georgian houses, bars and dance halls, *Girl with Green Eyes* successfully captures the book's atmosphere. Given that O'Brien's books were banned and subject to public burnings in the republic, this was quite a brave decision to take. O'Brien writes exclusively from a woman's point of view about unsatisfactory and sexually difficult relationships and the plot provides many sharply-drawn moments. The uproar that Kate causes with her family when she starts seeing Gaillard; a censorious priest laying down the law of the Church; the differences that rise between Kate and Gaillard about Catholicism (which she still embraces, up to a point); and the awkwardness within their relationship when he continues to correspond with his estranged wife. Eventually they split up, Tushingham and Redgrave's characters leave for London and the next, more hopeful stage of their life commences.

The film appeared in May 1964, and was a reasonable success. Liked by the critics, it provided Tushingham with her fourth consecutive starring role and gave Redgrave's career a significant boost. Desmond Davis and O'Brien reunited for *I Was Happy Here* (1966) in which the central female character returns to County Clare from London. It won best picture at the San Sebastian Film Festival and after separating from Gébler, Edna O'Brien managed to evoke the swinging sixties somewhat more successfully than Shelagh Delaney. She was one of the commentators giving her views about the scene in the 1967 documentary *Tonite, Let's All Make Love in London* and wrote two screenplays, *Three into Two Won't Go* (1969) and *Zee and Co* (1971). Like Delaney's *A Taste of Honey*, her earlier work retained its popularity with her TV adaptation of *The Country Girls* appearing in 1983, starring Sam Neill.

Emotional and sexual frustration were also evident in David Storey's 1960 novel *This Sporting Life*. A first reading of the book makes it seem a route one-angry-young-man piece. A chippy macho hero starts a relationship with a local widow in a northern town where power is in the hands of a tightly-knit group of well-to-do, well-connected men, whilst a predatory older woman circles in the background. On closer inspection it is clear it isn't a nihilistic beer, fags and football drama at all and with two central characters who struggle to express themselves, it is much more akin to *A Taste of Honey*.

Storey was from Wakefield and studied at Slade School of Art in the early 50s where one of his teachers was Lucian Freud. He also played Rugby League for Leeds RFC, who rated him so highly that they signed him to a 15-year contract. He could have been either an artist or a rugby footballer, but decided against both in favour of writing. *This Sporting Life* was his first book, and appeared when he was 27. Like all the classic Kitchen Sink works, its title had a resonance of its own, though in this case the author had borrowed it from a much-covered traditional country blues song. It sold well, and was suggested to Woodfall as a Richardson and Reisz project after the success of *Saturday Night and Sunday Morning*. They declined, and it ended up being produced by Independent Artists, the people behind *Tiger Bay*, with Lindsay Anderson directing, Storey writing the script and Rank agreeing a distribution deal.

Filmed mainly in Wakefield, its plot replicates that of the book. The central character, Frank Machin, is an ambitious rugby league footballer whose potential is spotted by the local team. The club's owner, Mr Weaver, is a powerful man in the town, and although not stated as such, it is signalled that he may be gay. His middle-aged wife takes an interest in the players he signs, often asking them around for afternoon tea in her husband's absence. Machin declines her advances and is living in lodgings with a widow and her two children. The widow is miserable, frustrated and eventually ill. They start a relationship, but it is unsatisfactory and Machin, trapped (and well-paid) as a popular local sportsman, eventually loses the woman and her children. The remorseless nature of everyday life for many people is stressed.

Anderson cast Richard Harris as Machin. He was perfect for the part, not least because as a teenager he played rugby for Garryowen, in Ireland. After which he caught the acting bug, appearing on stage in *A View from the Bridge* (with Mary Ure) and as part of Joan Littlewood's company in Lionel Bart's *Fings Ain't Wot They Used T'Be*. There were films too, notably *A Terrible Beauty* (1960), as an IRA man with Robert Mitchum and *The Long and the Short and the Tall* (1961), which Anderson had directed on stage.

He is supported by Alan Badel, giving a creepy performance as Weaver, and Rachel Roberts, excellent as the widow. Other parts are played by William Hartnell, Colin Blakely, Arthur Lowe, and Leonard Rossiter, all of whom are extraordinarily good.

A brilliantly-realized vision of the industrial north, it failed at the box office in February 1963. With a running time of 2 hours and 14 minutes it was on the long side and had a complex plot told in flashbacks. The film also came with a score from Roberto Gerhard that was not likely to appeal to mass audiences. A pupil of Arnold Schoenberg in the 20s and 30s, Gerhard was an innovative modern composer and pioneer of electronic music, whose soundtrack for this remained unreleased. Like Denys Coop's photography and Peter Taylor's editing, it was superb. The critics lavished praise: Rachel Roberts won a BAFTA to match the one she already had for *Saturday Night and Sunday Morning* and Harris won Best Actor at Cannes. It hardly mattered. John Davis, the head man at Rank, deemed the film 'squalid' and announced the company would not commission any more Kitchen Sink projects.

The truth was, by mid-1963, most of the major Kitchen Sink/ angry young man books and plays had either been committed to film, or deemed unworkable as such. But there was a sense that the times were changing after *Please, Please Me* reached No 2 in the UK pop charts and James Bond wowed US audiences. Black and white social realism, no matter how well done, suddenly seemed slightly passé. As far as cinematic adaptations went, this affected Storey's subsequent career. His second novel, *Flight into Camden* (1961), was supposed to be filmed with Glenda Jackson, only for the funding to dry up. His third, *Radcliffe* (1963), which Kenneth Halliwell was reading the night he murdered Joe Orton, centred on two men in an obsessive, controlling relationship and was probably too bold a study to be considered for any type of adaptation. Later works by him included the plays *In Celebration* (1969) and *Home* (1970), both of which Lindsay Anderson directed on the stage, and the novels *Pasmore* (1972) and *Saville* (1976), which both won literary prizes. Lindsay Anderson directed a film adaptation of *In Celebration* too, in 1975, but this is by far the least-known of his feature films.

Despite Rank's views, Keith Waterhouse's 1959 novel *Billy Liar*, which followed *This Sporting Life* into cinemas in August 1963, was a considerable success, possibly because audiences warmed to it as a comedy, rather than an exercise in stark realism. A *Daily Mirror* journalist from Hunslet, near Leeds, Waterhouse had earlier published *There is a Happy Land*, which like Cooper's *Scenes from Provincial Life*, Wain's *The Contenders* and Sillitoe's *Key to the Door*, was set in the 30s, a period often returned to by Kitchen Sink writers.

Response to *Billy Liar* was enthusiastic, resulting in a stage version being written by Waterhouse and his childhood friend and fellow writer, Willis Hall. It ran at the Cambridge Theatre, London from September 1960 with Albert Finney in the title role of Billy Fisher, and was directed by Lindsay Anderson.

Fisher is a day-dreamer. A would-be writer and lyricist, who cannot come to terms with reality and isn't brave enough to make a break and head for a better life elsewhere. He has multiple girlfriends and entertains violent fantasies about ridding himself of his enemies. The plot allows for a lot of clowning, some of which remains quite funny. Finney handed over the stage role to Tom Courtenay in June 1961 and a film adaptation became possible via producer Joseph Janni, with John Schlesinger directing, after their earlier partnership on *A Kind of Loving* (which Waterhouse and Hall wrote) produced a commercial and critical hit.

Courtenay and Mona Washbourne (playing Fisher's mother) were retained from the stage version. Wilfred Pickles was cast as Fisher's father. A hugely influential radio and stage actor stage from the 30s onward, he projected a good-natured and shrewd northern persona, to the extent that – for propaganda reasons – he was utilised as a BBC news reader during the Second World War. Rodney Bewes, as Arthur Crabtree, Fisher's friend, and Leonard Rossiter, as Emanuel Shadrack, his employer, give memorable support. The film is notable for co-starring Julie Christie as the third and most sophisticated of Fisher's girlfriends.

Much of it was filmed in and around Bradford and Leeds, with excellent camerawork by Denys Coop. Domestic audiences liked it, as did critics, though those in the US were quick to point out similarities to James Thurber's *The Secret Life of Walter Mitty*. It was nominated for six BAFTAs, with an immense amount of praise being – rightly – lavished on Christie. Onscreen for 12 minutes, she represents the possibilities of a glamorous life elsewhere, either down south or abroad, that Fisher ultimately doesn't have the confidence to pursue. Only 23 when she filmed *Billy Liar*, Christie soon became an international star after the impact she made in this role.

But the film belongs to Courtenay, whose performance seems to have chimed with something deep in the psyche of the film's audience. Which wasn't surprising: most people have memories of adolescent awkwardness, and everyone can reminisce about paths that weren't, but should have been, taken. Billy Fisher ultimately doesn't follow through on anything, and remains a mediocrity, but he is funny as a teenager, and on that basis, we indulge him. In the years that followed the character became something of an institution. There was a London Weekend TV series (1973, with Jeff Rawle and a Peter Skellern title theme) and a 1974 musical, scripted by Dick Clement and Ian La Frenais, with Michael Crawford, Elaine Paige and a John Barry score. Waterhouse wrote a sequel *Billy Liar on the Moon* (1975), with Fisher stuck in a dead-end local government job in a drab town and still prone to elaborate fantasies in his mid-thirties; there was even a 1979 US TV series with Steve Guttenberg.

The book, and its spin-offs, became Waterhouse's pension. Which was probably a good thing, as like many of the other Kitchen Sink writers his subsequent novels were somewhat less successful. He remained in some demand, though, for film and TV scripts and as such was a major beneficiary of the success that followed *Look Back in Anger* and *Saturday Night and Sunday Morning*. Both films encouraged producers to head north in search of new subject matter, and as a result existing writers, like Waterhouse and Hall, were often brought in to add authenticity to the screenplay.

One example of this came with *Whistle Down the Wind*, based on a 1958 novel by Mary Hayley Bell. Set on a farm in rural

England, its plot follows a group of children who find a stranger in a barn, and think he is Jesus. It transpires he is an escaped murderer, allowing the narrative to explore the issues of capital punishment, religious belief and the loss of innocence. A rather fey allegory, Bell was also Mrs John Mills and the film rights were duly purchased by Allied Film Makers, a company founded in late 1959 to make more realistic films. With Bryan Forbes directing, Richard Attenborough producing and Rank distributing, Waterhouse and Hall were hired to provide a script. The action was switched to the north, with much of it filmed in and around Clitheroe and Burnley.

Alan Bates played the convict on the run who is mistaken for Christ, Hayley Mills was the oldest of the children and Bernard Lee her father. Somewhat more robust than the novel, it was a box office hit when released in July 1961, being nominated for 4 BAFTAs. Unusually, the main title theme by Malcolm Arnold, a slightly jazzy instrumental piece, came out as a single on Decca, credited to The Wayfarers. But as was the case elsewhere, no soundtrack album emerged, despite Arnold's immense popularity at the time. (Among other things, he did *Bridge on the River Kwai*.) The decision to cast Bates in a leading role paid off and the scale of the success pointed to the popularity of the Kitchen Sink style.

Waterhouse and Hall were in rather more familiar territory for *A Kind of Loving*, the 1960 novel by Stan Barstow. In this case the producer was Joseph Janni who embraced the genre after success with well-made entertainments like *A Town Like Alice* and *The Captain's Table*. For reasons that aren't clear, Barstow didn't do the script, Waterhouse and Hall being brought in to adapt the book. Janni hired John Schlesinger to direct, impressed by his transport documentary *Terminus* which achieved the rare distinction of being nominated for both a BAFTA and an Academy Award.

Barstow set his novel in a large Yorkshire town, either Wakefield or Leeds, and centred it on the relationship between a young couple (Vic and Ingrid) after they are obliged to get married due to an unexpected pregnancy. Without a place of their own, they end up staying with the girl's mother, which causes considerable stress.

A drama about life in the pre-contraceptive pill/pre-abortion era, and the unacceptable social pressures that arise from that, this is handled in a very realistic and down to earth fashion. There are none of the melodramatic scenes and shouting matches encountered with Osborne, Braine and Sillitoe.

Vic and Ingrid, are played by Alan Bates and June Ritchie respectively. Ritchie, 21, was straight out of RADA; for Bates this was a second consecutive leading role that established him as a major actor. Thora Hird is marvellous as the mother-in-law. Filmed in various locations in Lancashire – Blackburn, Bolton, Oldham and Preston – it was released in April 1962. *A Kind of Loving* won popular and critical acclaim in the UK and it also won top prize, the Golden Bear, at the Berlin film festival. The music, by Ron Grainer, also managed to get a commercial release, appearing on a Fontana single. Done in a quasi-trad jazz style, like his main title theme for *Steptoe and Son*, it had a sad and melancholy feel, matching the film perfectly.

A Kind of Loving could have been written a hundred years earlier, which is probably why it remains popular. It describes personal circumstances (a young couple struggling because they don't have a place of their own) which still have resonance today. Barstow wrote a sequel, *The Watchers on the Shore* (1966) in which Vic leaves Ingrid, and moves to London where he meets an actress. It was broadcast as a BBC radio play in 1971. Another novel, *A Raging Calm* (1968) became a 1974 Granada TV series with Alan Badel, after which Barstow reached back to the 30s adapting Winifred Holtby's *South Riding* for Yorkshire TV. But, as with the adventures of Joe Lampton and Billy Fisher, *A Kind of Loving* remained the work for which he was best known, being remade by Granada as a 10-part series in 1982, with Joanne Whalley as Ingrid.

Angry young men who reached university featured in both *Hurry on Down* and *Lucky Jim*. Jimmy Porter has also been there too, though not a prestigious one – 'not even redbrick, but white tile' as his wife, Alison says. A 1960 play, *The Tinker*, by Laurence Dobie and Robert Sloman, looked closer at this phenomenon, managing a decent run at the Comedy Theatre. Edward Judd, who had been in Lindsay Anderson's stage version of *The Long and the Short and the Tall*, was in the leading role. He played Harry Brown, a working-class undergraduate at a provincial university in the Midlands with strong, class-based views a la Colin Smith.

Although not a great success, a film version followed in 1962 starring Ian McShane, who was 20, and hadn't even graduated from RADA at the point he was cast. But, in terms of credibility, he ticked a lot of angry young man/Kitchen Sink boxes. He was born in Blackburn and his father – Harry McShane – had been a professional footballer at Manchester United under Matt Busby, winning a League Championship medal in 1952. You couldn't get more authentic than that. His co-stars were Samantha Eggar, 23, and John Hurt, 22. It was a first feature film for all of them.

Filmed in Lincoln, the action follows Harry (Ian McShane), his girlfriend Josie (Eggar) and Phil (Hurt), a shy roommate who shares lodgings with Harry. They live a run-of-the-mill student existence until, echoing *The Browning Version*, Harry starts a relationship with a professor's wife. The cuckolded professor is not prepared to seek a divorce due to the scandal it would cause, and the possibility that it might jeopardise his getting a knighthood. Eventually, Harry and Phil get involved in a rather stupid, and dangerous, 'Rag Week' stunt. Phil gets killed, and Brown is expelled from the university. His girlfriend realises that she was never that important to him, and he goes back to 'the provinces'.

This was a Rank film, with the company firmly in the driving seat. It was produced by Betty Box, and directed by Ralph Thomas, both of whom were known for *Doctor in the House* (1954), an NHS comedy and one of the UK's biggest ever commercial hits. The task of turning *The Tinker* into a screenplay went to Nicholas Phipps, who had also worked on *Doctor in the House*, and Mordecai Richler, a serious Canadian writer, whose 1959 novel *The Apprenticeship of Duddy Kravitz* had been adapted for TV by the BBC in 1961. Despite this, whatever rough edges *The Tinker* had on stage, on screen, where it was renamed *The Wild and the Willing*, what emerged was an adequate romantic drama.

Not only were the cast very young, the music, of which there was quite a bit, was entrusted to Norrie Paramor. Paramor had produced virtually everything by Cliff Richard and the Shadows, which makes one wonder if Rank's intention with *The Wild and the Willing* was to make a film for serious teenagers (aged, say 15 to 18) who might not have wanted to spend time watching *The Young Ones* (whose target audience was 10 to 14). The music itself includes an Ian McShane single, *Harry Brown*, a weird spoken word account of the plot done in folky-jazzy-country style, with strings, and an EP by the Mike Cotton Jazzmen, one of a plethora of trad-jazz bands around then. Both were released to coincide with the film in October 1962 and although none of the records charted, the film itself seemed to receive a good reception. A very pop version of the Kitchen Sink, its overall approach and emphasis on youth and music, was possibly indicative of how things were changing.

The gradual expansion of higher education to embrace working-class students, and the increase in social mobility that resulted from this, were also a key feature of the first episode of *Coronation Street*. This introduced viewers to Ken Barlow, who, having reached academia and met seriously middle-class people for the first time, finds his own background, and parents, something of an embarrassment.

The series was created by Tony Warren, an actor from Pendlebury, Lancashire. Inspired by the nineteenth-century industrial environment of Salford, he came up with the idea of setting all the action in a single street of tiny houses, with a corner shop at one end and a public house at the other. Granada TV, based in a brand-new office building in Quay Street, Manchester were interested, and in 1960 commissioned 13 episodes from him. He was 24 years old at the time.

The first episode – introducing Barlow and his class consciousness – was broadcast on 9th December 1960. The critics were unconvinced, and for a week or two there were doubts that the series would be extended beyond its initial run. But viewers loved it, identifying immediately with the ordinary, matter-of-fact characters, and the use of local dialect throughout the script. This last point should not be underestimated, given the omnipresence then of 'Received Pronunciation' (RP) throughout the media. *Coronation Street* gave millions of viewers a simple, universal setting that they could relate to.

But it was not *quite* the first to do so. On radio the BBC had run *Mrs Dale's Diary* from 1948 and *The Archers*, from 1950; and on TV *The Grove Family*, from 1954. All were lengthy series, with ensemble casts and micro-drama plots. *The Grove Family* even had theme music by Eric Spear, later composer of the *Coronation Street* theme music. All were Home Counties, middle class and aspirational. Until Warren got the green light from Granada no one, apparently, had thought of doing likewise within a northern, working-class milieu.

It undoubtedly helped that there was a tradition of locally-made and distributed films in the north, with one studio, Mancunian Films, functioning from the 30s through to the mid-50s, making popular features with leading variety and music hall figures like George Formby, Frank Randle, Jimmy Clitheroe and Sandy Powell. One of these, *Cup-Tie Honeymoon* (1948), starred Powell with a youthful Pat Phoenix as a co-star. It wasn't that big a step, then, to do something similar, albeit not comedic, on TV. And of course, the network of professional repertory theatres that existed, as can be seen from the work of Jack Popplewell, provided a ready supply of actors for any such project.

With one exception, the leading roles in *Coronation Street* went to actors and actresses that northern and provincial audiences would have been familiar with. The exception was Ken Barlow, played by William Roache, a privately-educated former Captain in the Royal Welch Fusiliers. Otherwise in the early years, among those appearing on a nightly basis was Bryan Mosley, whose CV later included supporting roles in a run of films from *This Sporting Life* to *Charlie Bubbles* to *Get Carter*. Pat Phoenix had two extended periods playing Elsie Tanner from 1960, her last appearance being in 1984 – but she had been memorable as a prostitute in 1962's *The L-Shaped Room*. Also, Kenneth Cope, Jed Stone in 'Corrie', was one of the company in Shelagh Delaney's second play, *The Lion in Love* and Arthur Lowe, left 'The Street' for the stage run of *Inadmissible Evidence* and a succession of bigger projects. The cast also had more female roles than male: of those appearing in 100 or more episodes in its first five years, the majority were women.

Women were also prominent behind the camera, directing many episodes (notably Pauline Shaw, who produced the 1982 Granada remake of *A Kind of Loving*) and writing them too, particularly Adele Rose, who later worked on *Z-Cars*. In the circumstances it was hardly surprising that by March 1961 *Coronation Street* was the most widely viewed programme in the UK, with 75 per cent of those who had a TV tuning in, a level of popularity that rivalled Rank's *Doctor in the House* seven years earlier.

The series is still running, with Roache, now a nonagenarian, the only survivor of the original cast. The theme music *Lancashire Blues*, survives too. Eric Spear's quasi trad-jazz piece was composed in two weeks before the first episode's transmission, for a payment of £6 (about £300 today) and remains probably the best-ever evocation of the north of England at that time. Amazingly, despite the immense popularity of the programme, his version was never released, the best that could be managed being its appearance (as re-recorded by Charles Blackwell) on *Coronation Street Monologue*, the B-side of a June 1962 Pat Phoenix single. Akin to a stream of consciousness poem, with lyrics consisting of phrases and statements that emphasise the homely and supportive nature of a traditional working-class environment, it makes for a fascinating comparison with *Beasley Street*, John Cooper Clarke's fierce observation about the destruction of the same communities some twenty years later.

None of which should suggest that the north consisted mainly of *Coronation Street*-type locations. After 1945 most of the major cities and towns outside London had bomb-damaged areas that required rebuilding together with extensive (and yet to be completed) slum clearance programmes that had been commenced pre-war. Two major strategies were pursued to address this: a government programme of building new towns and local authority-built housing estates, many of them in 'overspill' areas outside their boundaries.

One example of this was Liverpool Corporation's development of Kirkby, whose population rose from a few hundred in the 30s to 60,000 three decades later. It was a process that was not without its issues. Construction of the housing took place at a much greater speed than the provision of community facilities and shops, and many of those who moved there came from the poorest inner-city areas of Liverpool. The idea of setting a police drama TV series in the area came from Troy Kennedy Martin, who wrote scripts for the BBC. Named Z-Cars, after the radio call signs used by the police patrol vehicles, that were heavily featured, it was set in Newtown, a fictional town based on Kirkby.

As with Coronation Street, Z-Cars had clear antecedents. Regional crime dramas had become more common through the 50s and beyond, with films like Hell is a City (1960) and Payroll (1961) being particularly popular. The former was set (and filmed) in Manchester and was based on a novel by Lancashire writer Maurice Procter, who had originally been a local police officer. Payroll was filmed in Gateshead and Newcastle and had a marvellous jazz-instrumental main title theme, by Reg Owen and his Orchestra, that came out as a single on Palette. Billie Whitelaw, a key Kitchen Sink actress, appeared in both films, whilst Tom Bell, from Liverpool and a rising figure in what was being dubbed the British New Wave, co-starred in Payroll.

The first episode of Z-Cars appeared in January 1962 and had a noticeably harder, and more realistic feel to it compared with the somewhat gentler approach of Dixon of Dock Green, the most popular TV police drama up till that time. A resolutely male affair, it was directed by John McGrath, from Birkenhead and later a noted exponent of Joan Littlewood-style theatre. The cast was led by Stratford Johns, best known at that time for having appeared in some of Lindsay Anderson's productions at the Royal Court Theatre. The supporting actors – Frank Windsor, Joseph Brady, James Ellis, Brian Blessed and Robert Keegan – were all regulars in TV plays and provincial repertory theatre.

It was hugely popular, and ran until 1978, with a major rejig in 1966 when Johns and Windsor left to star in another TV police drama series, *Softly, Softly*. Interestingly, Adele Rose arrived the same year as a regular scriptwriter from *Coronation Street*. Perhaps its most remarkable legacy was the *Theme from Z-Cars*, which appeared as a single on the Piccadilly label a month after the first episode went out. It was performed by Johnny Keating, at that point a major arranger and producer for Adam Faith and Eden Kane, and like Reg Owen a former sideman in the Ted Heath Big Band. The *Theme from Z-Cars* probably exceeded everyone's expectation for a tune from a cop show by climbing to No 8 in the UK charts. Musically it was an instrumental reworking of *Johnny Todd*, a traditional folk song attributed to Liverpool children, and possibly Irish in origin. Recorded by Ewan MacColl on his 1955 LP *The Singing Sailor*, it was also part of the repertoire of Protestant marching bands in Ulster and adopted, from 1963, by Everton FC as the music played at home games when their team ran onto the pitch. Like *The Big Ship Sails on the Alley-Alley-O* from *A Taste of Honey*, it is immensely evocative of that era. The success of something that was so Liverpool-centric may even have been a factor in the rise of The Beatles, namely a recognition by London-based record companies that signing an act from Liverpool was no longer a risk – it was in keeping with the mood of the time.

DON'T KNOCK THE ROCK

Films about juvenile delinquency were a feature of US cinema for many years before 1945, with *Dead End* (1937) an early example. Based on a Sidney Kingsley play and set in a milieu of slum housing, petty crime and social realism, it was a critical and commercial success and provided Humphrey Bogart, who appeared in it as a gangster, with a key role. Whilst Kingsley, and writers like him, would be expunged from Hollywood during the McCarthy years, its success proved that an appetite clearly existed for films about teenage misbehaviour, violence and poverty.

Many of these portrayed outsiders, such as the Marlon Brando biker film, *The Wild One* (1953), which remained banned in the UK up till 1967, due to its characters being enthusiastic hooligans. A particularly famous example was *Rebel Without a Cause*, with James Dean as a tortured middle-class adolescent. Released in October 1955, a month after Dean's death at the age of 24, it did astonishingly well at the box office and was nominated for three Academy Awards, two of which were for Dean's co-stars, Natalie Wood, 17 and Sal Mineo, 16. It made an equal impact in the UK from January 1956, with Dean nominated posthumously for a BAFTA.

By the mid-50s, following Dean's meteoric rise and the appearance of Elvis Presley, the US was turning out many similar, albeit less distinguished films. Some of these were musical dramas with a featured band or singer, or in some instances little more than juke box musicals with 'putting on a show' type plots. Three that enjoyed particularly high box office takings were *Rock*

Around the Clock, Don't Knock the Rock and *Rock, Rock, Rock,* all of which crossed the Atlantic in 1956. To which should be added *The Girl Can't Help It,* a full-blown satire on the music business, and its connection to organised crime, with proper actors (Jayne Mansfield, Tom Ewell, Edmond O'Brien) and brilliant musical performances (Little Richard, Eddie Cochran, Julie London, Gene Vincent), directed in perfect pop-art style by Frank Tashlin.

Understandably, UK producers sought to replicate these trends at home. Given the emphasis on youth and its rejection of social norms, some of the films that appeared overlapped with angry young men and Kitchen Sink themes, even if most of them lacked a literary origin. The first such effort came from Herbert Wilcox, an ultra-conventional but successful filmmaker. He put together *My Teenage Daughter,* a UK response to *Rebel Without a Cause,* as soon as the original started making waves in the US. Shot in and around London, it was notable for featuring Kenneth Haigh – a couple of months before he was cast in *Look Back in Anger* – as an atypical delinquent resident in Mayfair and driving a Bentley. A success on its appearance in June 1956, Wilcox decided to head to Liverpool for *These Dangerous Years,* a second take on the genre.

Written by the prolific Jack Trevor Story, this centres on the tribulations of Dave Wyman, a young singer and gang leader. Set in Dingle in the south of the city, it was made at almost the same time as *Violent Playground* and also made good use of authentic locations. Wilcox wanted Diana Dors to star, but she was in Hollywood and declined, so her role was taken by Carole Lesley, who had just finished *Woman in a Dressing Gown.* Another one of J Lee Thompson's early efforts in social realism, this was a drama about marital infidelity and was one of the big British films that year.

Frankie Vaughan, a 29-year-old Liverpudlian, was cast as Wyman in *These Dangerous Years.* With a career trajectory similar to David Storey's, the teenage Vaughan had considered becoming a boxer but opted for singing after a spell at art school. This led to bookings on the variety circuit, where he refined his act, and was advised to adopt a dandyish appearance by veteran male impersonator Hetty King.

With his top hat, cane and retro-Edwardian clothing he clicked with audiences. Vigorous, energetic, Latin-looking, he moved around a lot on stage, which at that time was generally considered bad form. He had his first hit in 1953, the year the singles chart started, with 26 more up until 1968, of which his 1956 big band version of *Green Door*, which Joe Meek engineered, was particularly fine. In many ways he was a typical early 50s phenomenon, emerging similarly attired at the same time as the Teddy Boys, and performing music in keeping with their tastes, which were for big band swing a la Ken Mackintosh and Ted Heath. The UK media, with its characteristically loose grip on teenage realities, regarded him as a rock 'n' roll singer. He wasn't, but his loud, brash style certainly provided a template for Tom Jones.

The film's plot is simple enough. After various misadventures, Vaughan's character is called up to do National Service and finds that the army reforms him. He sings three songs, including the main theme, later released as a single. As an actor he does better than one might have thought and the film seems to have been a success on its July 1957 release. This encouraged Wilcox and his partner, actress Anna Neagle, to cast Vaughan in four further films over the next two years, all of which were middlebrow comedies, with bits of music. They were sufficiently bankable to earn him a ticket to Hollywood where in 1960-1961 he made *Let's Make Love* with Marilyn Monroe and Yves Montand and replaced Elvis in *The Right Approach*, an interesting adaptation of a play by Garson Kanin, the renowned author, screenwriter and film director.

The last two films Vaughan made for Wilcox before crossing the Atlantic co-starred Anthony Newley. Famous at 17 for playing the Artful Dodger in the 1948 David Lean version of *Oliver Twist*, Newley spent the years that followed working his way up through supporting roles, embracing music in the 1955 revue *Cranks* which ran in the West End before transferring to Broadway. A considerable success, it had him appearing alongside jazz-singer Annie Ross, amidst sets designed by artist John Piper. Whilst filming for Wilcox he was offered the starring role in an adaptation of William Camp's 1958 novel *Idle on Parade*.

Forgotten now, Camp was a lesser figure among the Kitchen Sink scribes, whose first novel *Prospects of Love* (1957) had been favourably reviewed. His own background was decidedly middle-class and included a spell in the Coldstream Guards, and standing, unsuccessfully, as the Labour candidate in Solihull in the 1950 General Election. As written, *Idle on Parade* concerns an intellectual who is conscripted into the army. Adapted by John Antrobus, whose other credits included writing scripts for the *Goon Show*, the central character becomes Jeep Jackson, a rock 'n' roll singer, as the film producers Irving Allen and Albert R Broccoli milked the publicity around Elvis Presley's military service (which began in March 1958) for all it was worth. The title was duly changed to *Idol on Parade* and the tone became mercilessly comic.

At 28 Newley was too old to be a conscript, and also too old to be plausible as a rock 'n' roll singer, but he attacks his part with gusto. Sidney James puts in a brilliant performance as his agent. The farcical nature of military life is stressed, with Jackson being generally feckless and disruptive. Newley sang five songs, several of which were released with the film in March 1959. One of these, *I've Waited So Long*, reached No 3 in the UK charts, and an accompanying *Idle on Parade* EP (which contained the marvellous parody, *Sat'day Night Rock-a-Boogie*) hit No 13. It started Newley on a string of musical comedies, all of which built on his persona as a full-blown, sharply dressed wideboy, steering an amoral path through life. He also racked up ten Top 30 hits, with a penchant for reworked street slang versions of traditional nursery rhymes like *Strawberry Fair* (1960) and *Pop Goes the Weasel* (1961). Executed in an unashamed cockney accent he influenced many, not least David Bowie.

Vaughan and Newley made entertaining films, even if they had only a smidgeon of social realism. This was more than could be said about most of the UK's genuine rockers who were resolutely neutered by showbusiness and given juvenile projects. The half-dozen films made by Tommy Steele wobbled between low-budget music dramas and children's entertainments; though a war comedy, *Light up the Sky!* made with Benny Hill, was somewhat better. Terry Dene fared even worse, making one appearance in a flimsy second feature called *The Golden Disc* just before his career folded whilst Billy Fury was probably the most underused. Hailing from Dingle, Fury might almost have been one of Frankie Vaughan's gang in *These Dangerous Years*, and made his debut on TV before releasing any records, in *Strictly for the Sparrows*, an October 1958 hour-long episode of ITV *Television Playhouse*. Other cast members included Kenneth Cope and Pat Phoenix, both *Coronation Street* stalwarts a few years later, as well as Vanda Godsell, Mrs Weaver in *This Sporting Life*. One is left thinking Billy Fury could have done more, but it was not to be. Only Michael Winner's lightweight pop musical *Play it Cool* (1962) came remotely near capturing his charisma, and it was not until his cameo in *That'll Be the Day* (1973) that audiences saw him in an intelligently-scripted film.

The first attempt at featuring an exciting rock 'n' roll singer in an adult drama came with *Serious Charge*. Adapted from a Philip King play that ran at the Garrick Theatre in 1955, this was about a well-meaning, unmarried clergyman who runs a youth club. Eventually a local delinquent accuses him of sexual assault. Reckoned a daring work in its day, a film version followed. Neither Patrick McGoohan, who played the vicar on stage, nor Laurence Harvey, who was also approached, were available and the leading role went to Anthony Quayle, heading a completely new cast. Amongst these, playing the unstable young man who makes the allegations was Andrew Ray, who later replaced Murray Melvin in the Broadway adaptation of *A Taste of Honey*.

Terence Young directed, and with the setting switched to a New Town, the plot was expanded to include a gang of teenagers led by Cliff Richard and Jess Conrad. Both were better ages for their roles than Vaughan and Newley: Conrad 22 and Richard, 18. Born Harry Webb in Lucknow, India, Richard arrived in the UK as a child, living with his family on an overspill estate in Cheshunt, Hertfordshire, where he was bullied at school on account of having noticeably darker skin than his peers. He seems to have been brought into *Serious Charge* straight after his debut single, *Move It*, hit No 2 in the UK charts. Naturally, he sings in the film too, performing *Living Doll*, a Lionel Bart song (Bart also wrote for Vaughan, Steele and Newley) done here in noticeably rockier fashion than the version that appeared as a 45.

Released in May 1959, the film was rather uneven in tone, either because of the strictures of censorship, or due to it being an odd mix: Philip King usually did comedies (like *Sailor Beware!*) and Terence Young would later become famous directing three Bond films. The conclusion is ambiguous, as we are left wondering if Quayle's character is gay, or if it has all been a misunderstanding, given he is 'rescued' and straightened out by the young woman he eventually marries. Perhaps this was the best that could be done in the mid-50s. But Richard is a powerful presence, glowering and looking moody. For decades there has been speculation about Richard's sexuality, so it is odd, now, to watch him in a film exploring the same topic so early in his career.

Living Doll, retooled as a harmless country and western style pop song, reached No 1 in the UK and even made No 30 in the US when released in July 1959. By then Richard was acting in his second film, *Expresso Bongo*. Adapted from an April 1958 stage musical co-produced by Oscar Lewenstein and written by Wolf Mankowitz and Julian More, it took a satirical, almost farcical, look at the English rock 'n' roll scene. By way of research Mankowitz and More had explored the coffee bars and venues of Soho, observing the desperate scrabbling by teenage singers and guitarists as they sought fame, and the predatory agents who circled them. Both had prior experience they could draw on. Mankowitz's novel, *A Kid for Two Farthings*, had been filmed in 1955 and nominated for the Palme d'Or at Cannes, and More had a stage hit with *Grab Me a Gondola*, a musical comedy set at the Venice Film Festival, with a cast of anxious starlets and film producers. It ran for two years in the West End, during which time he co-wrote the theme music for the BBC TV series *Six-Five Special*.

The combination of these ingredients produced *Expresso Bongo*, a strongly plotted piece with well-drawn characters, plenty of jokes about the class system and catchy songs. The story revolves around a small-time duplicitous agent (Johnny Jackson) who discovers a virtually talentless teenager (Bongo Herbert) who eventually outwits him and moves on to better things. Starring Paul Scofield and Millicent Martin, it proved immensely popular and had a good run, through to early 1959, with a BBC TV version – showing selected scenes only – screened on 11th December 1958. An original cast LP appeared on Pye and one wonders if it didn't in some way inspire John Osborne to write *The World of Paul Slickey*, his 1959 musical satire about gossip columnists, with big-ballad singer Dennis Lotis and a scene featuring a rock 'n' roll funeral.

A film was put together by Val Guest, with Laurence Harvey replacing Scofield and Cliff Richard cast as Bongo Herbert. Much of the social comment in the original was removed (including a song *There's Nothing Wrong with British Youth Today*) with the score being smoothly recalibrated by Norrie Paramor. But enough survives. Harvey is in fantastic form as Jackson, playing him as a streetwise spieler, living on his wits and constantly hustling for his own advantage. It seems impossible that his characterisation wasn't based on Larry Parnes, manager of Tommy Steele and Billy Fury; and is so similar to the demeanour of the late Malcolm McLaren, that one assumes McLaren must have seen the film. Sylvia Syms appears as a would-be actress, reduced to performing in a strip club, and Yolande Donlan (Val Guest's wife) is the Judy Garland type fading star who prises Herbert away by pointing out that as a minor – he is under 18 – he can't be under contract to Jackson.

Richard acquits himself well in this company. His trademark Elvis imitation, backed by The Shadows, comes early on and he extracted two hits from the soundtrack, *A Voice in the Wilderness* (No 2) and an *Expresso Bongo* EP (No 14). It had dance sequences by Kenneth MacMillan, later of the Royal Ballet (who also choreographed Osborne's musical) and an awful lot of casual nudity in the strip club scenes, so much that it is a surprise to note that it was granted an A certificate on its release in December 1959. A big commercial hit, and to this day reckoned to be one of the best UK musicals, it remains far superior to later attempts at the genre like *Absolute Beginners*. Interestingly, both the stage and film versions feature the song *I Never Had it So Good* sung by Jackson. Is this where Harold MacMillan found his catchphrase for the 1959 general election?

After a success like this, you would have expected an interesting succession of follow-ups from Richard. Instead, he opted for increasingly lightweight pop musicals built around his clean-living persona: *The Young Ones* (1961), *Summer Holiday* (1963) and *Wonderful Life* (1964). These were family entertainment, with nothing left to chance. Notably, Barbara Streisand was rejected for a co-starring role in the first, which might have given it some depth. Despite critical indifference, all three were staggeringly successful with tie-in LPs and hit singles that sold in monstrous quantities, but none are as rewarding as *Serious Charge* and *Expresso Bongo*.

The only other pop singer to make a successful transition to cinema was Adam Faith. Real name Terry Nelhams, and a trainee film editor from Acton, he was short, neatly dressed, working-class, and like Anthony Newley, projected a London wide-boy persona. In November 1957 he was noticed singing with The Worried Men skiffle group at the 2i's Coffee Bar in Soho, on the night the BBC and Jack Good arrived to film the proceedings for *Six-Five Special*. The evening ended with the cast, including Chas McDevitt, Laurie London, the King Brothers, Wee Willie Harris (noted for performing in a leopard skin leotard), Jim Dale, and Mike and Bernie Winters doing an ensemble rendition of *Rockin' at The Two I's*. Faith, 17, was immediately signed by HMV as a solo singer.

By April 1959 he'd met John Barry, who introduced him to Eve Taylor, one of the more intelligent agents who smartened up his image and thought that he should concentrate on acting at least as much as singing. The following month Faith duly confirmed these ambitions in an interview in *Disc*, saying that his ultimate ambition was to become an actor or even a director, rather than remain a singer. When he finally had a hit with the John Barry produced, faux-Buddy Holly, *What Do You Want?* in October 1959, he was immediately cast in *Never Let Go*, a tough crime drama, directed by John Guillermin, and produced by Independent Artists, the same company behind *Tiger Bay*.

This had a script by Alun Falconer, who co-wrote the nervy thriller *The Man Upstairs*, which had attracted attention in 1958. *Never Let Go* starred Richard Todd and Peter Sellers. The plot is about a crooked garage owner (Sellers) who runs a racket respraying and selling on stolen cars. One day a travelling cosmetics salesman (Todd) finds that his car has vanished. The police show less interest than expected, and unable to earn any money without it, he decides to investigate.

Filmed mainly around Bayswater and Paddington, the film has fine black and white cinematography by Christopher Challis. Sellers does well in a straight role and Faith plays the leader of the teenage gang carrying out his thefts. Carol White appears as the love interest. Faith and White combined are an interesting pair, and come across well in their scenes. As a portrait of a vanished working-class culture – shabby terraced streets, small cafés and so on – the film is well done and still holds some interest today.

Importantly, this was John Barry's first ever score, and he opted for a jazzy, big band approach. The main theme – a brilliant, menacing, instrumental underpinned by his characteristic loping bass guitar – was released as a single and grazed the Top 50, no mean achievement for a piece of film music. Faith sings a version of the American Civil War anthem retitled *Johnny Comes Marching Home* which reached No 5 in the charts when re-recorded and released as a single. His acting was not entirely accomplished, but it was more than adequate. Like Tom Courtenay he had a classic bone structure, and with his stylish French college-boy hair – eschewing the Brylcreemed quiff then thought essential – his appearance was iconic.

Never Let Go was a major production, distributed by Rank and with big established stars. Faith followed it a few months later with *Beat Girl*, which was decidedly more sensational. Today it appeals either to connoisseurs of camp or nostalgia buffs. Critics remain aloof, with Halliwell's short sign-off ('Risible exposé-style melodrama') being typical. It was written by Dail Ambler, a pseudonym used by Betty Uelmen, who had adapted Elleston Trevor's novel *The Pillars of Midnight*, about a smallpox outbreak in a provincial town and *Murder in Slow Motion*, a Boileau-Narcejac suspense drama about the Le Mans motor race. The latter were established French writers: both *Les Diaboliques* and Hitchcock's *Vertigo* were based on their works. This might lead one to expect something vaguely literary in *Beat Girl*, except that under another pseudonym (Danny Spade) Uelmen also wrote pulp fiction and this is where *Beat Girl* firmly belongs.

Directed by Edmond T Gréville, it resembles something John Waters might have done three decades later (such as *Cry Baby*) without the satire or parody. We follow Jennifer, a teenage girl, as she battles with the step-mother brought home by her father, an architect with plans to build City 2000, somewhere in South America. A student at St Martin's School of Art, Jennifer also spends her time hanging out in a coffee bar with Adam Faith, Carol White, Oliver Reed, Shirley Anne Field and Peter McEnery.

A great deal of ersatz beatnik dialogue is bandied about, the teenagers go to a gig in Chislehurst caves, and, inevitably, frequent deepest Soho (albeit shot entirely on set) where there are sequences in a strip club. This is run by Christopher Lee (channelling *Dracula*) and features a performance by Pascaline, an extraordinarily explicit Haitian dancer from the Crazy Horse cabaret in Paris. Jennifer narrowly avoids becoming an exotic dancer herself – clearly a fate worse than death – and is tearfully reconciled with her father and stepmother.

Just scraping an X certificate, the film appeared in August 1960. Jennifer was played by Gillian Hills, 15, who was being promoted by Roger Vadim as the next Bardot, whilst working with Serge Gainsbourg on a parallel singing career. She looks amazing. Faith sings *Made You*, a big hit for him, and for the first time a soundtrack album, credited to John Barry, Adam Faith and Shirley Anne Field, was released, reaching No 11 in the UK album chart. *Beat Girl* wasn't great stuff, but it was grown-up entertainment after a fashion and along with *Never Let Go* it meant Faith drew the attention of serious commentators.

Most memorably, this took the form of being interviewed for half an hour in December 1960 by former Labour MP John Freeman on *Face to Face*, a highbrow BBC TV programme that probed famous personalities about their lives, backgrounds, ambitions and careers. Wedged in between Victor Gollancz and Otto Klemperer, Faith gave a good account of himself (his favourite composers were Sibelius and Dvořák, apparently, and his favourite book *The Catcher in the Rye*). This was a significant appearance: as well as being the only pop singer featured in Freeman's series, he preceded both John Osborne and Albert Finney as one of Freeman's interviewees.

As a follow-up he was due to make *Girl on a Roof*: also featuring a John Barry soundtrack, this was a BBC TV film about a pop star pursued by a female fan. In the event, Faith had a change of heart and Ray Brooks replaced him. Faith next appeared in a comedy, *What a Whopper* (1961), which yielded another hit, *The Time Has Come*, before returning to serious drama with *Mix Me a Person*. Based on a 1959 Jack Trevor Story novel, this was about a hapless delinquent, Harry Jukes, who is convicted of murdering a police officer. It appears to be an open-and-shut case and he is sentenced to death, with even his defence lawyer assuming that he is guilty.

Repeating the image cinemagoers had of him from *Never Let Go* and *Beat Girl*, Faith's character, Jukes, hangs around coffee bars and strums a guitar. US actress Anne Baxter, playing a psychiatrist, eventually proves that the real killer was an IRA gunman, taking part in their border campaign and Jukes is reprieved at the eleventh hour. Efficiently directed by Leslie Norman, who also did the film version of *The Long and the Short and the Tall*, it was filmed in and around London, with a supporting cast that included Jack MacGowran and Anthony Booth. To tie in with the release, Faith did the title theme, composed by Les Vandyke, which appeared on the B-side of his August 1962 hit *Don't That Beat All*.

Though connected with the music business beyond the 60s, in 1971 Faith was cast as the lead character in the Keith Waterhouse-Willis Hall series *Budgie* and further film roles, and some quite respectable material followed: *Stardust*, *Yesterday's Hero* and *McVicar*. For many years he toured in rep in *Alfie*, and his 1959 comments in *Disc* about wishing to concentrate on acting remain pertinent when assessing his dual career.

Delinquency, and how to deal with it, was the theme of another Leslie Norman film, *Spare the Rod*. Based on a 1954 novel by Michael Croft - who later founded the National Youth Theatre - this was set in an inner city secondary modern school. The staff battle the pupils and the local education authority in equal amounts as they strain to keep order. Corporal punishment is liberally used, much to the dismay of a new supply teacher.

With similarities to *The Blackboard Jungle* and clearly pointing toward later material like *To Sir, With Love*, this starred Max Bygraves as the enlightened supply teacher, and Donald Pleasence, doing a solid turn, as a grimly pessimistic headmaster. For anyone familiar with his later light entertainment incarnation it is surprising to see Bygraves in such material. But, for a few years he considered a career as a straight actor, leading to appearances in both this and *A Cry from the Streets*, a 1958 drama about a social worker dealing with orphaned children after their father has been hanged for the murder of their mother. Based on Elizabeth Coxhead's novel *The Friend in Need*, *A Cry from the Streets* joins *Spare the Rod* in dealing with issues that mainstream cinema tended to avoid.

Both films provide reasonably interesting drama whilst featuring London landscapes that no longer exist. *Spare the Rod* forcefully argues against corporal punishment in schools, a common practice in the UK until finally abolished in 1998. Adapting Michael Croft's book for *Spare the Rod* had been thought too difficult, with the British Board of Film Censors regarding anything criticising teachers and showing violence in classrooms as X certificate material, much as they had done with *The Blackboard Jungle*. To ensure a wider audience, *Spare the Rod* is less sensational, but it failed to get its money back when released in May 1961. Unlike Adam Faith, Bygraves stuck to music thereafter.

In both his roles Bygraves, a kind of pre-rock 'n' roll Anthony Newley, was affable and earnest. The same qualities were evident in *Some People*, filmed around Bristol in early 1962, with Ray Brooks as the main miscreant. Set in a world of coffee bars, cafés, youth club dances, teenage boys doing a 'ton-up' on their motorbikes and trebly guitar bands, you wouldn't think The Rolling Stones were less than a year around the corner when this was being filmed, so resonant is it of the 50s.

Written by John Eldridge, who earlier in his career had made documentaries with Dylan Thomas, it was sponsored by the Duke of Edinburgh Awards and filmed in colour. Brooks, sporting a neat combination of jeans and donkey jacket that would be *de rigueur* with Dexys Midnight Runners two decades later, rides about on his motor bike, until he loses his licence. A local church warden, played by Kenneth More, encourages him to form a band. The plot revolves around their rehearsing and entering a competition. There is a bit of pushback against conformism, but nothing like the amount shown by Colin Smith in *The Loneliness of the Long-Distance Runner*.

Harry H Corbett appears as Brooks's father, and as directed by Clive Donner the film provides slick entertainment. Much of it is filmed out of doors, with improvised dialogue and everything moves along at a good pace. Today, it looks like a template for the work that Donner made his reputation with a little later, notably *Here We Go Round the Mulberry Bush*. Music played an important part in selling it to a young audience, and *Some People* had a Ron Grainer score featuring The Eagles, one of several guitar groups who tried to replicate the success of The Shadows.

Carol Deene released the main title theme as a single, and it reached No 25 in the charts. The film was a big hit, though the cast went in markedly different directions after its release: Ray Brooks was later seen in *The Knack* and *Cathy Come Home*, whilst the other members of his band, David Hemmings and Frankie Dymon, had careers that diverged sharply, Hemmings to immense acclaim in Antonioni's *Blow-Up*, and Dymon to an involvement with black power activist Michael X. Overall, *Some People* got fair reviews with *Kine Weekly* declaring it 'a laughable and holding working-class mosaic'.

A similar description might also apply to Joan Littlewood's stage production *Sparrows Can't Sing*. Written by Theatre Workshop actor Stephen Lewis, its genesis lay with Frank Norman's play *Fings Ain't Wot They Used T'Be*. Norman was a highly-rated novelist, with his reputation resting on *Bang to Rights* (1958) recording his time in prison, and *Stand on Me* (1959) about his life in Soho in the mid-50s.

Fings is about a gangster, Fred Cochran, attempting a comeback. He runs a gambling den frequented by various criminals, surrounded by the flotsam and jetsam of the surrounding streets: spivs, pimps, teddy boys and girls. Norman wrote it as straight theatre with lively dialogue that mixed rhyming slang, Yiddish and Cockney in equal amounts. He took it to Littlewood, who saw its potential as an ensemble piece. With Norman's agreement, Lionel Bart provided some songs, to give it a suitably Brechtian feel, and in its final form it could almost be seen as a companion piece to *Expresso Bongo*.

It opened at the Theatre Royal, Stratford in February 1959 with Glynn Edwards (later one of the soldiers in *Zulu*) playing Cochran and a supporting cast that included James Booth (also one of the *Zulu* soldiers) and Richard Harris. By January 1960 it was in the West End, starting a two-year run with Edwards and Booth joined by Miriam Karlin, Barbara Windsor and Paddy Joyce, nephew of writer James. It was astonishingly popular. Norman's characters lament the destruction of traditional working-class communities and its replacement by something dependent on consumerism. With so many city areas being redeveloped and their populations dispersed at that time, this was a theme with immense resonance for audiences.

Bart's songs helped, too. An original cast recording appeared as an album on Decca in March 1960 and reached No 5 in the charts. Max Bygraves took a cleaned-up version of the title song to a similar position in the singles chart. There was even a second recording of the songs, on an HMV LP later that year, featuring Bart with Adam Faith, John Barry and his Orchestra, Sidney James and others. Tellingly, there was no filmed version of the play by either BBC or ITV. Given the material – prostitutes, corrupt policemen and so on – a screen adaptation of any kind was unlikely.

Littlewood, though, clearly thought a similar format could be used for an original drama set in the East End. Lewis duly provided this, and *Sparrers Can't Sing* (as it was originally spelt) opened at the Theatre Royal, Stratford in August 1960, transferring to the Aldwych Theatre in March 1961. The plot follows a sailor in the merchant navy who returns from abroad to find his home demolished and his wife bringing up a baby he knows nothing about.

Lewis's script was somewhat milder than Norman's and a film version followed, directed by Littlewood herself. James Booth played the seaman and Barbara Windsor his errant wife. Roy Kinnear and Avis Bunnage co-starred, with smaller parts taken by George Sewell, Murray Melvin, Victor Spinetti and Yootha Joyce. Much of the action is shot outdoors and the transition from the old streets (being demolished) to the new high-rise flats is evident. The finale takes place in a large 'gin-palace' pub, with the proceedings presided over by Queenie Watts – a luminous character and something like a female Daniel Farson, she ran her own drinking establishment in Poplar, and recorded a jazz album with Stan Tracey whilst acting in film and TV.

Sparrows Can't Sing all works quite successfully. Released in February 1963, both UK and US reviewers claimed the dialogue was difficult to understand, leading to subtitles being added for the US release. This may seem strange now, but in an era of cut-glass RP accents it was – possibly – understandable. It came with less music than *Fings Ain't Wot They Used T'Be*, with only the title theme (a Bart composition) getting a commercial release as a single by Barbara Windsor. *Films and Filming* regretted that it took a comic approach, which, compared with Norman's work, it did, but it seems to have done well at the box office.

The same themes – social change, modern life not being all it was cracked up to be and a nostalgia for a recently vanished past – also featured heavily in *What a Crazy World*, another Theatre Royal/Littlewood production. This began life as a November 1961 pop song written by Alan Klein and released by Joe Brown and the Bruvvers, which Klein later said had been composed whilst he was travelling on a tube train.

It was a minor hit and Brown was noticed performing it on TV by Gerry Raffles, the General Manager of Theatre Workshop and Joan Littlewood's partner. He commissioned Klein, who was 22, to write an entire musical exploring the same themes. One of the songs composed for this, *A Lay-Abouts Lament*, appeared on the B-side of Joe Brown's next single, *A Picture of You*, in April 1962, and the completed work was staged at the Theatre Royal, Stratford in October.

Critics were not overwhelmed with *The Times* stating 'this musical appears a crude and amateurish echo of *Fings Ain't Wot They Used T'Be* and *Sparrers Can't Sing*', but it was popular. Robert Stigwood wanted to arrange a West End transfer, starring Mike Sarne, but a film version was undertaken instead, directed by Michael Carreras, a mainstay of the Hammer Films production line.

As was to be expected, changes were made to the stage production, which had primarily been about the conflict between a father and son in a typical working-class family in east London. In the film both these roles were recast, Harry H Corbett playing the father and Joe Brown Alfie Hitchens, his son. Avis Bunnage remained in place as the mother, but Susan Maughan, briefly famous for her cover of the US hit *Bobby's Girl*, was brought in to play Brown's girlfriend. Michael Ripper was inserted as 'the Common Man' a Greek chorus figure playing multiple roles. Marty Wilde – decked out in the same donkey jacket and jeans outfit modelled by Ray Brooks in *Some People* – appeared as a local gang leader, Michael Goodman as Brown's younger brother, and Grazina Frame as a second love interest. Wilde was a popular rock 'n' roll singer who had moved into stage musicals and both

Goodman and Frame had Lionel Bart connections – Goodman in *Oliver* and Frame via the musical *Blitz!* which was running whilst *What a Crazy World* was being filmed.

There is a sense here of things being overtaken by events. The world explored by Bart, Norman and others was recognisably 50s; drab, black and white and with the same moral choices presented in films like *The Blue Lamp*. By mid-1963 these parameters were collapsing as The Beatles became the predominant force in UK (and then global) pop culture, and film production moved into colour. This probably explains the importing of Freddie and the Dreamers, a Manchester group firmly associated with the 'beat boom' into *What a Crazy World*, where they do one of their predictable knockabout routines whilst performing at a local dance.

But, despite the changes, what remains is still an effective piece of street theatre, and a cut above most of the pop musicals of the period. A soundtrack LP was released when the film appeared in December 1963, which included another Klein written Joe Brown hit, *Sally Ann*. But the era of Joan Littlewood producing substantial theatrical successes was coming to an end. Delaney, Norman, and Klein all owed their big break to her staging early versions of their work at the Theatre Royal, Stratford, and it is interesting to note that they all struggled to follow up on their initial impact. What is being celebrated, particularly in *Fings Ain't Wot They Used T'Be* and *What a Crazy World*, is the strength and authenticity of working-class culture and values. Politics is not a central theme, and despite what the authors (and Littlewood) may have wished, many of the working class of the east end, and other inner cities, would prove within a few years to be perfectly at home with the views of Alf Garnett and his non-fictional counterpart Enoch Powell.

Whilst working on *What a Crazy World*, Klein was also busy recording for Joe Meek, releasing two singles, including the immortal *Three Coins in the Sewer*. Meek was an important figure pre-1963, and one who had distinct appeal to film producers. Firstly, he was successful, producing 15 hit singles and EPs prior to the emergence of The Beatles, including three that reached No 1, the biggest of which, *Telstar*, did likewise in the US, an unprecedented feat for a UK act then. Secondly, he was independent: you could deal with him without becoming involved in boardroom politics. Thirdly, he owned a studio, at 304 Holloway Road in London, which implied lower recording costs. Finally, he had his own stable of artistes and could, if required, produce sufficient music to adorn a pop film at short notice.

He entered films in 1960, having by that point produced six hits and released an early album of electronic music. Independent Artists engaged him to provide a main title theme for *Linda*, a second feature being directed by Don Sharp. A teenage drama set in London and Brighton, this starred Alan Rothwell, just before he joined *Coronation Street* (where he would appear in over 200 episodes) and Carol White. We know little more about it today, all the copies of the film having been lost, but contemporary reviews were largely positive and it was released in December 1960 as the supporting film for *Saturday Night and Sunday Morning*. Meek's contribution, sung by his latest star Michael Cox, a 20-year-old from Liverpool, appeared as a single on HMV.

Three years later Meek also provided the score for two pop films featuring his protégé Heinz. The first of these, *Live it Up*, was based on 'an idea' by Harold Shampan, a Tin Pan Alley-type figure involved with Billy Fury's *Play it Cool* and a slew of lesser musicals. The 'idea' seems to have been to build a film around a quartet of GPO messenger boys as they get a group together.

Heinz, naturally, leads the band which includes David Hemmings and Steve Marriott, later of Small Faces fame. Jennifer Moss, another *Coronation Street* actress appears too, and was recording for Meek at this point as were others we encounter, notably Gene Vincent. Kenny Ball and his Jazzmen were brought in to give it a bit of additional selling power, even though trad-jazz was expiring by this point as a commercial force. They are seen performing a bowdlerized version of Mozart's *Rondo*, which reached No 24 in the UK charts. Some of the dramatic interplay between Heinz, Hemmings, Marriott, Moss and John Pike (the fourth band member) is good, but they are collectively wasted on such a flimsy plot. Still, it did quite well on its release in November 1963. There was a Heinz *Live it Up* EP which sold well and a Joe Meek-assembled soundtrack album.

A month later Meek and Heinz were back with *Farewell Performance*, a slightly weightier affair about a murdered pop star. Harold Shampan was involved with this too, as 'music associate' and David Kernan, who appeared in *Mix Me a Person*, as well as being one of the regulars on the TV satire show *That was the Week that Was*, played the pop star. Meek supplied Heinz and The Tornadoes (who perform their hit *Ice Cream Man*) but otherwise, we know little about it. After being distributed around cinemas by Rank, copies were left in a vault somewhere, and subsequently went missing. All that survive are a couple of tracks of music that made it out onto vinyl and some lobby cards. Like *Linda*, it is regarded as a 'lost' film by the British Film Institute, with only a faint chance of being recovered, presumably at a car boot sale or house clearance.

The angst experienced by teenagers, and their appetite for films crowded out with bands and singers, was met in its simplest form by a string of pop musicals with almost zero plot. The best of these, *It's Trad, Dad!* appeared in March 1962 and was a decidedly trans-Atlantic affair, being produced by Milton Subotsky, the man behind *Disc Jockey Jamboree* and *Rock, Rock, Rock*. Arriving in the UK in 1960, he quickly became a panellist on *Juke Box Jury* prior to forming Amicus Productions. *It's Trad, Dad!* was their first film.

The script, by Subotsky, exists solely for the purpose of stringing together as many different acts as possible, and is a repetition of the kids-putting-on-a-show-whilst-battling-squares plot that went back at least as far as the 1939 Judy Garland-Mickey Rooney musical *Babes in Arms*. In this instance teenagers, led by pop singers Helen Shapiro and Craig Douglas, fight the local mayor after he has turned off the jukebox in their local café. They drum up support by touring clubs and lobbying DJs. Eventually the show happens, the mayor repents and everyone enjoys the music.

Where it scores, and repays viewing, is in the handling of the musical sequences by director Richard Lester. Lester had worked

with The Goons, directing Spike Milligan and Peter Sellers in the
1956 TV series *A Show Called Fred*, and in a 1959 short, *The Running
Jumping & Standing Still Film* (co-directed with Sellers), which was
nominated for an Academy Award. Lester had also completed
a music documentary, *The Sound of Jazz*, with drummer Tony
Kinsey. Consequently, the editing and camera angles are fresh
and the staging inventive, particularly during two numbers by
The Temperance Seven. A group of art school students (there were
actually eight of them, sometimes nine) The Temperance Seven
played antique jazz, dressed like it was 1925 and were popular on
radio and stage, where their work included appearances on *The
Goon Show* too. Finally, Derrick Guyler, used in *It's Trad, Dad!* as
a narrator to explicate the non-existent plot, had also appeared on
the celebrated comedy programme.

What emerges is a slightly surreal, edgy collection of early pop
videos. Gene Vincent is particularly fine, and even the Brook
Brothers are interesting, coming across like a proto-Wham. The
film fits in the major UK trad-jazz acts – Chris Barber (with vocalist
Otillie Patterson), Acker Bilk, Kenny Ball and Terry Lightfoot – at
exactly the point that music was peaking. The various US artists
are done in a less interesting fashion and it may be that their slots
were filmed elsewhere and edited in later.

It was a huge hit, and a soundtrack LP, on EMI Columbia, did
just as well, reaching No 3 in the charts. A year later, Subotsky and
Amicus followed it up with *Just for Fun*, a vaguely satirical effort
with a slightly firmer plot. The premise is that UK teenagers have
been given the vote, a general election is being held and, whilst
seeking re-election, the Prime Minister cuts airtime devoted to pop
music. Outraged teenagers – led by singer Mark Wynter – form
their own political party and fight it out with the establishment.

An attempt to emulate the success of *It's Trad, Dad!*, *Just for Fun*
was made in colour and the Prime Minister was played by Richard
Vernon. Trained at the Central School of Speech and Drama,
Vernon specialised in authority figures in his character acting
career and filmed his scenes whilst appearing in Henry Livings's
Kelly's Eye at the Royal Court with Nicol Williamson, Sarah Miles

and Arthur Lowe. (He also starred in the 1961 TV series *Stranger on the Shore* the theme music for which provided Acker Bilk with a colossal transatlantic hit.) Other acting roles are limited, with everything going from one comic scene and song to another via DJs and clubs, in much the same way as Lester's film. 28-year-old Gordon Flemyng, coming in from TV, directed and helped by the young Nicolas Roeg's cinematography, the action zips along.

Most of the performers were under contract to Decca, and to coincide with the films February 1963 release a soundtrack album appeared, put together by Dick Rowe. It reached No 20 and included contributions by Brian Poole and the Tremeloes, the band he famously signed in preference to The Beatles. Had he opted for Epstein's group, this would have been their big screen debut, presumably with Pete Best still on drums. As we now know events took a rather different turn.

Forgotten today, *Just for Fun* had a curious afterlife via Screaming Lord Sutch, who also recorded for Decca, whilst being produced by Joe Meek. He isn't in the film, but after its commercial success he launched his own Teenage Party in August 1963. Starting at Stratford-upon-Avon in the by-election caused by John Profumo's resignation, he was still standing for Parliament, without success, in 1997, representing an early and raucous version of the anti-establishment, 'anti-politician'.

The pop revue headed for an unlamented oblivion with *Every Day's a Holiday* (1964), *Be My Guest* and *Dateline Diamonds* (both 1965). The former was directed by James Hill, and represented something of a comedown for a man who'd won an Academy Award a few years earlier for *Giuseppina*. Ron Moody, Mike Sarne and Grazina Frame appear with music by Freddie and the Dreamers and Liverpool band The Mojos. It's lively enough with photography by Nicolas Roeg, and was praised, but is scarcely essential viewing. The latter two were produced by Harold Shampan. *Be My Guest* reunited Steve Marriott and David Hemmings in a caper about a seaside hotel in Brighton, whilst *Dateline Diamonds* had Marriott, by now lead singer and guitarist in The Small Faces, appearing alongside many other acts in a drama partially filmed on board the pirate radio ship Radio London. Jeremy Summers directed, having previously worked with Tony Hancock on *The Punch and Judy Man*.

It only remains to record the journey that UK TV took during this period as it came to terms with the rise of the teenager. When it first appeared, rock 'n' roll was seen as something non-serious, mainly for children, and the approach to it adopted by *Crackerjack!* would be typical. A BBC comedy and quiz programme that ran from 1955, this went out at 5.15 pm ('tea time') and had a music slot where acts would perform or mime their latest hit in front of a pre-adolescent audience. ITV put out *Cool for Cats* a year later, on which records were played, commented on, and interpreted by a team of dancers. Aimed at teenagers, though hardly any over 16 would have watched, each episode lasted only a quarter of an hour.

Slightly better, and more fondly remembered, was *Six-Five Special*, which appeared in February 1957 on the BBC. Most of the episodes were produced by Jack Good, an Oxford graduate and former actor, and managed to convey a degree of excitement that was lacking elsewhere. It was sufficiently popular to generate a film version, released in March 1958. In an echo of the plot lines of so many Kitchen Sink and angry young men dramas, this was set on a train going to London, where one of the passengers is a young woman heading south to seek stardom. Various people perform songs, and its pleasant enough. But this is showbiz, not rock 'n' roll. Some of the material manages to be unintentionally weird, including Jim Dale doing *Train Kept A-Rollin'*, later Led Zeppelin's set opener. Also on board are Mike and Bernie Winters, regulars in the TV show, where the most commonly featured acts were Dale (often as presenter), and band leaders Ted Heath and Humphrey Lyttleton.

Which is why Jack Good decided to switch channels. Between 1958 and 1960 he did three ITV series, *Oh Boy!*, *Boy Meets Girls* and *Wham!!*, concentrating on the music and avoiding the BBC's avuncular public service ethos. All the major figures from the early years of British rock 'n' roll were featured – Vince Taylor,

Billy Fury, Cliff Richard, Marty Wilde, Adam Faith, Johnny Kidd, Joe Brown – as well as some of the Americans, notably Gene Vincent and Eddie Cochran during their last, fateful tour. Then, as a record producer, he did the Billy Fury albums *Billy Fury* and *The Sound of Fury*. The second of these was an astonishing effort, an authentic, completely self-written set that was years ahead of the field at the time. It was also popular, reaching No 18 in the nascent album charts. Another Good credit was the 1962 release *R&B from the Marquee*, by Alexis Korner's Blues Incorporated, the first British electric blues album. Throughout this period, he also wrote a weekly column for *Disc*, commenting intelligently on the music scene, which, like Adam Faith's appearance on *Face to Face*, was a sign that pop culture was now being taken seriously.

By the time Merseybeat made its critical impact Good was in the US, and TV had taken a huge step forward in the way it presented pop music, moving on from rival panel shows like *Juke Box Jury* (BBC) and *Thank Your Lucky Stars* (ITV). *Ready Steady Go!* went on the air in August 1963: informal and youth-orientated, it looked fabulous with set design and graphics that echoed much of the Pop Art of the period. The BBC responded in January 1964 with *Top of the Pops*, broadcast from the old Mancunian Films studio, presumably on the basis that many of the new chart acts at that point were either from Manchester or Liverpool. It finally went down to London in 1966.

This completed pop's journey from the Kitchen Sink to Swinging London. The best films built around this subject combined vibrancy with respect for the music, the latter not always a feature of mainstream cinema. For once, teenagers were being taken seriously and not patronised. Discounting the clean young men in suits who were centre stage in *It's Trad, Dad!* and *Just for Fun*, this was the era of Newley, Brown, Klein, Faith and Marriott. Their sarcastic, working-class demeanour, marked them out as angry young men too, even if it wasn't as extreme as that paraded by Tom Courtenay and James Bolam in *The Loneliness of the Long-Distance Runner*.

PUNCH AND JUDY MEN

Challenging convention and defying the status quo weren't attributes solely confined to serious drama and literature. Comedy took a different turn in the 50s too, becoming much sharper and less restrained.

Before this it had been heavily class-based, with an almost hermetically-sealed barrier separating the working-class comedy of Max Miller, Sandy Brown and Frank Randle from the genteel middle-class comedy found on stage and in many films. Both types revolved around the day-to-day tribulations of their characters, within the parameters of their respective social classes, and although many of the situations and assumptions involved difficulties with the authorities, in neither case were entire institutions sent up and mocked.

The war changed this. Many regarded the conduct of the UK's political class prior to 1939, particularly the appeasement of dictators, and the subsequent record of the British officer class, presiding over a string of defeats between 1939 and 1942, as risible. After 1945 writers, actors and comedians emerged who had been in the forces during the conflict and were happy to debunk areas of society previously considered sacred.

Consequently, there were novels, plays, radio shows and films that strongly questioned how heroic life in the army had actually been during the war, many of which used comedy to make a point. Other targets were foreign policy, colonial issues, industrial relations, academia and petty small-town bureaucracy, before finally reaching a crescendo with the full-blown state of the nation critique provided by the 60s satire boom. Two figures were important to this process: Tony Hancock and Peter Sellers. Both served in the RAF and had done stand-up routines between semi-nude floorshows at the Windmill Theatre, Soho before graduating to BBC Radio.

Hancock became a household name with *Hancock's Half Hour*, a weekly series that transitioned successfully to TV in 1956 and ran until 1961. Written by Alan Simpson and Ray Galton, it avoided the traditional quick-fire jokes and knowing patter format of radio comedy, replacing it with carefully written situations, commenting on everyday events. Expertly played by an ensemble cast including Hattie Jacques, Kenneth Williams and Sidney James, it attracted an immense audience.

This remained so even after Hancock discarded his co-stars, and reflected the fascination listeners had for his character. Fatalistic, unsuccessful, living in reduced circumstances amongst people he feels are his social inferiors, the comedy here arises in how he tries to maintain his pretensions only to see them flattened, time after time. In some ways it provided the public with a prism through which they could view the UK's class system and Hancock may have been helped in his ability to convey this by having been to public school. Importantly he developed the persona of the little man, the shabby failure, wearing slightly obsolete 'respectable clothing' from a recently bygone era (such as a homburg hat) who proclaims that he lives in East Cheam, a place that doesn't exist and was presumably one of the dreary, semi-industrial suburbs then found just to the west of Croydon.

The scripts had a literary feel, and Hancock's importance in the zeitgeist was reflected in his appearance on *Face to Face*, the intellectual chat show that had also welcomed Adam Faith. Such was the impact of Hancock at the time, selected episodes of his show were kept available by the BBC for broadcasting in the aftermath of a nuclear attack, when it was expected that they might be useful in raising morale.

Peter Sellers became famous in *The Goon Show*, which ran from 1951 to 1960 and more or less started the guying of the officer class and officialdom generally. Whilst retaining some of the routines of variety comedy, it was absurd, manic, zany and occasionally improvised. Selected episodes were very inventive and the programme was interspersed with jazz and deadpan announcements, clearly setting it apart from more conventional fare. Chiefly written by Spike Milligan, it was immensely popular, spawning four films, three hit singles and a couple of hit albums. Later related examples of it included *The Telegoons*, a TV series (done with puppets), a comic satire of *Bridge on the River Kwai* (considered in very poor taste and eventually released as *Bridge on the River Wye* in 1962) where Milligan and Sellers were joined by Peter Cook and Jonathan Miller from *Beyond the Fringe*, and *How to Win an Election* (1964).

After 1960 Milligan attempted to go straight and starred in a couple of mainstream films that tried to contain his edgy persona. When these failed to take off, he concentrated on TV, becoming a considerable influence on the rise of *Monty Python* and alternative comedy. He also co-wrote a play with John Antrobus, *The Bed-Sitting Room* (1962), about the bizarre world that might exist after a nuclear war. As with most of his output, no one would claim that this was social realism.

Sellers, however, flourished as a screen actor and quickly became one of the UK's leading stars. He rarely had the same persona twice in his many appearances and was dependent to a large degree on the quality of his material. But he was clearly a comic actor of some brilliance. Once established in cinema, he appeared in adaptations of George Bernard Shaw, Marcel Pagnol, Kingsley Amis, Jean Anouilh, Vladimir Nabokov and John Mortimer, and made two films with Stanley Kubrick. Sellers won two Best Actor Academy Award nominations (for *Dr Strangelove* and his final film, *Being There*), while he was nominated five times for a BAFTA.

His first BAFTA was for *I'm Alright Jack*, a 1959 satire on UK industrial relations, directed by John Boulting and produced by his twin brother Roy. Both had been involved in the British film industry since the 30s and were left-leaning politically, John volunteering as an ambulance driver for the Republican cause in the Spanish Civil War. Their reputation grew steadily and was helped post-war by *Fame is the Spur* (1947), adapted from Howard Spring's novel about the rise and fall of a north country Labour MP, and *Brighton Rock*, an adaptation of Graham Greene's best-selling thriller. By the mid-50s they had sufficient funds and standing to embark on their own projects and did so with a series of satirical studies of British society.

The first such was *Private's Progress* which introduced the character of Stanley Windrush, who stumbles through the Second World War from one mishap to another. Surrounded by fools, skivers, and quietly corrupt superiors, the plot ends with Windrush getting arrested for supposed involvement in an art fraud. Based on a 1954 novel by Alan Hackney, Ian Carmichael played Windrush and Terry-Thomas, memorably, his commanding officer. Getting it filmed proved problematic. At the time it was sacrilege to suggest that the UK armed forces were anything less than heroic and the War Office refused to cooperate. But audiences loved it, and after its release in February 1956 it wound up being the second most popular UK film of the year, behind the Douglas Bader/Battle of Britain hagiography *Reach for the Sky*. This suggests that the British public had, on the one hand a tremendous appetite for the war, whilst also being on the other hand fully aware of its inglorious side.

From here the Boultings, Carmichael and Thomas proceeded to *Brothers in Law*, which took a similar approach to the legal profession. Taken from a novel by Henry Cecil, a county court judge who published fiction, it did well and, after their adaptation of Kingsley Amis's *Lucky Jim* (see below), they followed it with *Carlton-Browne of the F.O.*, a diplomatic farce about an obscure British colony whose valuable mineral deposits attract the attention of the US and Soviet Union. Thomas reappears as the useless upper-class civil servant Carlton-Browne, and Peter Sellers plays the colony's Prime Minister. As a comic study of British decline, it was effective and paved the way for *I'm All Right Jack*.

This celebrated satire was based on *Private Life*, Alan

Hackney's sequel to *Private's Progress* and follows Windrush, now a management consultant, as he blunders through industrial relations, nudism and crooked arms deals with an unnamed Middle Eastern country in what amounts to a full-blown critique of the nation. Carmichael and Thomas repeat their earlier characters, but the star is undoubtedly Sellers. Cast as Fred Kite, the ultimate opinionated shop steward with such overweening power that his actions ripple through the unions so that the country is brought to a halt over an otherwise obscure dispute. With a fleeting resemblance to Hitler, with his toothbrush moustache, Sellers gives an extremely sharp and well-observed performance. *I'm All Right Jack* remains an excellent comic study of the UK class system, and also highlights the essentially trivial and exploitative role the mass media have in promoting stereotypes.

Released in August 1959, it was the most successful British film of the year, with Sellers deservedly winning his BAFTA. But it proved a tricky subject to explore further. Industrial disputes increased in number through the 60s – though, contrary to how it was reported domestically, they were never as widespread as those experienced by some other countries – and the polarising effect this had on society made it difficult to extract comedy from such circumstances. It is interesting to note that as late as 1984 Alan Hackney, who like John Braine had moved sharply to the right politically, was trying – and failing – to get *I'm All Right Jack* adapted as a stage musical.

The final institution the Boultings poked fun at would be the Anglican Church in *Heavens Above!*. This was based, ironically, on an idea from Malcolm Muggeridge, a journalist, satirist and former deputy editor of *The Daily Telegraph* who, though an agnostic at this point, would convert to Catholicism in few years later.

Heavens Above! was put into production with Sellers (by then well on his way to becoming an international star), firmly centre stage with Thomas absent and Carmichael reduced to a much smaller role. The script was by Frank Harvey and John Boulting, two of the team that penned *I'm All Right Jack*. It follows the mishaps, confusion and anger caused by a uniquely good and blameless clergyman (Sellers) who, due to his having exactly the same name as an upper-class cleric (Carmichael), is accidentally assigned to a prosperous English market town that the Anglican hierarchy had intended for his namesake.

Smallwood/Sellers instigates, from the best of intentions, various situations which duly outrage local church-goers. He helps house an extended traveller family (led by Eric Sykes, with Steve Marriott as his son) who live in an abandoned railway carriage, appoints a black dustman as his churchwarden and starts his own food bank, to the chagrin of shopkeepers. Eventually the mix-up over the names is sorted out with Smallwood/Sellers being sent to a remote Scottish island and Smallwood/Carmichael finally arriving at his rightful berth. The film ends with Sellers being blasted into space in an early British moonshot, broadcasting a sermon as he goes into orbit.

Like the preceding Boulting satires, *Heavens Above* has a huge ensemble cast. It is well-made without being laugh-out-loud funny, and was one of the UK's top box office films of 1963, with Sellers' understated performance much admired. Watching it today, one wonders whether anyone now would portray the Anglican Church and well-to-do elements in a prosperous part of middle England as class-bound hypocrites. Some argue that the Boultings' critique inclines more to the political right than left, but a close viewing of their work shows it to be even-handed. The upper classes usually appear as semi-comic idiots, the middle classes are blinded by petty aspirations and the working classes are damned for skiving, being content with beer, fags and football whilst remaining uneducated. 'Good' characters crash ineffectually against these barriers. If anything, their work is a cry of despair – similar to that voiced by Sillitoe's and Storey's anti-heroes – at a society slowly going bad.

In the middle of this purple patch, between *Brothers in Law* and *Carlton-Browne of the F.O.*, the Boultings made a film adaptation of *Lucky Jim*, Kingsley Amis's 1954 novel. Amis had more strands to his career than any other writer associated with the Kitchen Sink or dubbed an angry young man. After war service, he became a lecturer at Swansea University, writing a volume of poetry in 1947, the first of several. The publication of *Lucky Jim* was a great literary event, quickly regarded as a landmark and starting point for a new type of fiction. It ran into numerous editions, was translated into many languages and its overwhelming success allowed Amis to expand into writing political essays, beginning with *Socialism and the Intellectuals* (1957, for the Fabian Society), whilst also editing science fiction anthologies. Finally, he maintained a scholarly interest in jazz, beginning a regular column on the subject in *The Observer* in April 1956.

Like John Wain's *Hurry on Down* and David Storey's *This Sporting Life*, *Lucky Jim* took its title from a popular American song, an 1896 ragtime 'mock ballad' written by Charles Horwitz and Frederick V Bowers. First released on a wax cylinder in 1904, it had been strummed on the ukulele or banjo by generations of young men. It was a humorous, and slightly wistful account by a singer who believes his rival in love, and life, to be 'luckier' than he, until a sudden twist of fate proves the opposite. The tone fits Amis's plot perfectly. This is centred on Jim Dixon, a junior lecturer at a provincial red-brick university who dislikes the petty pretentiousness of academic life and has an unsatisfactory relationship with his girlfriend.

It's a sharply observed comedy, with farcical set pieces. What makes it unusual is that Jim's situation and relationship are based on those of another writer, which was never the case in work by Osborne, Braine, Waterhouse, Sillitoe and others. Lurking in the background of *Lucky Jim* is Amis's friendship with Philip Larkin. Like Amis, Larkin was a published poet and had written a couple of novels in the 40s, one of which *Jill* (1946) concerned a student from the north of England who finds being at Oxford an awkward experience. Larkin's long-term girlfriend, Monica Jones, was Amis's model for Dixon's difficult partner, and Larkin worked at Leicester University, which is clearly a candidate for the setting of *Lucky Jim*.

In the film Ian Carmichael was cast as Dixon. An established comic actor he was adept at playing rather hapless individuals (in the 60s he would be a memorable Bertie Wooster on TV), and despite his screen demeanour came from Hull. Terry-Thomas appeared as his snobbish rival, with Hugh Griffith as a vague and slightly peculiar professor reputedly modelled on J R R Tolkien. The script, mainly written by Irish humourist Patrick Campbell, is genial rather than cutting and played for laughs. At the conclusion Dixon departs for London by train to start a new life with his new girlfriend.

The film didn't match the commercial success of the book but did well enough and remains worth watching, particularly when one understands the nuances behind the characters and dialogue. Ian Carmichael recorded and released the title song as a single on the HMV label in September 1957, and like Joe Lampton and Billy Fisher, Jim Dixon had an ongoing existence. There was a 1967 TV series, *The Further Adventures of Lucky Jim*, written by Dick Clement and Ian La Frenais, with the action shifted to Swinging London and a title theme by Alan Price. The series was remade in 1982, and as late as 2003 a new adaptation of the book appeared starring Stephen Tompkinson.

Given this level of impact, it was hardly surprising that Amis's following novel, *That Uncertain Feeling*, was also optioned for a film. Renamed *Only Two Can Play* and set in a fictionalised version of Swansea, it is about a local librarian, John Lewis, who starts an affair with a glamorous, well-connected, local woman who offers to fix a job interview for him. Lewis disapproves of such petty machinations, breaks off the affair and (in the book) takes a job in a colliery office instead. Work on the film began in 1961 with Sidney Gilliat directing and Bryan Forbes writing the script.

As in *Lucky Jim*, this is an exploration of class, and the pretensions of Welsh culture from Amis's point of view. Swansea is sent up as a prim and proper place with 'small-town' values, although it is the second largest city in Wales. Peter Sellers, giving a well-rounded, solid, performance, starred as Lewis, with Swedish actress Mai Zetterling as the object of his adultery, which remains unconsummated on screen. (The ending is changed too, with Lewis opting to work in a mobile library, rather than a colliery office.) Despite the alterations, this was a highly praised and commercially successful film when released in 1962, and the avoidance of farcical situations, a feature of *Lucky Jim*, allows for more serious explorations of character and circumstance.

It is rather remarkable that few of Amis's other novels were filmed, despite their usually healthy sales figures. *Take a Girl Like You* (1960) took a decade to reach the screen and his post-Ian Fleming James Bond novel, *Colonel Sun* (1968) still awaits an adaptation. This is puzzling, given the extent to which plots involving 007 are at a premium.

Despite the runaway success of his eponymous radio and TV series, Hancock fared markedly less well than Sellers. By 1960 his standing was so high that he was also shifting immense amounts of vinyl, with albums like *This is Hancock* and *Pieces of Hancock* enjoying lengthy chart runs. When he finally moved into cinema it was probably a bit late: many other comedians might have done so sooner, but Hancock waited until his longstanding scriptwriters, Ray Galton and Alan Simpson provided him with *The Rebel*.

For his debut in a leading role on film, Galton and Simpson built the story around the persona he had perfected: an unhappy, frustrated little man in a dead-end job, attempting to break out and make good. The opening scenes are filmed in Addiscombe (another possible candidate for East Cheam?) as Hancock, a bank clerk, awaits his morning train surrounded by dozens of identically dressed fellow commuters. Later, in an act of defiance he quits his job and takes himself off to Paris to live a bohemian life as an artist. But here too he is surrounded by identically dressed beatniks – only they are all earnestly discussing existentialism. Hancock nevertheless blends into the *milieu* and comes within touching distance of artistic immortality, feted by the art world up until the crushing revelation that it's all a case of mistaken identity and it was his flatmate who was the genius after all. His dreams shattered, at the end of the film Hancock is back in his dingy lodgings in Addiscombe.

Plenty of money was put into *The Rebel*. Shot in colour, with location shooting in Paris, it had a fine supporting cast led by George Sanders as a polished, aristocratic art dealer and Paul

Massie as the fellow bohemian flatmate with the artistic talent.
Robert Day directed, fresh from directing the Peter Sellers
comedy *Two-Way Stretch* the year before. It remains an interesting,
intermittently funny film, with Galton and Simpson's script
ridiculing the pretensions of the English middle class and sparing
no mercy with those deemed pseudo-intellectuals.

Rather as Amis mocks academia in *Lucky Jim*, a considerable
amount of fun is had at the expense of modern art and its
adherents, though whether we are supposed to be laughing at
them or just at the general absurdity of the situation isn't entirely
clear. We see Hancock execute an 'action painting' in the same
way demonstrated by William Green in a 1957 Pathé newsreel,
and compose rudimentary compositions – dubbed 'the Infantilist
School' in the film – that resemble work by the Kitchen Sink artists
Alistair Grant and John Bratby. This might seem a low blow, but
as an approach it was not without admirers: Lucian Freud was
said to regard *The Rebel* as the best film made about modern art,
presumably due to its depiction of the gallery system, and the
rogues that speculate on the futures of individual painters.

The film appeared in March 1961, and was one of that year's
most popular releases in the UK. Audiences were clearly taken
with the cheerful philistinism of Hancock's character and the
heroic failure of the simple, mistaken man 'having a go'. Hancock
was nominated for a BAFTA, but it wasn't enough for him.
Continually analysing his character, the situations it was put into
and trying to establish the point of his humour, he sacked Galton
and Simpson (and his agent Beryl Vertue, who also represented
Spike Milligan), and struck out on his own.

He hired writer and journalist Philip Oakes to help him produce
an original screenplay. Oakes had less experience than Galton and
Simpson, but was no novice and had helped devise the 1958 ABC
TV series *The Sunday Break*, which featured earnest discussions
between a teenage audience and clergy about moral issues of the
day interspersed with musical interludes from selected chart acts.
(Shades here of *Serious Charge* and *Some People*.) What emerged
from his endeavours with Hancock was *The Punch and Judy Man*,

in which Hancock finally ditches his eponymous character. Filmed in Bognor Regis, Hancock plays beach entertainer, Wally Pinner, who crosses swords with bossy local councillors. The plot also dwells on his lacklustre marriage to a socially ambitious wife. Billie Whitelaw was originally cast in this role, but dropped out to appear in the Keith Waterhouse and Willis Hall satirical stage revue *England Our England*, Sylvia Syms replacing her.

Shot in black and white, Jeremy Summers directed and familiar faces from Hancock's TV and radio series, notably John Le Mesurier and Hugh Lloyd, had prominent roles. The public was also keen, with two thousand local people volunteering as extras, an indication of how high Hancock's standing was at that time. It all moves along well enough, with brawling at a civic function turning into a food fight and an ending that has Pinner and his wife reconciled and moving to another town. But, rather like Woody Allen's *Stardust Memories*, it isn't funny. Hancock's character remains misanthropic and self-deprecatory and viewed today, the film, while adequate entertainment, is more interesting as a study of what it might have been.

There were no follow-ups, and after doing a poorly received series for ITV, Hancock tried, and failed, to get Galton and Simpson to return. Having been jettisoned so brusquely by him, they declined. The duo had already adapted the ideas that underpinned *Hancock's Half Hour* into a drama about two men, eking out a marginal existence in a battered inner city setting. Echoing the writing of Beckett and Pinter, which challenged theatrical convention just as much as Osborne's *Look Back in Anger*, when Tony Hancock made his overtures, in mid-1963, they were now enjoying renewed critical and popular acclaim with *Steptoe and Son* which began life as *The Offer*, an episode of *Comedy Playhouse* broadcast in January 1962. Directed by Duncan Wood, who had also done the Hancock TV series, it focussed on a father and son, working as rag and bone men, and their love-hate relationship against a backdrop of accumulated rubbish and general urban deprivation. Today this might seem somewhat contrived but it was a typical setting for the time: dowdy, semi-derelict inner London. Galton and Simpson apparently drew their inspiration from walking around the streets surrounding the BBC HQ in Hammersmith, with much of the external location footage being shot in north Kensington.

Watching it in the twenty-first century, it really *is* like viewing a comedic cross between *The Caretaker* and *Waiting for Godot*, particularly the latter, which after its limited run at the Arts Theatre in 1955, became a BBC Third Programme radio play in April 1960, with Patrick Magee and Wilfrid Brambell (as Estragon) and was then adapted for BBC TV in June 1961 with Jack MacGowran. Even if Galton and Simpson weren't consciously copying – or emulating – Beckett, parallels were visible and would have been recognized by their commissioning editors. They duly liked *The Offer* and agreed a series: *Steptoe and Son* was first transmitted in June 1962.

It starred Harry H Corbett and Wilfrid Brambell. No more than seven episodes were broadcast per year, and even allowing for later additions, only 57 were filmed up to 1974. Whatever the plot, the conclusion rarely varied: Harold (the son) fails in his attempts to extricate himself from his dependent relationship with Albert, his canny, grasping father. Like Hancock it was astonishingly, almost compulsively, popular. Its hopelessness appealed to millions, with massive audiences laughing at the doomed characters. TV viewing figures were immense and the theme music, *Old Ned* by Ron Grainer, became one of the most recognised bits of music of its time, up there with the *Coronation Street* theme. Albums of extracts from the shows (*Steptoe and Son, Steptoe & Son* and *More Junk*) all charted, as did a November 1963 EP *At the Palace*.

With *Hancock's Half Hour* and *Steptoe and Son* on their CV, Galton and Simpson were the hottest scriptwriters of the day. Offers came thick and fast, the first being *The Wrong Arm of the Law*, a 1963 Peter Sellers crime caper written with John Antrobus. This co-starred Lionel Jeffries and Bernard Cribbins who, with Sellers, had been in *Two-Way Stretch*, a not dissimilar film from three years earlier. The inclusion of Cribbins confirmed his burgeoning popularity at the time. Despite being from Oldham, like Anthony Newley, Alan Klein and others he projected a cockney layabout persona that he marketed successfully on vinyl with three hit singles *Hole in the Ground, Right Said Fred* and *Gossip Calypso.* He also made an album *A Combination of Cribbins*, produced by George Martin.

The *Wrong Arm of the Law* was a commercial success and their next venture, between *Steptoe* series, was *The Bargee*, designed to establish Harry H Corbett as a major star. It follows Hemel Pike (Corbett) a British Waterways Board canal boat worker as he delivers cargo between London and Birmingham with his cousin, Ronnie (Ronnie Barker). There is a great amount of jack-the-laddery involving women and the film, which was shot in colour, records (semi-accidentally) what is now a completely vanished way of life as within a few years British Waterways dropped their public delivery service.

Pike eventually accepts marriage (to Julia Foster) and unlike Harold Steptoe, is a character capable of breaking away from his circumstances. Duncan Wood directed and, as with *The Rebel*, it had music by Frank Cordell, a fascinating figure who mixed avant-garde art – he was part of the *This is Tomorrow* exhibition at the Whitechapel Gallery in 1956 – with composing film soundtracks.

Released in April 1964, *The Bargee* seems to have done reasonably well. Galton and Simpson went on to *Milligan's Wake*, a Spike Milligan TV series, and Corbett to a film version of Charles Dyer's play *Rattle of a Simple Man*. Dyer's play was a big deal in its time, enjoying a lengthy West End run with Edward Woodward from September 1962 and even managing a Broadway transfer. The film rights were purchased, the idea being that it would be the next Peter Sellers hit, only for the leading role to fall vacant when Sellers went to the US. Corbett replaced him with Diane Cilento co-starring.

As written, it is a two-hander. Corbett's character is Percy, a middle-aged, sexually naïve football supporter 'down from the North' in Soho; Diane Cilento is Cyreene, an experienced sex worker he spends the night with. Most reviews agreed that the play managed to convey the awkward situation with a degree of pathos and charm. The film however is opened out to include scenes with

Percy's mother, Thora Hird, and as directed by Muriel Box, opts for a conventional lads-on-the-town approach. It's all very gauche by today's standards, even if it had an X certificate by virtue of some strip club scenes with Ingrid Anthofer, who can be seen doing similar in *It's All Over Town* and *Life at the Top*.

To be fair, Corbett does quite well with a northern accent, but on its release in September 1964, reviews were only moderate and he found starring roles difficult to come by in the years that followed. Oddly, whilst the film remains dated (it was shot in black and white, emphasising the feeling that one is watching something that will shortly be old hat) the play continued to be popular. It was revived in 1980 with John Alderton, and even staged at the Comedy Theatre as recently as 2004 with Michelle Collins, from *EastEnders*, and Stephen Tompkinson.

Sellers, in his various guises, Hancock and Steptoe were all characters that audiences laughed at, their oddness cloaked in comedy. Whilst their popularity was immense and enduring, they were only part of a disparate spectrum of work that explored quirky, non-standard situations and individuals. An early oddity was *The Man Upstairs*, a September 1958 film made by ACT Films, the company set up by the Association of Cinematograph, Television and Allied Technicians, the trade union that represented film and TV production staff.

Noting the difficulty in getting uncommercial and marginal subjects filmed, the union established a film-making arm in 1950, subsequently completing 22 features and second features up to 1962. *The Man Upstairs* was one of the better examples of their work and was co-written by Alun Falconer (author of the *Never Let Go* script), who started out in the National Coal Board Film Unit, and probably influenced the documentary-style approach. The plot is about a man with a loaded gun (Richard Attenborough) who suffers a nervous breakdown and eventually barricades himself in his room in a dingy London boarding house. The treatment is stark – there is no music and the action takes place in 'real' time – but it retains considerable dramatic impact. Specifically, the film shows the benefit of treating mental illness sympathetically, rather than using a gung-ho approach employed by the police before the Attenborough character is taken to hospital for treatment.

Critics generally thought it a good piece of work, and, despite its subject, regarded it as part of the police thriller/suspense thriller canon. This was certainly not the case with the 1960 ATV series *The Strange World of Gurney Slade*, which presented viewers with a series of absurd and surreal situations. Limited to six episodes, it was directed by Alan Tarrant who, like Duncan Wood, had worked on the *Hancock's Half Hour* TV series, and written by Anthony Newley. Newley also plays the leading role – Gurney Slade, a comic actor – whose day-to-day life involves him moving through completely artificial environments and encountering weird people whilst being trapped inside a studio and unable to break away from 'performing'. It's an interesting example of the direction Tony Hancock's career might have taken had he been able to restrain his destructive impulses. Its inner monologues and free association dialogue meant, however, that audiences found it hard to place and its viewing figures were insufficient to justify a second series. Such diffidence did not extend to its theme music, a jazzy flute-led instrumental by Max Harris, which proved extremely popular. Released as a single it reached No 11 in the UK charts.

Newley followed it up with a stage revue co-written with Leslie Bricusse, *Stop the World – I Want to Get Off*, in which he appeared as Littlechap. Anna Quayle co-starred (later replaced by Millicent Martin) and it ran in the West End from July 1961, where it was a big critical and commercial hit, something it repeated when it transferred to Broadway. The plot retains elements of the *Gurney Slade* approach, namely a set-based examination of the main characters life and artifice, to which it added Marcel Marceau-style mime and Chaplinesque pathos. An original cast recording album reached No 8 in the UK and No 3 in the US, with its most covered song, *What Kind of Fool Am I?* becoming a transatlantic hit for Sammy Davis Jr. Having written, directed, starred, sung and mimed in the show, it was a triumph for Newley, whose influence was cited in later years by David Bowie. It is interesting to note how Newley, with his cockney persona, 'broke America' before The Beatles, albeit with very different material.

The Man Upstairs and *The Strange World of Gurney Slade* were about individuals. A notable piece with two inadequate characters came in 1957 with John Mortimer's *The Dock Brief*, a radio play that became a long-running West End success. Both early incarnations starred Michael Horden. The subject was serious, and by no means easily playable as comedy: a hopeless barrister trying (and failing) to defend a pathetic and inept murderer at a time when the death penalty was in force.

The title comes from the legal tradition of barristers who are unattached to a case awaiting instructions at the Court from unrepresented defendants, and being paid at public expense once they accept these. It must be doubtful if a murder case would ever reach the trial stage without barristers already being appointed, but that is the point of the drama here: the barrister is a long-standing failure with no work, and the defendant is undoubtedly guilty and uninterested in trying to defend himself.

In the film version Peter Sellers plays Wilfred Morgenhall, the barrister, and Richard Attenborough is Herbert Fowle, the shabby, emotionally limited murderer. Beryl Reid appears as Fowle's wife and victim. Morgenhall goes on to lose the case, Fowle is sentenced to death, and then reprieved on the grounds that his defence was completely inadequate. The film ends with the two lonely little men becoming friends and walking off together.

Pierre Rouve wrote the script: he had co-produced the Sellers film *The Millionairess* and was the screenwriter for another Sellers vehicle, *Mr Topaze* (1961) based on Marcel Pagnol's play. Rouve opted to open up the play, which was set in a cell beneath the Old Bailey, to include flashbacks, showing why Fowle murdered his wife. Director James Hill managed to dissuade Sellers from playing his part in a northern accent, and though undeniably well done, what emerges is slightly too affable in tone for the material. It was released in September 1962 to reasonable reviews and earned Attenborough, who had developed a line in seedy characters since playing Pinkie in *Brighton Rock* 14 years earlier, a BAFTA nomination.

Mortimer was a solid, rather prosaic writer, who published six novels before making his name with *The Dock Brief*. His characters – despite their oddness – are accessible and their dialogue follows normal, theatrical conventions. Very little of the conventional was found in the work of Harold Pinter, whose career makes for an interesting contrast with that of John Osborne.

Like Osborne he began in minor roles in repertory, appearing under the name of David Baron. A capable actor, like Osborne he also aspired to be a playwright, presenting his first play, *The Room*, in Bristol in 1957. Neither *The Room* or *The Birthday Party*, first staged in London the following year, made any headway. But, then, like a dripping tap whose effect seems non-existent only to result in the collapse of a ceiling many days later, there was a deluge of his work in the opening months of 1960. In short order, he had a double bill of *The Room* and *The Dumb Waiter* playing at the Royal Court Theatre, followed by *A Night Out* (with Tom Bell) on BBC TV, after which *The Caretaker* premiered in the West End. It ran for over a year and was a critical and commercial success.

The plot of *The Caretaker* centres on three characters Pinter had observed whilst in lodgings in Chiswick: two brothers and an older man, possibly a tramp, who seemed to have taken up residence in their house. Avoiding the verbal heroics of Porter, Seaton and Smith, it was presented with gnomic minimalism, the dialogue like fragments of conversation heard on the street: disjointed and expressed with either a threatening or a defensive emphasis. As with *Look Back in Anger*, this was another comprehensive defeat for Received Pronunciation, confirmation that this was how many people spoke and articulated their emotions.

In the play, Donald Pleasence, an actor of immense skill, was Davies, the tramp. The brothers were played by Alan Bates, as Mick and Peter Woodthorpe (Estragon in the original 1955 stage production of *Waiting for Godot*) as Aston, the slower of the two. By the end of 1961 it had transferred to Broadway, with Robert Shaw replacing Woodthorpe. *The Caretaker* closed in February 1962 and given Pinter had by then written two more TV dramas, *Night School* and *The Collection*, as well as contributing material to the Peter Cook stage revue *One Over the Eight* (along with Lionel Bart, John Mortimer and N F Simpson) a film adaptation beckoned.

Except... none of the major production companies or distributors were willing to invest in such a project. It's unlikely that this was because the material was too difficult or experimental. By 1962 there was plenty of Absurdism around. Apart from Beckett, plays by Jean Genet and Eugène Ionescu were running in London, with the latter particularly popular. (His *Rhinoceros* was staged at the Royal Court by Orson Welles in 1960, with a cast led by Laurence Olivier and Joan Plowright.) It's more likely that this diffidence came down to cinema being seen as a cut above TV and a world apart from theatre.

Instead, alternative arrangements were made. Most of the funding needed to kickstart the film came from £1,000 donations made by noted celebrities – among whom were Elizabeth Taylor, Richard Burton, Harry Saltzman, Peter Hall, Leslie Caron, Noël Coward and Peter Sellers – with the producer, director and stars agreeing to work for nothing against a share in the profits. Shot in black and white, on a tiny budget, it was filmed in Hackney, on Pinter's home streets, the characters accurately reflecting the flotsam and jetsam then found there. Clive Donner directed – quite a step change from *Some People* – with Nicolas Roeg as cameraman and Ron Grainer contributing a non-musical soundtrack composed entirely of sound effects.

Pleasence is brilliant, while Shaw underplays in a dazed stupor, as befits the recipient of a frontal lobotomy. The only question mark is Bates, who seems to be consciously acting a part rather than naturally inhabiting a role that requires a hum of ill-educated menace beneath the surface. But it works well. *The Caretaker* made Pinter's reputation, is constantly revived and has been a set text in schools for half a century. By the time the film appeared in June 1963 he was working on the screenplay of *The Servant* and the angst about funding *The Caretaker* turned out to be a fuss about nothing.

Pinter's drama can be read baldly as an account of how family members repel a predatory outsider and is a study of marginal figures in seedy surroundings, providing sharp scenes of social realism in the interplay of the three characters. Pinter's contemporary, N F Simpson, went even further, with Absurdism possessing an extended cast. Various points about social organisation arise, but whereas in Europe Absurdism was often used (by Kafka and others) to convey political messages in repressive circumstances, Simpson's UK version seems more akin to the nonsense writings of Edward Lear.

The appearance of work like this in mainstream theatre still pushed boundaries, though, and Simpson's play *One Way Pendulum*, which ran in the West End from 1959 surprised many by becoming a notable success. Its main character (Mr Groomkirby) was played by Roddy Maude-Roxby, a performance artist and contemporary of Peter Blake at the Royal College of Art. His later, eclectic career included a spell in *Rowan & Martin's Laugh-In* and working with Terry Jones and Michael Palin on the pre-Python *The Complete and Utter History of Britain*.

Delineating *One Way Pendulum*'s plot is a somewhat complicated process. Suffice to say that at its conclusion the family living room has become the main court at the Old Bailey with Groomkirby on trial for various fantastic offences. A filmed version of the play was screened by the BBC on 10th July 1961, after which Woodfall acquired the film rights.

For the first time, they elected to film on sets rather than carry out a preponderance of location shooting, the intention being to enhance the artificiality of the experience. With one exception (Alison Leggatt, retained as Mrs Groomkirby) they also opted for a completely different cast, led by Eric Sykes.

Sykes was a noted comic writer and performer, having worked with The Goons, Hancock and Galton and Simpson. He does sterling work here, delivering everything in resolutely deadpan fashion. Directed by Peter Yates – a left-field choice for him after *Summer Holiday* – it received good notices in the UK on its release in January 1965. Kenneth Tynan liked it, but *One Way Pendulum* was inexplicable to US audiences and the film lost money despite being made on a very low budget.

Today one can admire the professionalism with which it is executed, and the nonsensical intricacies of the plot, but it remains unclear what it was being absurdist about. Authority? The sad limitations and peculiarities of people trapped in little houses in suburbia? Possibly the latter, as there is a strong suggestion in both the film and play that the setting is a typical residential area. Leaving aside Hancock's lodgings in East Cheam, by the end of the 50s, discerning observers (like J G Ballard) had noted a new England emerging from the suburbs, often with sinister undercurrents, as displayed in Pinter's work.

David Turner's 1962 play *Semi-Detached* was another example of this, a grim comic satire about petty, little people – the Midway family – determinedly pursuing one-upmanship. A considerable success, with a cast that included Laurence Olivier, Mona Washbourne, John Thaw and James Bolam, it was directed by Tony Richardson and produced by Oscar Lewenstein. For various reasons Woodfall missed out on the film rights and Granada TV only brought a version to the screen in June 1970, retitled *All the Way Up* and starring Warren Mitchell.

More eccentricity was on display in *The Madhouse on Castle Street*, described by *The Times* as a 'strange free-wheeling piece about a man who has said goodbye to the world and simply shut himself up in his room'. From an original script by Jamaican poet Evan Jones, this was directed by Philip Saville and broadcast as an hour-long BBC TV *Sunday Night Play* in January 1963.

All the action takes place in a down-at-heel boarding house. One of the tenants, Lennie, played by David Warner, locks himself in his room, leaving a note saying that he will remain there until the world changes its ways. The other lodgers, and his sister, attempt to change his mind whilst being unclear what the problem is. In an extraordinary apparition, almost in keeping with its fashionable Absurdism, Bob Dylan plays one of the occupants, a folk singer (Bobby) who performs songs like a kind of Greek chorus to elucidate the unfolding plot.

Dylan was almost completely unknown at this point, his debut album, *Bob Dylan*, having been released to limited sales in March

1962. But he had been seen performing by Philip Saville in New York a few months later and invited to come across to London to appear in the play, despite having zero acting experience. He arrived after completing most of the sessions for *The Freewheelin' Bob Dylan*.

He performed four songs in the play, two adapted from traditional numbers: one, *Ballad of the Gliding Swan*, written by Evan Jones and *Blowin' in the Wind* – at that stage unknown but shortly to be his first really big international hit. It was used over the opening and closing credits, which together with the storyline of a man wanting to keep away from the world suggests – possibly – that Jones's script may have been written during the Cuban Missile Crisis of October 1962.

The key word here is possibly. Because, having been filmed over five days and broadcast nine days later, the negative was placed in storage. The play was never repeated and in 1968 the 35 mm master was thrown away... even though Dylan was now internationally famous. Like Joe Meek's *Linda* and *Farewell Performance*, we have no idea what the finished article looked like. All that remains are some positive reviews, still photographs and the memories of the few remaining participants.

Moving beyond studies of individuals, couples and families, Arnold Wesker's 1957 play *The Kitchen* provided audiences with a general critique of society. Like Pinter, Wesker was from Hackney, Jewish and fiercely political. Unlike Pinter, this latter element often showed in his work. Set in a restaurant, somewhere in the West End, *The Kitchen* jettisons a conventional plot, consisting instead of over 30 different characters representing the staff, interacting with each other, the restaurant owner and a tramp during the course of a day.

The employees are from different nations and of various ages. Their variety gives a democratic veneer to proceedings. There are other factors too: the cooks, who have very exact specialities, are almost exclusively male and the waiting staff, exclusively female. They argue, fight, bicker, move in and out of clouds of steam, engage in petty theft and at one point dance between shifts.

Wesker clearly intended this to be some sort of allegory about how the population ('the workers' in his kitchen) cope with their lot in a capitalist system. It works well, and remains an entertaining piece that has been revived on several occasions.

As with *The Caretaker*, there was trouble interesting mainstream production companies in a cinema adaptation. Eventually, it was made by ACT films, and released in August 1961, with an X certificate due to a scene where one of the waitresses has a miscarriage. Directed by James Hill, prior to *The Dock Brief*, it was adapted by Sidney Cole, a producer and writer whose credits stretched back to J B Priestley's 1944 study of utopia *They Came to a City*. It is extremely well made, and can be seen occasionally on TV. There are no stars or leading roles, it is a true ensemble piece, rather like one of Joan Littlewood's productions. Tom Bell, Sean Lynch and James Bolam appeared and Adam Faith did the song *Something's Cooking* that the cast danced to during one of their breaks. Despite Faith's commercial standing, and an arrangement by Johnny Dankworth, the track is still unreleased.

It only remains to record how Absurdism, comedy and satire concluded. A decade after The Goons began blowing the doors off deference, the BBC broadcast *That Was the Week That Was*. In a clear line of descent from the Boultings' films, the last of which had wrapped (but not yet been released) when *That Was the Week* hit the airwaves in November 1962, the satirical programme was mostly written and performed by actors. Its genesis, though, lay with *Beyond the Fringe*, whose West End success from May 1961 persuaded BBC producer Ned Sherrin that something similar could be made for night-time transmission.

An immense number of scriptwriters were recruited, among whom were *Beyond the Fringe* star Peter Cook and critic Kenneth Tynan. Others included Roald Dahl, best known then for his work in US TV, Eric Sykes, Frank Muir and Dennis Norden, all of whom were part of the Milligan-Sellers-Hancock generation. In a clear sense of the baton being passed on, the younger contributors included John Antrobus, Keith Waterhouse and Richard Ingrams (editor of *Private Eye* magazine, partly-owned by Cook). Also involved were John Bird, who had been Assistant Director of the stage production of *One Way Pendulum* and two Labour party political hopefuls, Gerald Kaufman and Dennis Potter (Potter having published *The Glittering Coffin*, a sweeping Osborne-style condemnation of UK society in 1960). Finally, there was a trio of Cambridge graduates, Graham Chapman, John Cleese and Bill Oddie. This roll call of talent was almost entirely university-educated, with political and social views formed by the Suez debacle, the accelerating collapse of the British Empire and the attacks on class and privilege that had been made so energetically since the appearance of *Lucky Jim*.

The programme started with a song, *That Was the Week That Was*, sung by Millicent Martin to music by Ron Grainer, with lyrics that varied according to whatever was in that week's news. The cast, including Martin, Roy Kinnear, Kenneth Cope, David Kernan, Lance Percival and Willie Rushton (another *Private Eye* figure) then acted out the material with the proceedings refereed, and linked, by David Frost, a former Rediffusion TV trainee who had developed a sideline hosting cabaret at the Blue Angel night club, Berkeley Square.

Among the targets were Prime Ministers Harold Macmillan and Sir Alec Douglas-Home, the Home Secretary Henry Brooke, who had barred Lenny Bruce from re-entering the UK in April 1963 after he had performed at Peter Cook's club, The Establishment. Other targets were the Church of England, the monarchy, capital punishment, nuclear weapons and much else. All of which was a huge step-change from how the BBC usually handled such subjects, even within the domain of comedy. Audiences loved it, with up to 12 million tuning in, and an LP of selected excerpts peaking at No 11 in the UK charts in February 1963.

The programme's transmission as the Profumo affair was unfolding made for attractively subversive viewing and the show's influence on societal values has been seen as a contributory factor to the unravelling of Macmillan's government.

Despite this, *That Was the Week That Was* came to an end quite suddenly, the final episode being broadcast on 28th December

1963. Officially this was because 1964 was an election year: the BBC were obliged to be impartial, and remorseless attacks on the government were in breach of that. Alternatively, it could just have easily been the case that Douglas-Home was a less liberal PM than Macmillan (who had been equable about attacks on himself) and wanted to use any means at his disposal to try and stay in office.

After the election was over, and Harold Wilson was installed in 10 Downing Street, there were no attempts at reviving *That Was the Week That Was*. Fondly remembered, it begat an array of successor shows over the following decade. In the immediate aftermath of its demise, though, two films appeared both of which clearly owed something to its approach.

The first of these was *It's All Over Town*, a 55-minute long second feature shot in colour that appeared in January 1964. The plot is childishly simple: a stagehand and his friend (Lance Percival and Willie Rushton) fall asleep and dream of visiting a string of fashionable London establishments. Satirical monologues, in the style of *That Was the Week That Was*, introduce each segment. Various musical acts are encountered, including Frankie Vaughan, who gets to perform five songs. No attempt is made at realism with it being clear that the action is taking place on sets. But a lot of talent is crammed into the film, including appearances by Dusty Springfield and The Hollies.

The supporting cast includes Ivor Cutler, a practitioner of Absurdist humour from the mid-50s onwards, and quite the equal of Spike Milligan; ballet dancer April Olrich and stripper Ingrid Anthofer, whose routine in Paul Raymond's Revuebar is so risqué it is surprising the film managed an A certificate. The combination of this, the music and the satirical asides probably seemed very grown-up at the time, and was a reflection of the changing times. Douglas Hickox directed, having previously made a TV documentary, *Stop Laughing, This is England*, a montage of photographs taken by Henri Cartier-Bresson in the north of England, set to an ironic commentary.

The second *That Was the Week* offshoot was *Nothing But the Best*, which began life as the 50-minute play *The Best of Everything*, transmitted on ITV in August 1961. A shrewd and humorous analysis of the UK class system, it was adapted by novelist Frederic Raphael from a short story by US writer Stanley Ellin. Gary Raymond played the amoral central character. The play was much admired and a feature film was set up by David Deutsch (whose father owned the Odeon cinema chain) with Raphael retained to do the script and Clive Donner hired to direct immediately after he completed *The Caretaker*.

In what can only be described as poetic justice, given what happened when *Look Back in Anger* was filmed, Alan Bates replaced Raymond in the leading role of the working-class clerk who is determined to advance through society at any cost. He finds his family embarrassing, lives in a rented room in a large sub-divided house and constantly calculates how to play situations to his advantage via inner monologues, in the style later used in *Alfie*, which the audience, but not the other characters, hear. Cynically, he befriends a useless sponging ex-public schoolboy (Denholm Elliott) who shows him the ropes, and the two cruise through parties, balls and nights at the theatre with Bates's character learning the nuances of social climbing.

Eventually, having disposed of Elliott and sent his family to Australia on an extended holiday, he marries the boss's daughter, and succeeds in his quest for a life of luxury. *Nothing But the Best* is an entertaining, well-made film, shot in colour (by Nicolas Roeg) and making good use of glamorous locations. It also includes a band, The Eagles, who were involved in Donner's earlier film *Some People*. Harry Andrews does a fine turn as the boss and Willie Rushton appears as an idiotic upper-class hanger-on. The film also scores in having two key female roles: Millicent Martin, as the woman Bates marries, and Pauline Delaney as Mrs March, the landlady who quietly demands sexual favours from him in exchange for assistance with his endeavours. Both are shown as having a depth, and agency, that was usually lacking in the characters women portrayed on screen at that time.

Ron Grainer was contributing his third score for Donner after *The Caretaker* and *Some People* and Millicent Martin performed the title theme. Released in March 1964, there is a clear resemblance to *Room at the Top*, with its sexual manoeuvrings and underlying message that aspirational values trump everything and should be embraced by everyone. But this is a long way from Joe Lampton's Yorkshire, and the 60s were almost in full swing.

THE FRIGHTENED CITY

One of the aspects of 'otherness' that the Kitchen Sink mined was the seam of sex and violence that passed through Soho. Here could be found all manner of crime and dissipation, even the occasional murder. Soho was a most un-British place, a foreign-looking corrupting landscape that sucked in innocents and destroyed them.

Visions of Soho were usually nocturnal, like a Whistler palette: black and white with night and fog and buses looming in and out of the rain amidst neon signs. Villains were run to ground by police (some of whom had dubious morals themselves), and then despatched to prison to fester with marginal groups of all types – homosexuals, immigrants, and thieves – before being washed up in bedsit land.

Its alien characteristics were so complete – even the food was foreign – that UK filmmakers rarely deigned to visit. When its cinematic possibilities were explored, it was in the footsteps of foreign directors and stars. Notable examples are *Night and the City* (1950), *Street of Shadows* (1953) and *Passport to Shame* (1958). The latter was typical. Mainly shot elsewhere in London, it featured Diana Dors who had less screen time than Odile Versois and Eddie Constantine, both of whom were big in French cinema. In fact, it plays rather like a *film de flic* washed up on Shaftesbury Avenue.

Much the same was true of *Too Hot to Handle* (1960) made by Terence Young after his work on *Serious Charge*. A crime thriller, much of it was shot on sets and concerned two rival strip club owners, a blackmailer and a journalist writing 'an exposé of sexy, sordid Soho, England's greatest shame'. Jayne Mansfield starred as a main attraction at one of the clubs, with Carl Boehm as the journalist. Christopher Lee and Barbara Windsor both had supporting roles. There were censorship issues – basically the film was designed to show Mansfield in as little clothing as possible – and much coverage in *Playboy* magazine. The final version was released uncut in France but with cuts in the US and UK, where a version in black and white was inexplicably preferred. Its fate seemed to confirm that Soho would remain B-picture territory, at best. But, whilst big name British directors and stars tended to avoid such settings, Michael Powell proved an exception.

As early as 1954 he and his partner Emeric Pressburger announced they would make *Miracle in Soho*, with much the same high production values that had characterised their famous productions of *The Red Shoes* and *The Tales of Hoffman*. In the end, Pressburger alone worked on the *Miracle in Soho* screenplay as well as producing the film, which was not a success. In the meantime, Powell had travelled to Spain to make the ballet drama *Luna de Miel* (1959), which got him nominated for the Palme d'Or at Cannes, before he returned to London to begin work on *Peeping Tom*.

Avoiding the whimsicality and romanticism that characterised his earlier work, this was a study of voyeurism, sadism and pornography. It was written by Leo Marks and based on his recollections of living above Marks & Co, a bookshop run by his family at 84 Charing Cross Road, London. The main character, Mark Lewis, is part of a film crew and aspires to be a director. He takes pornographic photographs of women in his spare time (for sale under the counter at selected newsagents), is shy, reclusive, has few friends and lives at his deceased father's house in the old Edwardian suburb of Cricklewood, where he rents out spare rooms to lodgers. He is also a serial killer targeting women, preferably prostitutes. The plot follows his actions as he films himself murdering three women, and concludes when he is cornered by the police.

This was a major change of direction for Powell, who tried and failed to get either Dirk Bogarde or Laurence Harvey for the leading role. (Harvey accepted, but quit prior to the start of shooting to make *The Alamo* in the US with John Wayne.) Eventually the part went to Carl Boehm, who started immediately he had finished *Too Hot to Handle*. Other cast members included Anna Massey and Shirley Anne Field. Expertly made, in colour, a great deal of it was filmed around Fitzrovia, the neighbourhood that immediately adjoins Soho and has (or had then) a similarly raffish reputation.

Peeping Tom premiered in April 1960 to generally poor reviews and failed to be the success that Powell had hoped for. There were a number of possible reasons for this. Having a young blond sadistic serial killer with a German accent was, with hindsight, a risky option at a time when UK cinema was still replete with war heroics, often featuring stereotypical Nazis. It is also interesting to note its similarities to *Cover Girl Killer*, a September 1959 supporting feature about a repressed (and completely English) killer of glamour models, played by Harry H Corbett. This attracted much less opprobrium, and though it's an inferior film, its existence rather makes one wonder to what extent *Peeping Tom* was a completely original work.

Perhaps its failure at the time was due to it having a leading character (Lewis/Boehm), who although pathetic at the end, is motivated by sexual gratification, a psychological complication that UK films avoided. The comparison has often been drawn between *Peeping Tom* and Alfred Hitchcock's *Psycho*, which appeared two months later. This too has a mentally unbalanced killer, who lives in his dead parent's house and carries out gruesome murders. Unlike *Peeping Tom*, though, *Psycho* was a runaway success and was nominated for four Academy Awards.

Part of this might be explained by Hitchcock releasing his film straight to the public without any press previews. Powell had a preview and was dogged by poor reviews. It may also have come down to the UK having a more censorious attitude to violence, and certainly not being ready in 1960 for serial killer fare. Whilst it was deemed acceptable then to show full frontal (female) nudity (which *Peeping Tom* does when Lewis claims his third victim, Pamela Green), it was also deemed essential that the camera cut away rather than show victims being hacked or stabbed to death.

Powell's intention in *Peeping Tom*, even allowing for it being implied in some scenes, was to show extremes of sex and violence that had hitherto been kept off screen in the UK. If he thought this radical approach would ensure a commercial success, he miscalculated badly.

As did Albert Finney, some years later, when exploring similar territory in *Night Must Fall*, a project that he got involved with after rejecting *Lawrence of Arabia*, and failing to raise money to film *Ned Kelly* in Australia. With *Psycho* a success he and director Karel Reisz, opted to remake Emlyn Williams's 1935 play about a psychopathic murderer. Mona Washbourne and Susan Hampshire co-starred, with Finney playing his part with a restrained, nihilistic intensity.

His character adroitly insinuates himself into various roles – hotel bellboy, butler – that provide him with proximity to his victims, whilst also carrying on affairs with two separate women. The violence depicted here is pointless and extreme with no discernible motive. Shot in black and white, Finney's make-up (his face, capped with blond hair, has a ghostly Roy Orbison-like pallor) heightens the terror, and the film ends with him cowering on a lavatory floor as the police arrive.

As written by Clive Exton, this was a radical rework of Williams's original, and went down badly with critics and audiences, particularly given the ongoing popularity of the original play in repertory theatre. The film was a failure and may well have influenced Finney's 3-year break from cinema, as he recharged his batteries at the National Theatre.

Thus, for the immediate future, explorations of depraved and sadistic situations were confined to a smaller canvas. A classic example of this was *Jungle Street*, written by Alexander Doré and released in March 1961. Doré had previously adapted Jean de Létraz's French bedroom farce *Moumou* for Paul Raymond, which toured through the repertory circuit in 1956 and was later restaged as *Pyjama Tops* in the West End from 1969. *Jungle Street* is part of the same direction of travel. Much of it takes place in the Adam and Eve Club – whose proprietor, played by actor Brian Weske looks amazingly like Raymond – where a procession of dancers and strippers entertain an audience of old men.

One of these, Sue (played by Jill Ireland) has a delinquent boyfriend, Terry (David McCallum), a petty criminal from a limited working-class background, who is given to waving a gun about much as he does in *Violent Playground*. With his sidekick, Kenneth Cope, he plans a robbery but it miscarries and after shooting dead a couple of people he is dragged off screaming by the police. Everything about it is resonant of Britain before The Beatles. Particularly the main title theme, a brooding, guitar heavy instrumental, released as a single by The Planets on the HMV label.

Equally small and intense, *Rag Doll* appeared the same month. The plot here is about Carol, 17, played by Christina Gregg (formerly Miss ABC Television 1956), who leaves her job as a waitress in a transport café to escape from her alcoholic stepfather, Patrick Magee. She pitches up in Soho where she works in a coffee bar and meets pop singer Joe Shane. Jess Conrad plays Shane, having gravitated to a starring role after hanging around in the background in *Serious Charge*. He'd also just broken into the charts at this point and the film exploits this with music scenes by Jack Good featuring an early version of the Dave Clark Five.

It turns out that Conrad, like David McCallum in *Jungle Street*, dabbles in crime and he eventually goes on the run with Carol after shooting dead her predatory boss. The film concludes with him collapsing and dying in a field somewhere outside London. Directed by Lance Comfort, this is an above average supporting feature whose co-stars Hermione Baddeley and Kenneth Griffith have dialogue – as Auntie and Mort – that is so stylised, parts of it might almost be lifted from Pinter's *The Birthday Party*.

A slightly bigger entry in this field, by virtue of having recognisable stars like John Gregson and Herbert Lom, was *The Frightened City*, released in August 1961. Lom had been visible in

Soho-set dramas since *Night and the City* and *Passport to Shame*, generally playing suspect 'foreigners' of unspecified nationality. Gregson was one of the stalwarts of UK cinema: he had a string of popular successes after the release of *Genevieve*, though his career was now in decline. Here he plays Detective Inspector Sayers, battling against a protection racket run by a consortium of local gangs.

Much of the action occurs in and around The Taboo Club, whose owner employs an Irish enforcer played by Sean Connery. The plot follows the creation of a crime syndicate, where legitimate businesses act as a front for less than savoury activities, something being undertaken by the Kray brothers at around the time the film was made. Audiences are also shown the police as being prepared to cheat, which they justify by citing their higher duty to clear the streets of crime and secure convictions. Such thinking was nowhere to be seen in 1950's *The Blue Lamp*, but it was certainly one that was common by the end of the 60s, and in that respect *The Frightened City* is a forerunner of things to come.

That it remains watchable is probably due to its script, which was largely the work of Leigh Vance, whose prior credits included two other crime dramas, *The Shakedown* and *Piccadilly Third Stop*. In the 70s he quit the UK for Hollywood where he produced various cop drama series for US TV. The film also had a classic guitar instrumental, by The Shadows, as its main title theme. Written by Norrie Paramor, it was duly released as a single making No 3 in the UK charts in May 1961.

Another step up came with *The Boys*. Written by Stuart Douglass – whose previous work included the Ray Brooks TV play *Girl on a Roof* – this was directed by Sidney J Furie, probably best known at that point for Cliff Richard's *The Young Ones*. Filmed in and around Soho, Paddington and the railway lands of Kings Cross, it follows a gang of delinquents on a night out that ends up with them facing charges of murdering a nightwatchman.

Much of the film takes place in the court room where the quartet end up on trial for their lives. As they, and various witnesses, are cross examined we see flashbacks of how events occurred, and explore the background of the four youths. They are all shown as insecure individuals, whilst the adults giving evidence against them make assumptions about their guilt based on their appearance and age. It's well-made, and like many UK court room dramas quite engrossing in a stagey kind of way.

As with *The Frightened City*, some big-name stars were involved. In this case Richard Todd and Robert Morley, both appearing as barristers. Like Gregson, Todd was a huge star in the 50s whilst Morley's career involved a great deal of theatre work, often as an actor-manager. The delinquents, played by Dudley Sutton, Tony Garnett, Ronald Lacey and Jess Conrad, represent an interesting cross section of the talent emerging at that time. Sutton (who glowers like a satanic cherub throughout), Garnett and Lacey had appeared in TV and theatre productions by Brendan Behan, David Mercer, Henry Livings and Arnold Wesker and the supporting cast, containing Wilfrid Brambell, Roy Kinnear, Patrick Magee and Carol White is also strong.

The denouement sees one acquitted and three declared guilty. Two are under 18 and are therefore 'detained at Her Majesty's pleasure', Sutton's character is over 18, and sentenced to death. The epitome of the pre-swinging London crime drama, *The Boys* did well commercially on its release in September 1962. As did an EP of music from the film performed by The Shadows, despite the incongruity of the material being performed in their jaunty, cheerful style. After all, this was a drama about the iniquities of the death penalty, and young people being put on trial for their lives at an age when they couldn't even vote. A darker sound would have probably been infinitely preferable.

Anthony Newley now made an entrance into this genre with the March 1958 BBC TV Play *Sammy*, in which the solitary character, Sammy (Newley), sat alone in a room making increasingly desperate phone calls to try and raise £200 (about £8,500 today) to pay off gambling debts. Written and directed by Ken Hughes it was a great success, with a US version, starring Mickey Rooney, following a few months later. When Newley became a transatlantic star with

Stop the World – I Want to Get Off, funding was raised to expand *Sammy* into a feature film, with Hughes remaining in situ behind the camera and rewriting the script.

Reprising his role in *The Small World of Sammy Lee*, Newley is the compere at the Peep Show Club whose embarrassing patter between acts is listened to in silence by the bored male audience. He gambles and owes money to unsavoury characters, runs around frantically and returns to Whitechapel to try and borrow from his brother, played memorably by Warren Mitchell. There is no happy ending, and no wider social point is being made. Sammy/Newley is a hustler who is out of his depth, a failure at work, in life and in love. The message is that Soho collects people like this, who find themselves unable to relate to 'normal' life outside and are eventually dragged down and destroyed.

Newley's co-stars were Julia Foster, 20, playing a girl he tries to shield from corruption only for her to succumb and become a dancer/stripper, Robert Stephens and Wilfrid Brambell. The soundtrack was done by Kenny Graham, one of the key UK jazz players in the 50s and 60s. It has a haunting, elegiac quality, but remained unissued until 2013. Released in April 1963, *The Small World of Sammy Lee* lost money and led to Hughes briefly struggling to find work. Newley left the UK for Hollywood shortly afterwards and *The Small World of Sammy Lee* rapidly receded from public memory. Seen today, in black and white, accompanied by Graham's score, it stands up rather well.

The East End of London, which shared many of Soho's seedy attributes, was explored in some detail in *A Place to Go*, one of a series of socially-conscious films made by Basil Dearden and Michael Relph. Like their earlier *Violent Playground*, this was a study of alienated youth, based on Michael Fisher's 1961 novel, *Bethnal Green*. Set in a London of trolley buses, tenements, dog racing tracks and a huge amount of war damage, its cast of characters was referred to by one reviewer as being 'worthy descendants of Hogarth's people'.

The plot revolves around a relationship between factory worker Ricky and his independently minded girlfriend Cat. As in *Sparrows*

Can't Sing, they live in an area in an era of upheaval, where terraces are being demolished and new flats are being built. They want to move on as well, but finding legitimate channels frustrating, Ricky helps plan a robbery. He ends up in court, but is let off with a fine, after which he and Cat plan their future.

Rita Tushingham, then appearing in *The Knack* at the Royal Court Theatre, was cast as Cat. For Ricky, the producers opted for Mike Sarne, which on paper may have looked like an accident waiting to happen: in May 1962 he had recorded *Come Outside*, a comic cockney pop dialogue with actress Wendy Richard which reached No 1 in the UK charts. Projecting the same demeanour as Newley, Cribbins, Faith, Klein and Brown, the idea that he would perform convincingly in a major dramatic role would normally have been regarded as unlikely.

Except, as the press release from Parlophone records made clear, his family name was Scheuer, he was studying Russian Literature at the University of London, could speak six languages fluently, came from a German/Slovak family and had a father who was an art historian. And, he was also an actor, having made several TV and film appearances, often uncredited, and usually as a German officer, since 1960. On this basis his career escalated. Raconteur and cultural sophisticate Daniel Farson, sensing a happening phenomenon, had Sarne and Wendy Richard on *Dan Farson Meets*, an ITV version of John Freeman's *Face to Face*. By the time Sarne's next hit appeared – another comic dialogue, *Will I What?*, with Billie Davis – he had started filming *A Place to Go*.

He acquitted himself well and the film today remains quite effective, particularly in its chronicling of a vanished Haggerston and Bethnal Green. Released in July 1963, it had a score composed by Charles Blackwell, a mere 23 years old at the time. Formerly connected with Joe Meek, he was responsible for many hits by Billy Fury, Jess Conrad, John Leyton and Jet Harris, making him one of the hottest young producers in the UK. Mike Sarne released the main title theme as a single in April 1964, which was really a bit late in the day, and the film is little-known today.

A *Place to Go* was followed into cinemas by two Soho-set crime dramas, *Girl in the Headlines* and *The Informers*, both of which were released in November 1963. The former was adapted from *The Nose on My Face*, the debut novel by actor Laurence Payne. It was the first in a series he wrote about Inspector Birkett and his colleague Sergeant Saunders, played here by Ian Hendry and Ronald Fraser. They investigate the murder of a glamorous model, meeting a faded opera star addicted to drugs and visiting various seedy locales, including a gay club (possibly the first time one was shown openly on screen) and a John Aspinall-type gambling casino. Filmed around the same time as the Profumo scandal, it had a script by Patrick Campbell, allowing, as in his earlier work on *Lucky Jim*, for a humorous feel to certain scenes. It also featured an early appearance, at 17, from Jane Asher, playing Birkett's daughter. The opening title sequence by Robert Ellis is impressive, very Pop Art, and set to cool jazz by John Addison, who had recently completed the soundtrack for *Tom Jones*. It was released to generally positive reviews but again, is seldom seen today.

The Informers was also based on a novel, in this case *Death of a Snout*, by Douglas Warner, a pseudonym used by John Currie and Elizabeth Warner. Like *The Nose on My Face*, this was the first in a series, one of which was filmed for US TV by Hitchcock. It's an odd, but interesting, mixture of the old and the new. After *Dick Barton* style intro music, we meet Nigel Patrick, very suave as Chief Inspector John Johnnoe, in overcoat and trilby. Johnnoe is indiscriminate in the use of informers and, heedless of warnings, he even continues to do so after one of them is murdered. As he closes in on the film's villains, he is framed and sent to prison. The film follows his restoration to civilian life after his wife enlists the support of the murdered man's brother.

The Informers was produced by William MacQuitty and Earl St. John, both associated with the Rank Organisation. St. John's credits include *Sapphire*, *No Love for Johnnie*, *Flame in the Streets* and *The Wild and the Willing*, suggesting a willingness to explore social issues on film. Forgotten today, his reputation might have been higher had he not declined to film *Look Back in Anger* in 1957 after purchasing the rights, or been able to raise enough money to make *Saturday Night and Sunday Morning*.

Directed by Ken Annakin from a script by Alun Falconer (and Paul Durst) after his work on *The Man Upstairs* and *Never Let Go*, *The Informers* is a very efficiently made and entertaining film. The cast are outstanding: Colin Blakely is an Irish scrap metal dealer and Frank Finlay plays the villain, both using their own accents (Ulster and Bolton, respectively). Derren Nesbitt also makes an impression as the sadistic, positively Wildean head of a Soho gang. The fight sequences are realistic, and a plot where policemen take bribes and get framed was pushing boundaries in 1963.

Apart from relatively straightforward 'police procedurals', there were also films that attempted to plumb the depths of criminal psychology, particularly of those deemed to be 'outsiders'. The best was probably *The Criminal*, released in October 1960 and starring Stanley Baker. Like *Peeping Tom*, its funding was secured, at least in part, from producers Nat Cohen and Stuart Levy, whose role in backing key productions during this period is somewhat underestimated.

As the title suggests, this was about a career criminal, Johnny Bannion, and was directed by Joseph Losey who had quit the US in 1951 during the McCarthy era. Arriving in the UK via Italy, he was adept at hard-boiled, intelligent thrillers. The material here, written for the screen by Alun Owen, certainly provides that quality, confirming the potential Owen had shown with his acclaimed plays, *Progress to the Park* and *No Trams to Lime Street*. The latter was so popular that three different versions of it were made for television.

Like a lot of Owen's work, *The Criminal* explores the meaning of identity. Baker/Bannion is a lapsed Catholic, and makes for an interesting comparison with Pinkie in Graham Greene's *Brighton Rock*. He is involved with two different women, drives a fancy car and has a swish London apartment. With his US partner, Mike Carter (played by Sam Wannamaker, like Losey a US exile) he takes part in a robbery at a racetrack – shades again of *Brighton Rock* – but gets caught and sent to prison. After being transferred to another jail he escapes, but is cornered by gangsters who have double-crossed him, and are holding his principal girlfriend hostage. Despite shooting one of them dead, he is shot in return and dies, clutching a religious medallion he wears around his neck and begging God for forgiveness. He knows he is a bad man, and probably damned, but repents in his last moments, having saved the woman who loves him.

There is an awful lot of Catholicism on show here. A key scene occurs during a Latin Mass inside prison in which Chief Warden Patrick Magee is also revealed to be a scrupulous believer. The film was banned in Ireland because so many of the criminals and prisoners depicted were Irish Catholics, notably O'Hara (played by Eugene McCarthy), Kelly (Kenneth Cope) and Flynn (Tom Bell). In fact, jail is shown as a place where the outcasts of society end up. Apart from the Hibernian contingent, other inmates include Caribbean (Tommy Eytle), Italian, Maltese and gay (Murray Melvin) characters.

The jazz soundtrack by Johnny Dankworth was released as an EP and the main title theme *Thieving Boy*, sung by Cleo Laine and co-written by Owen, appeared as a single on Fontana, with *Let's Slip Away*, from *Saturday Night and Sunday Morning*, finally getting an airing on the B-side. One wonders if this combination of crime and jazz was another conscious emulation of Louis Malle's *Ascenseur Pour L'échafaud*. With excellent photography by Robert Krasker, winner of an Academy Award for *The Third Man*, the film was a commercial success, particularly in Paris, where co-stars Grégoire Aslan and Margit Saad were familiar to audiences.

Jazz and refugees from the House Un-American Activities Committee were also prominent in *All Night Long*, released in February 1962. This had origins that could be traced to the 1959 John Cassavetes film *Shadows*. Distributed by British Lion and set in Beat Generation New York, this explored race relations via three characters, two of whom are sufficiently light-skinned to 'pass' as white. Nominated for two BAFTAs and an award-winner at the Venice Film Festival, it also had a notable jazz soundtrack featuring bassist Charles Mingus.

The reception to *Shadows* drew Paul Jarrico, an American screenwriter who'd been blacklisted in 1950, back to Hollywood trying to raise funds for a modern-dress, mixed-race version of *Othello* replete with a jazz soundtrack. He got as far as discussions with United Artists who wanted the mixed-race angle dropped and Lena Horne cast in the main female role. Jarrico, and his co-author Nel King, declined and headed instead for London where Bob Roberts (blacklisted in 1951, and former business partner of John Garfield) set up a distribution deal with Rank. Nel King, a friend of Mingus, brought him across for the film which was now set in London, with a screenplay attributed to Peter Achilles (a Jarrico and King pseudonym).

Because Bob Roberts hadn't actually produced a film since leaving the US, Rank insisted on Basil Dearden directing and Michael Relph producing, their suitability for this being their involvement with the 1959 race drama *Sapphire*. As well as replicating the commercial and critical success of *Shadows*, there was even the chance of selling some records, too, given that Rank, as Top Rank, ran their own record label between 1959 and 1962.

Anyone familiar with Shakespeare's *Othello*, will recognise the plot, which takes place here over a single evening. A husband and wife, Aurelius and Delia, celebrate their wedding anniversary. Aurelius (Paul Harris) is black, Delia (Marti Stevens) white, and both are US jazz musicians living in London. A party is thrown for them – in a huge warehouse flat near London Bridge – by an admiring jazz promoter, Rod (Richard Attenborough).

The guests assemble and smoke cannabis whilst jazz musicians Charles Mingus, Dave Brubeck and Johnny Dankworth circulate and play. There are machinations going on involving two musicians in Rex's band, drummer Johnny (Patrick McGoohan) and saxophonist Cass (Keith Michell). These involve detaching Delia from Rex and the evening implodes in violence and mistaken allegations. Unlike the play, no one is murdered and the film ends with Rex and Delia still a couple, Cass en route to hospital and Johnny frantically drumming away.

McGoohan made this whilst simultaneously working on the first series of *Danger Man* and tackles his role in an intense and manic fashion. Harris, Stevens and Michell all had experience in musicals and Attenborough once again burnishes his CV with a capable performance in an interesting film. Also in the cast is US actress Betsy Blair as Johnny's wife – she was also blacklisted and would shortly marry Karel Reisz, making the UK her home.

Though not a crime drama, *All Night Long* was an interesting study of sociopathic behaviour and jealousy, with a louche background and characters. Critics were lukewarm at best (presumably because any tampering with Shakespeare was frowned on), and in some cases rather missing the point of what is being shown on screen. *All Night Long* was made at a time when jazz, allied with folk and blues, was thought by some to be the music of the future, with London its epicentre. The urban avant-garde jazz depicted in *All Night Long*, together with modern art and design (which avant-garde jazz album sleeves often utilised) was seen as part of a bold new world. We know today that events did not quite turn out that way, and there is a feeling when watching the film now of a path not taken.

Anyhow, the film restricted Dankworth and Mingus to a single track each, and Brubeck to two (*It's a Raggy Waltz* and *Blue Shadows on the Street*) both of which were included on his album *Time Further Out*, which reached No 12 in the UK in May 1962. The remaining tracks were put together by Philip Green, who worked consistently with Dearden and Relph, and includes the title theme from *Sapphire* as one of his pieces. The musicians involved – Johnny Scott, Ronnie Ross, Tubby Hayes, Keith Christie, Bert Courtley, Colin Purbrook, Ray Dempsey, Kenny Napper and Allan Ganley – were the cream of the UK scene, ensuring that this is one of many quality UK jazz albums to appear at that time.

McGoohan was also seen in the 1962 film version of Brendan Behan's 1954 play *The Quare Fellow*. An austere, claustrophobic portrait of Ireland in the middle of the De Valera era, and a powerful polemic against the death penalty. It was staged successfully by Joan Littlewood at Stratford in 1956 before a West End transfer followed, enlivened by Behan attending the theatre and joining in the dialogue from the stalls. (Prior attempts by him to enter the UK in 1950 and 1953 both ended with his deportation, due to his having served eight years in prison for bombing and attempted murder offences during his time in the IRA.)

The plot takes place within a prison where a murderer, 'the Quare Fellow', is awaiting execution. His case is discussed by the inmates who compare him favourably with 'the Other Fellow' an inmate imprisoned for gay offences. A new warder, Crimmins (McGoohan), has just started and is naïve and accepting of authority. He comes from Inishbofin, a small island off the coast of Galway, and his character is that of an innocent plunged into a world where he has limited experience. The arbitrary nature of justice – another convicted murderer is reprieved, but not the Quare Fellow – is explored, as are attitudes to sex, religion and politics.

Various film companies were interested in adapting it, but in the end the rights were purchased by Arthur Dreifuss, a German director long resident in Hollywood, for £2,000. Backed by independent producer Anthony Havelock-Allan and the Irish Film Finance Corporation, the business of writing a script commenced. Initially Behan turned to James McKenna, a sculptor and author of *The Scatterin'*, a rock 'n' roll ballet successfully staged at the Dublin Theatre Festival in 1960. Instead, Dreifuss, working with Jacqueline Sundstrom, who had translated and adapted Kafka's *The Trial* for the stage in 1949, revised the material and it is their names that appear on the credits.

The new script moves some of the action outside the prison, and introduces the character of Kathleen (Sylvia Syms), the Quare Fellow's wife, who is portrayed as a promiscuous woman. The drama is enlarged to allow her to meet Crimmins, thus enabling Crimmins to place the murder in the context of surrounding events – i.e. Kathleen was sleeping with her husband's brother – and to see that the world is more complicated than he realised.

Scenes in lodging houses and a local bar have a grim authenticity
and the film concludes with the execution of the Quare Fellow –
who is never seen – being carried out.

It appeared in October 1962 to quite reasonable reviews and
was noted for its use of the song *The Auld Triangle*, later covered
by Bob Dylan, The Pogues and many others, over its opening
scenes. There were attempts to enter it into the Venice Film
Festival as a British production, but these were declined by the
organising committee due to its Irish/European origination.
Notwithstanding that, its texture and subject matter, as well as the
shabby urban background it is set against, place it firmly within
the Kitchen Sink oeuvre.

The dingy old houses that regularly appeared in these dramas
provided readers and audiences with a setting that enabled the
introduction of multiple characters (as well as locations familiar
from everyday life). The whole scenario of 'going down to
London' involved arriving at one of these, having a room (or two)
of your own, and striking out on the great adventure of living
independently. Later in the 60s, this would become the 'bedsit
land' terrain familiar to watchers of TV series like *Take Three Girls*.
Before that though a classic early example was Lynne Reid Banks's
1960 novel *The L-Shaped Room*.

Banks had been an actress in the early 50s, in the same
repertory company as John Osborne at one point, before working
as a TV journalist. Her play, *It Never Rains* was broadcast by the
BBC in 1954, and after a few similar efforts, her novel appeared
to some acclaim, attracting the attention of film producers. Like
Shelagh Delaney's *A Taste of Honey*, it is told from a female point of
view, following Jane, 27, who decides to live alone in a run-down
boarding house in Fulham after finding out she is pregnant. At a
time when abortion was illegal (and expensive even if you could
arrange one with a Harley Street consultant) and the contraceptive
pill not yet available, this was a life-defining situation. From a
comfortable, middle-class family, her civil servant father wants her
out of the house when he learns she is pregnant. (The similarities
here with Alison, in Osborne's *Look Back in Anger* are striking.)

Sloane Square, 1956: theatrical history being made by Kenneth Haigh and John Osborne (in cravat) as the angry young man and kitchen sink genre gets under way in *Look Back in Anger*.

Alan Badel, as Mr Weaver, the powerful owner of a northern rugby league team, admires new signing Frank Machin (Richard Harris) whilst Arthur Lowe looks on in the 1963 film adaptation of David Storey's *This Sporting Life*.

Liverpool 1957. David McCallum strikes a pose as
the UK's first authentic juvenile delinquent in *Violent Playground*.

Absolutely typical kitchen sink imagery. Newlyweds June Ritchie, Alan Bates and
mother-in-law Thora Hird battle it out in the 1962 film of Stan Barstow's *A Kind of Loving*.

The Soho scene, with its decadence and exotic possibilities featured in many of the taboo breaking films of the period. *Beat Girl* (1960) was typical. From left to right Peter McEnery (later in *Victim*), Gillian Hills, Adam Faith and Shirley-Anne Field.

Too odd to be successful, TV series *The Strange World of Gurney Slade* (1960) confirmed the emergence of Anthony Newley as a major talent.

The Johnny Dankworth Orchestra in full flight circa 1960. Note Dudley Moore on piano at the rear. They scored 7 films and 3 TV series between 1958 and 1964.

Girl with Green Eyes was the 1964 film of Edna O'Brien's 1962 novel *The Lonely Girl*. Rita Tushingham and Peter Finch as Kate and Eugene starred as the couple in emotional difficulties.

Rachel Roberts, Shirley Anne Field and Albert Finney enjoy a drink at the premiere of *Saturday Night and Sunday Morning* (1960).

Dudley Sutton and Colin Campbell: two young men sharing a bed, what could possibly go wrong? From *The Leather Boys* (1963) an early UK look at same sex relationships.

The Beatles took the train down to London in 1964 in *A Hard Day's Night*. Written by Alun Owen, it surrounded them with much kitchen sink era talent, including Wilfred Brambell (seen here), Norman Rossington and an uncredited Kenneth Haigh.

Author John Braine in his natural surroundings at around the time that his novel *Room at the Top* took off.

Alan Bates and Joan Plowright in the splendour of Morecambe, from the 1960 film of John Osborne's *The Entertainer*.

**Producer Joseph Janni on set with star
Tom Courtenay** during the filming of
Keith Waterhouse's *Billy Liar* in 1963.

Joan Littlewood, the pioneer of Brechtian,
participatory ensemble theatre, on location directing
the 1963 film version of *Sparrows Can't Sing*.

Helen Shapiro and Richard Lester on the set of *It's Trad Dad!* (1961)
One of the best of many UK films that provided a portmanteau of pop performers.

David Storey with his father in Wakefield,
just after the publication of *This Sporting Life*, 1960.

An image from Michael Winner's 1963 film *West 11*.
Alfred Lynch gets to know Kathleen Breck during a break in dancing.

A night out that goes badly wrong in 1962. Ronald Lacey, Jess Conrad, Tony Garnett (later a major
TV producer) and Dudley Sutton get ready to enjoy themselves in the 1962 film *The Boys*.

In her new home she meets a frustrated young writer, Toby, who is struggling to complete his debut novel; John, a West Indian jazz guitarist; two women who entertain male clients in their basement room and Mavis, an elderly spinster, living alone with her cat. The film, co-produced by the Woolf brothers after their earlier success with *Room at the Top*, was directed by Bryan Forbes who wrote his own adaptation of the script. This shifts the location to Ladbroke Grove, deletes Jane's father (a major part of the novel), changes the identity of the angry young writer from Jewish to Yorkshireman, and switches John's instrument from guitar to trumpet.

Much of it was filmed in black and white on location in and around Paddington and Westbourne Park, giving it an agreeable authenticity. It was a significant production. Leslie Caron, as Jane, was a major star, famous for appearances in musicals with Gene Kelly and Fred Astaire. She had also played the title role of *Gigi* on the London stage and starred in a film of Jack Kerouac's *The Subterraneans*. Not an obvious choice – she was French, but so was Simone Signoret in *Room at the Top* – her performance here was highly regarded, and won her a BAFTA and an Academy Award nomination. Tom Bell, confirming his position as a young northern actor ascending in the wake of Finney, Bates and Courtenay, co-starred as Toby, the fraught novelist.

In supporting roles, Forbes assembled Avis Bunnage as the boarding house owner, Bernard Lee as her boozy casual partner, Pat Phoenix as one of the working girls in the basement and Brock Peters, a US actor-singer of some significance (he'd released four albums and been in *Carmen Jones* and *Porgy and Bess*) as John, who eventually turns out to be gay. They perform effectively, but all of them are upstaged by Cicely Courtneidge, a trooper and veteran of Edwardian comic operas as Mavis, the closet lesbian. The whole package – angry young man + gay musician + Pat Phoenix – was catnip to 80s pop star Morrissey, who later used a clip of Courtneidge singing *Take Me Back to Dear Old Blighty* in the ramshackle Christmas Day party scene to introduce The Smiths 1986 album *The Queen Is Dead*.

For a film with such a strong cast, and one clearly pitched at audiences beyond the UK, a soundtrack album might have been expected. None emerged despite John Barry being brought in to provide music for a jazz club scene. He composed a wonderful instrumental *T-Shaped Twist*, which remained unreleased in its original form, though a cover of it, by The Jazz Messengers, appeared on their 1963 US album *Heat Wave*. Instead, the main title theme, an adaptation of Brahms's Piano Concerto No 1 in D minor, was released by Johnny Pearson on Parlophone, its gloomy resonance catching the film's mood perfectly. The critics were effusive on its release in November 1962, and Forbes and his producers, had a success on their hands. But Banks – rather like Delaney – had trouble repeating this. By the mid-60s she was living in a kibbutz in Israel, eventually returning to the UK to publish two sequels *The Backward Shadow*, 1970 and *Two is Lonely*, 1974. Neither were filmed and she was better known in later years for children's fiction.

The same locations that feature in *The L-Shaped Room* provide the setting for *The Comedy Man*. This too was written by a working actor, in this instance Douglas Hayes, who appeared in repertory and managed to accrue, through the 50s, a fair number of minor roles in TV productions. He published *The Comedy Man*, his second novel, in 1960, its jacket proclaiming it 'a bawdy, rumbustious novel of low-life London'. Sales were good enough for it to be optioned for a film by Jon Pennington, who'd previously been involved with *Expresso Bongo*.

Both book and film portray the desperation and penury of bohemian life. The shabby bedsits, unemployment offices and array of characters hoping that something will turn up... actors who are too old, but can't quite retire, actors who are perennially unlucky, some on whom fortune shines and some who become suicidal. They audition, party and have relationships whilst largely arbitrary factors determine their fate. The plot centres on Charles 'Chick' Byrd who, after being sacked from his job in a provincial repertory company for misbehaving with the producer's wife, takes the train down to London to try his luck there. Renting a room in a ramshackle house near Paddington Station, he eventually strikes it lucky by landing the main role in a series of TV commercials for breath fresheners. At which point his conscience kicks in, and preferring legitimate theatre he quits London to return to the provinces.

Directed by Alvin Rakoff, whose credits included a lot of TV drama, and *Passport to Shame*, Byrd was played by Kenneth More, who like Richard Todd, Laurence Olivier and John Mills was interested in appearing in contemporary material, rather than repeating himself in the sort of roles that had made him a household name. As with *The L-Shaped Room* and *All Night Long*, the supporting cast was strong, with Billie Whitelaw, Cecil Parker, Norman Rossington, Edmund Purdom, Alan Dobie and Dennis Price all helping create the generally seedy atmosphere.

Due for release in mid-1963, and granted an X certificate, for reasons that aren't clear it ended up on the shelf for a year, during which period literary critic Julian MacLaren-Ross extolled Hayes's virtues as a novelist in *The London Magazine*, ranking him above Kingsley Amis. The film finally appeared, on a double-bill with *Lord of the Flies*, in September 1964. Reviews were good, *The Evening News* calling it 'a merciless and accurate picture of the brave band of actors who live from hand to mouth and commute between the Salisbury Arms pub and the Poland Street Labour exchange' but it failed to give More the career boost that he sought, despite being his favourite role. He would appear in character roles from now on while Hayes remained an obscure writer in spite of MacLaren-Ross's lavish praise.

Nearly a year earlier, in a final echo of this pre-swinging London scene, came *West 11*, based on Laura Del-Rivo's 1961 novel *The Furnished Room*. Convent school-educated, and impeccably middle-class, Del-Rivo 'dropped out' in the mid-50s, gravitating to Soho where she became part of the bohemian set circulating around the angry young men writers Colin Wilson and Bill Hopkins. Wilson would maintain a reputation of sorts after the runaway success of his first book, *The Outsider*. Hopkins, though, would not. His nihilism seemed disturbingly like proto-fascism and he would never recover from the critical dismissal of his debut novel *The Divine and the Decay*. Del-Rivo's own writing took time to coalesce, but was praised when it appeared. The publishers strap line for *The Furnished Room* was 'A novel of the young and lost in modern London' and Colin Wilson endorsed it as 'one of the significant novels of the 1960s'.

The Furnished Room tells the story of Joseph Ignatius Beckett (Joe) who lives in a bed-sitting room somewhere between Notting Hill and Earl's Court. Joe has moved from the provinces some years earlier, having abandoned teenage plans to be a Catholic priest. Misanthropic, and given to mystical speculations, he eventually encounters Dyce, a sinister ex-army officer. Dyce wants an elderly aunt killed so he can inherit her estate. Unemployed and impoverished, Joe agrees to do this, in exchange for £10,000. In the book his motive is simple: he is told his mother has an incurable illness, and he wishes to fund a trip to Lourdes for her. In the film his mother dies, making his reasons for getting himself wrapped up in a murder plot somewhat vaguer. In both he loses his nerve, the old lady is killed in a fall after a struggle with him, Dyce denies everything and Joe ends up in police custody. There is no neat conclusion.

The narrative revolves around loss of faith, and specifically the role of will in determining outcome. This was also a popular theme with Wilson and Hopkins, and interestingly both Del-Rivo's book and subsequent film adaptation have a scene where Joe attends a fascist rally. Critics were kind and the film rights were acquired by Daniel Angel, whose father-in-law owned the Windmill Theatre. Associated British came on board as well. They had cash to spare after backing Hancock's *The Rebel* and Cliff Richard's *The Young Ones* and their involvement here reflected the enthusiasm in UK cinema by 1962 – given the success of *Saturday Night and Sunday Morning*, *A Taste of Honey* and *A Kind of Loving* – for all things Kitchen Sink.

Willis Hall and Keith Waterhouse were recruited to write a script with the intention that Claudia Cardinale would star and Joseph Losey direct, probably based on his work on *The Criminal*.

After Losey quit and Cardinale opted to make *The Pink Panther* instead, the film took about a year to set up, with Michael Winner given the director role. Winner's recollections of the film revolved around casting rows, with Daniel Angel rejecting suggestions to hire Sean Connery for the lead role, Julie Christie to replace Cardinale and James Mason to play Dyce.

Winner settled on Alfred Lynch, who'd made his name at the Royal Court with *The Long and the Short and the Tall* and at Theatre Workshop with *The Hostage*, as Joe. Sarah Miles was cast as the female lead and Eric Portman, a distinguished theatre and film actor, was Dyce. Diana Dors also returned from Los Angeles where she was working in TV with Alfred Hitchcock, to play Georgia, an older woman with an abundance of male friends. Finally, just before shooting began, Miles left to make *The Servant*, and was replaced by Kathleen Breck whose main credit, at that point, had been appearing in the TV play *Collect Your Hand Baggage* with Kenneth More. Had the film been made with any of those rejected by Angel, it is likely that *West 11* would enjoy a higher cachet today – even so, the film remains as of some interest. The cast play their parts well (particularly Dors and Portman) and the cinematography of Otto Heller, who also shot *Peeping Tom*, perfectly captures the shabbiness of London's battered Regency terraces.

This is a film with as much Catholicism as *The Criminal*, and as much jazz as *All Night Long*. The title theme, by Acker Bilk, is excellent and there are appearances by the Tony Kinsey Quartet and Ken Colyer's Jazzmen. Both are filmed at Studio 51, 10-11 Great Newport Street, London. Kinsey and his band are cool, have US college-boy haircuts and Brooks Brothers suits. They bop along quite nicely. Colyer's band are older, with beards and tweed jackets. They play authentic 'trad'. As well as this footage, Winner also includes shots of the famous Troubadour coffee bar in Earls Court.

Both Studio 51 and the Troubadour were critical in the rise of the London music scene. Colyer – who worked his passage to New Orleans on an oil tanker in 1952 so he could buy every available trad-jazz record – launched Studio 51 on his return to London. Hosting jazz, blues and rock for the next twenty years, by the time Winner was filming, The Rolling Stones, then a six-piece rhythm and blues band led by Brian Jones, had a residency there, but hadn't yet released a record.

West 11 opened to moderate reviews in October 1963. Whatever its qualities, it was resonant of a black and white, social realism era that was receding, and as a result was quickly forgotten. Winner for one grasped the opportunities of the changing times. By the summer of 1966 he was making *The Jokers*, in colour, with Michael Crawford and Oliver Reed skidding around London in a Mini Moke, in a caper about borrowing the Crown Jewels. In contrast, like many of her fellow writers, Laura Del-Rivo struggled to repeat her initial success. After a follow-up, *Daffodil on the Pavement* (1967), she later supported herself by running a clothes stall on Portobello Market whilst producing the occasional short story.

THE END OF EMPIRE

The second world war cast a long shadow over Britain. On the one hand there was the obvious damage to visual surroundings, particularly in towns and cities, much of which remained unresolved for many years. On the other, there was the personal and psychological impact on the population: loss, bereavement, physical and mental impairment, together with a loosening of social constraints, more divorces and separations.

For anyone born between 1945 and 1960, the experience of growing up during the post-war period – which effectively lasted into the mid-70s – meant living in a world where every family had anecdotes about life and death situations they experienced in the recent past. Every child had a father, uncle or elder sibling who had served in the forces, some of whom had died or been injured. Even when peace came, the trappings of war lasted a long time: rationing until 1954, and National Service – an exclusively male affair – until 1960. The last National Service conscripts were only demobilised in early 1963 and it wasn't until 1968 that a year passed without a member of UK armed forces being killed on active service.

Throughout this time the UK was a highly militarised society. A warfare state, as much as a welfare state, to quote contemporary historian David Edgerton. During the peak years of the British Empire, the UK typically spent about 3-3.5 per cent of its GDP (Gross Domestic Product) on defence. It exceeded this comfortably through the 50s and 60s, peaking at 11 per cent in 1952, and not dipping back to its pre-war levels until 1998. (In 2023, it stood at

1.9 per cent.) It was this abundance of funding that allowed Britain to maintain a massive network of overseas bases, to which its hundreds of thousands of conscripts were sent, policing immense territories that were still, to a large degree, governed directly from London.

For most of the public, having kith and kin abroad, taking part in military service or even a shooting war, was part of day-to-day life in the two decades after 1945. It was a continuation of how they had lived during and before the war and was regarded by many with pride. The UK was the only Allied country to fight all the way through the conflict from September 1939 to August 1945. It had paid an immense financial price for doing so, and the public view was that it should celebrate its achievements.

Thus, it comes as no surprise to find that after 1945 British cinema produced a body of work celebrating critical events in the war from a fiercely patriotic point of view, even if they only ever constituted a sizeable minority of what was being presented. Interestingly, it took some time for this trend to become noticeable. In the first years of peace, films set during the conflict like Powell and Pressburger's *A Matter of Life and Death* (1946) and *Small Back Room* (1948) tended towards restraint, or were even anti-heroic. It wasn't until 1950, with *Odette* and *The Wooden Horse* that newly polished accounts of wartime events started to emerge in appreciable numbers. From then on, through to *Battle of Britain* (1969) a steady stream appeared and it is interesting to note how this occurred as British power and influence declined. A number of these (*The Cruel Sea*, *The Dam Busters*, *Reach for the Sky* and *Sink the Bismarck!*) were huge UK successes, even if in most cases they failed to stir overseas audiences.

For actors this meant an awful lot of work in uniform. Indeed some, like John Mills, Jack Hawkins and Harry Andrews, hardly seemed to appear in anything else. For others it was simply a rite of passage: getting cast in a good part in a war film established you with the public, and was something that you might still be doing – lucratively – into middle age. Nor was this just about refighting battles against Germany, Italy and Japan. A few post-

1945 conflicts featured as well, notably in *A Hill in Korea* (1956), a rare British look at a war where their forces were only a minority of those committed and *Yangtse Incident: The Story of H.M.S. Amethyst* (1957) about the heroic defence of a Royal Naval frigate after it was attacked defending free navigation and trade on a river deep inside China.

The end of Empire was explored too, usually in a highly circumscribed manner. *Guns at Batasi* (1964) was set during the mutiny against continued British involvement, post-independence, in the armed forces of East Africa, and *The High Bright Sun* (1964) took place in Cyprus. US magazine *Variety* commented on the latter 'this sits firmly on the fence and makes virtually no attempt to analyse the troubles, the causes or the attitudes of the cardboard characters' – which accurately sums up the inadequacy of most of these attempts at conveying the background of colonialism, and the motives of those who opposed the Empire.

There wasn't much in this oeuvre that Arthur Seaton or Joe Lampton would have identified with. As late as 1969 the commercial success of a film like *The Virgin Soldiers*, set during the Malaya Emergency in the 40s and 50s, was an indication of the majority point of view about this era. The Kitchen Sink writers were, therefore, isolated in their cynical outlook. For them the British Army was not necessarily heroic, its officer class was usually incompetent and the Empire itself rife with brutalities. For them the debacle of Suez was critical, and the maintenance of conscription long into peace time was something to oppose.

The consequences of decolonisation, particularly the arrival after 1948 of substantial numbers of migrants from the non-white Commonwealth were also explored. Although the UK had always had small Asian, African and mixed-race communities in key ports, they rarely if ever featured in novels, plays or films. Now they were shown as characters with an agency of their own and their existence in post-war Britain was accepted and contrasted with the anti-immigrant views that many of the white working class exhibited.

Interestingly, production of traditional British war films peaked *after* Suez, with 13 appearing in 1958, including such immense successes as *Carve Her Name with Pride, Dunkirk, I Was Monty's Double* and *Ice Cold in Alex*. One other was *The Camp on Blood Island*, a grim, account of life in a Japanese prisoner-of-war camp, described (accurately) in *Halliwell's Film Guide* some years later as 'Dubious melodrama parading sadism and brutality as entertainment'. Released in April 1958, it was a significant box-office hit for its producers, Hammer Films. A novelisation by scriptwriter J M White sold millions of copies in paperback, but not everyone liked it, and as if to atone Hammer optioned a BBC TV play, *Yesterday's Enemy*.

Broadcast in October 1958, it had been written by Peter R Newman and directed by Chloe Gibson, one of the few women allowed behind the camera at that time. Reflecting Newman's own war service, it was a bleak and ultra-realistic account of an isolated British army unit being wiped out by the Japanese in Burma in 1942. It had no music and was filmed entirely on a studio set: the resulting claustrophobic atmosphere making it an effective piece.

The tone is defiantly anti-heroic and shows the British, led by Captain Langford, murdering local people they have taken hostage. This was an important point, and not included solely for dramatic effect, as reports from Malaya during the 50s, when the UK put down a rebellion, suggested that British forces had done just that on at least one occasion. The play makes it clear that local people see themselves as trapped between two equally bad options: colonial rule by the British or brutal exploitation by the Japanese.

To direct the film version of *Yesterday's Enemy*, Hammer appointed Val Guest, who had handled *The Camp on Blood Island*, and brought in Stanley Baker to play Langford. His character is very different from how officers were usually shown. This is a man with no upper-class, public school ethos, who happily breaks the Geneva Convention. The supporting cast includes Richard Pasco, from the original stage production of *The Entertainer*, and Gordon Jackson, who also appeared in the TV screening. Guest decided against 'opening out' the action with additional scenes and characters and it retains its visceral power. The film concludes, after the Japanese have shot the surviving British soldiers, with an image of the Kohima war cemetery in North East India, the site of one of the critical battles in the Burma campaign. It was a brave attempt at expressing the futility of war, but it was subject to some criticism on its release in July 1959.

The Long and the Short and the Tall, staged at the Royal Court Theatre in January 1959, was almost as bleak. Written by Willis Hall (who, like Alan Sillitoe, had served in Malaya in the late 40s) this revisited the disastrous events surrounding the fall of Singapore, focussing on a small patrol of UK soldiers who end up stranded in the jungle. Originally staged at the 1957 Edinburgh Festival, where it was known as *The Disciplines of War*, it was directed at the Royal Court by Lindsay Anderson. Robert Shaw and Albert Finney were originally cast in the two leading roles, but Finney got appendicitis just prior to opening and was replaced by Peter O'Toole. Others appearing included Edward Judd, Ronald Fraser and Alfred Lynch.

Like *Yesterday's Enemy*, the tone is anti-heroic, and the action takes place exclusively on a single set. There are no female roles and the outcome is suitably grim, though in this case a couple of the British soldiers survive to become prisoners. The critics liked it and BBC TV broadcast a version in April 1959. After Rank turned down the chance of acquiring the film rights, they were purchased by Associated British who brought in Leslie Norman to direct and Wolf Mankowitz to redraft the script. It was also completely recast. Richard Todd and Laurence Harvey replaced Shaw and O'Toole, Richard Harris and David McCallum co-starred. Only Ronald Fraser (and Kenji Takaki as a Japanese soldier) survived from the play. Released in February 1961, it became one of that year's most popular UK films, and remains watchable today, even though its theatrical origins are rather obvious.

Despite similarities to *Yesterday's Enemy*, a significant appeal of Leslie Norman's film seems to have been the dialogue – one might almost say banter – between the British servicemen and the use of a refrain from a World War 1 song, '*Bless 'Em All*' as its title. Later popularised by George Formby, '*Bless 'Em All*' expressed a weary fatalism about the prospects of serving somewhere east of Suez, sentiments the wider public were aware of and probably shared. The original play proved popular in repertory (one version touring Scotland early on with a cast that included Michael Caine and Terence Stamp) and there was a BBC remake in June 1981 with Michael Kitchen and Mark McManus. There were other lasting effects as well.

Willis Hall had been at school with Keith Waterhouse, and the huge success of his play led to Waterhouse suggesting they adapt *Billy Liar* for the stage. Subsequently they collaborated on many other projects for cinema, TV and theatre, including such seminal works as *Whistle Down the Wind, A Kind of Loving* and *That Was the Week that Was*.

Leaving aside revisionist accounts of wartime debacles, the tribulations of National Service were also examined. For most of those conscripted it was an experience marked more by boredom than danger, but during the retreat from Empire some lost their lives in a string of colonial conflicts. Typical of these was the 'Cyprus Emergency' in which several hundred UK service personnel were killed between 1955 and 1959. This was the setting for *Private Potter*, broadcast as an hour-long episode of ITV *Playdate* in April 1961.

It was directed by Caspar Wrede and written by Ronald Harwood, the same team that made the much-liked *The Barber of Stamford Hill* for ITV *Television Playhouse* a year earlier. The plot of *Private Potter* is deceptively simple: a soldier has a vision of God on the battlefield, jeopardises an important operation and is then court martialled. This leads to a debate between the commanding officer, medical officer and padre about whether the soldier is mad, suffering from delusions and requires hospital treatment, or failing as a soldier and deserving of military punishment – or whether he really has had a genuine religious experience.

Potter was played by Tom Courtenay, who was cast whilst part of the Old Vic company. It brought him to the attention of mass audiences and was a defining role for him: physically slight, working-class, refusing orders, put-upon, puzzled, striking out on his own, defiant: every inch an outsider. MGM's UK subsidiary liked what they saw and acquired the film rights, keeping Courtenay in the main role, Wrede as director and Harwood as scriptwriter. To increase the running time an extra character – Yannis, a Greek nationalist – was worked in, but otherwise it remained a straightforward reshoot of the TV play.

The problem was there was no audience appetite for a film that presented events in Cyprus in such an even-handed way. Press previews were fair, at best, and it eventually went out as a supporting feature. By that time the United Nations had sent a peace-keeping force to the island to separate the warring Greek and Turkish communities.

Prior to that, Wrede, Harwood and Courtenay made *The Lads*, another effort set in Cyprus, which was screened on ITV *Playhouse* in August 1963. Hard to categorise, this followed a group of young soldiers 'on the lookout for girls' prior to manoeuvres, with all the action in the plot developed by songs a la *What a Crazy World*. Trevor Peacock, a confrère of Jack Good's, and writer of pop hits for Jess Conrad, Bernard Cribbins, Joe Brown, Adam Faith and The Vernon Girls, provided the lyrics. John Thaw co-starred with Coral Atkins and Tom Courtenay even released an EP and single on Decca containing the material.

One wonders if this wasn't an attempt, given Courtenay's chippy acting style, to turn him into a pop star like Mike Sarne or Anthony Newley. If so, he didn't succeed, though the best of the songs, *Mrs Brown You've Got a Lovely Daughter*, subsequently reached No 1 in the US when covered by Herman's Hermits in March 1965. Trying to gauge the intention behind *The Lads* is difficult due to its non-availability: like *The Madhouse on Castle Street*, *Linda* and *Farewell Performance* it appears to be a lost work.

Whilst *Private Potter* was being filmed, Arnold Wesker's play *Chips with Everything* was running at the Royal Court Theatre. A study of how class is maintained by authoritarian means, and his fifth consecutive success, it was directed by John Dexter, whose distinguished stage career included the Waterhouse/Hall satirical revue *England our England* and, a little later, *Half a Sixpence*, the musical based on H G Wells's *Kipps* novel.

As with *The Kitchen*, Wesker deploys an ensemble cast, following a group of conscripts making their way through the RAF, in which Wesker himself served in the early 50s. One of these, Pip Thompson, is comfortably well-off but determined to avoid the compromises of becoming a commissioned officer. He believes himself to be a socialist, providing a line of dialogue about the 'squalor' of London's East End, typified by greasy cafés offering 'chips with everything' from which the play draws its title. In many ways it is a typical service drama. Some of the recruits are stronger than others; one is weak and bullied easily by the others; there are unpleasant, disciplinarian NCOs, sarcastic, supercilious officers and so on. But none of this is played for laughs in the way it would have been in a more conventional production. The plot shows, instead, how the officers eventually force Pip to conform and join their ranks.

The play starred Frank Finlay and Corin Redgrave. Ronald Lacey played the unfortunate 'Smiler', a recruit who can't stop smiling, and John Kelland played Pip. It drew approval from Kenneth Tynan and after an August 1963 BBC TV screening it transferred to Broadway, where Finlay and Kelland were replaced by Alan Dobie and Gary Bond. The play remained popular in repertory, and with schools, for decades afterwards. It was adapted for radio and had a major revival at the National Theatre in 1997.

Chips With Everything is one of a few works to look seriously at conscription. Another, David Lodge's fine 1962 novel *Ginger, You're Barmy* never got as far as being filmed for either TV or cinema. National service was something young men had a love-hate relationship with. Whilst the experience may have been disagreeable, particularly when it involved any fighting, its trappings and routines tended to be regarded in later years with nostalgia. Reflecting this, writers usually avoided analysis of its role in maintaining British power abroad, and of the ludicrous class-based structures within the forces themselves in favour of a comic approach. This was the case as early as 1957 in the TV series *The Army Game*, with the same approach being followed in John Dexter's film version of Leslie Thomas's 1966 novel *The Virgin Soldiers*, and the 1975 ITV drama *Get Some In*, which ran for six series until 1978.

Whilst conscripts, whose tenure in the services was usually 2-3 years at most, might have looked back with fondness, the continued reduction in the size of the military had graver consequences for those who had thought it might offer them a lifelong career. Quite suddenly, certainly for the first time in living memory, officers who assumed they would enjoy lengthy postings abroad with a substantial pension to follow, were finding themselves being made redundant. The literary possibilities of this were explored by John Boland in his post-Suez 1958 novel *The League of Gentlemen*.

This appeared after the 1957 Defence White Paper had halved the size of the Army, and its plot revolved around the newly redundant Lieutenant-Colonel Hyde, whose career has been blameless. He wants to get back at officialdom for ending his employment. To do so he recruits a group of ex-officers, all of whom have left the army, to rob a bank in the City of London, with each of them getting 10 per cent of the proceeds.

The novel sold well, and the film rights were purchased by Basil Dearden and Michael Relph. Produced by Allied Film Makers, it preceded *Whistle Down the Wind* and *Victim* in their schedule, and had a strong cast led by Jack Hawkins as Hyde. His colleagues, Nigel Patrick, Roger Livesey, Bryan Forbes, Richard Attenborough, Kieron Moore, Terence Alexander and Norman Bird, are a very louche and seedy group of failed military types. One (Moore) is gay, a former fascist and works in a boxing gym as a masseur. Another (Livesey) is impersonating a Catholic priest whilst selling pornography and the others give off the same aroma as Eric Portman in *West 11* – as chancers.

To carry out the robbery they steal weapons from an army camp in Dorset, posing as Irish telephone repairmen on the basis that the authorities will then suspect the IRA of the theft. (As Hyde explains, one nationality to whom the British never give the benefit of the doubt is the Irish.) The plot rocks along efficiently, they steal the money, make their escape and meet to divide the proceeds. It appears they have succeeded, but the police capture them one by one as they leave their safe house and they end up in custody. The ending was changed – in the book Hyde shoots himself once the game is up – but this is a very droll and urbane film, in the tradition of highly-civilised British comedies like *Kind Hearts and Coronets*.

Released in April 1960, it attracted good reviews, and was one of the most successful films of the year in the UK. The only downside, and it is a minor point, is Philip Green's title music which opts for a martial, stirring *Dam Buster*-style approach when something a bit left-field might have worked better. It is too conventional for an unconventional film. Still, it remains entertaining, which makes it strange that neither of Boland's sequels, *The Gentlemen Reform* (1961) and *The Gentlemen at Large* (1962) were filmed. Instead, like *Room at the Top*, *Saturday Night and Sunday Morning* and *The Loneliness of the Long-Distance Runner*, the book's title passed into common parlance, being borrowed by two different, and unrelated, bands, a 60s mod-soul outfit and an early 80s Robert Fripp project, a 1997 radio (and later TV) series and a 1999 comic book franchise, which yielded two different and unrelated films: *The League of Extraordinary Gentlemen* (2003, which starts with a bank robbery) and *The League of Gentlemen's Apocalypse* (2005). The connecting thread appears to be the phrase being a general symbol of English quirkiness.

Such qualities are not apparent in *A Prize of Arms*, an October 1962 film about a Captain Turpin (Stanley Baker) who seeks revenge after being cashiered from the army for black market activities in Hamburg. His solution is to rob an army payroll van with a couple of accomplices whilst disguised as Military Policemen. Based on an original story by Nicolas Roeg and Kevin Kavanagh (who regularly worked together as a cameraman and focus puller, though not on *A Prize of Arms*), it was directed by Cliff Owen, and 'presented by' Bryanston, independent film producers who operated between 1959 and 1964. Like *The Entertainer* (also part of the Bryanston stable, along with *A Taste of Honey* and others), it is set in 1956, as a British army unit is preparing to depart for Suez.

With almost no female roles, it stars Stanley Baker (as Turpin) and Tom Bell. The plot proceeds effectively toward a brutal climax. Cornered in a garage, the crooks change out of their army uniforms and make a run for it, with their loot (£100,000 in cash) in an army lorry. Baker, displaying the same attributes that he brought to his role in *Yesterday's Enemy*, uses a flamethrower to clear their path, only for the truck, which is on fire as well, to explode killing them all before they reach safety. The film received good notices from the critics, but didn't perform particularly well at the box office.

The Army's decline in size was due to the retreat from Empire, which began with Indian independence in 1947. Following a pause, it continued at some speed from 1957. As territory after territory became independent, the number of overseas military bases diminished and so, eventually, did the size of Britain's armed forces. Concurrent with this, and to the surprise of many in the UK, significant numbers of immigrants began arriving from the Commonwealth and settling in British cities. This occurred both before and after the independence of their places of birth, and they were fully entitled to do so because of the 1948 British Nationality Act, which created, in a moment of largesse from a Labour government, a single category of citizenship for the UK and its colonies, with all who qualified enjoying freedom to move, live and work throughout the Commonwealth.

No particular concern was attached to those who arrived from the largely white 'old Commonwealth' (Canada, South Africa, Australia, New Zealand). The opposite was true for 'new Commonwealth' immigrants, most notably those who came from the West Indies and East Asia. Though limited in size by the standards of later years, by the mid-50s non-white communities were visible in cities throughout the UK, rather than just a few specific locations, and a sense of grievance was taking root in some sections of the UK's indigenous population about access to employment, housing and social amenities. Eventually race riots erupted, the most notable of which took place in the St Anne's district of Nottingham and Notting Hill, London in the summer of 1958.

With hindsight it is striking how rapidly the artistic and cultural community responded to these events. Within a month Laurence Olivier, Johnny Dankworth, Tommy Steele, George Melly, Cleo Laine, Lonnie Donegan and Humphrey Lyttleton had founded the Stars Campaign for Inter-Racial Friendship, who distributed newsletters and launched the first-ever UK Carnival, at St Pancras Town Hall in early 1959.

A play, *Hot Summer Night*, also appeared. Written by Ted Willis, it opened in repertory in late September 1958, reaching the New Theatre, St Martin's Lane two months later. A study of an interracial romance within the family of a trade union leader, its treatment of the issues was interesting: the trade union leader, Jacko, played by John Slater, was committed to upholding workers' rights, but found it difficult to come to terms with his daughter's relationship with a black colleague. Andrée Melly, sister of jazz singer George, appeared as the daughter, and Lloyd Reckord as her suitor.

Something of a *succès de scandale* (there was an interracial kiss between Melly and Reckord, the first ever on a UK stage) a TV version, directed by Ted Kotcheff, was broadcast in February 1959 as part of ABC-TV's *Armchair Theatre*. Rank then bought the film rights, hired Roy Ward Baker to direct and had Willis rewrite the script, moving the action to 5th November and changing the title to *Flame in the Streets*. It was shot in colour with a completely new cast. John Mills played Jacko and Sylvia Syms his daughter with Johnny Sekka as the boyfriend. The plot remained the same, albeit with the addition of a brawl at the end, and the emergence of Jacko's wife (Brenda de Banzie) as a racist remains shocking. It premiered in London in June 1961 to good reviews and remains a generally worthy attempt at putting a difficult subject on screen. Willis's script was nominated for a BAFTA award and a novelised version of the screenplay, by John Burke, was also published.

Whilst Willis was toiling on *Hot Summer Night*, Rank commissioned Janet Green to write *Sapphire*. This began filming in the autumn of 1958 and starts on Hampstead Heath where children discover the body of a young woman who has been stabbed to death. The police – in post-war regulation raincoats and trilbies – arrive and eventually identify her as Sapphire Robbins. The plot then follows their efforts to trace her family and friends and discover her murderer.

It quickly emerges that she was mixed-race, but could 'pass' as white. They visit the Tulip Club, a West Indian shebeen she frequented, and interview her (black) brother, a GP in Birmingham. The police are divided in their approach to the crime. The senior officer Superintendent Hazard (played by Nigel Patrick) is open-minded, whilst his younger colleague, Inspector Learoyd (played by Michael Craig) is biased about the victim and her acquaintances.

An autopsy shows Sapphire was pregnant when killed, and further enquiries lead them to David, her fiancée, an architecture student from a respectable, but ultimately racist family. It turns out she was killed by David's sister who was motivated by hatred of her for lowering the family's social standing. Case solved, the police arrest the sister and the film ends with Superintendent Hazard acknowledging that such events are part of a much bigger social problem, and that the police 'didn't solve anything... We just picked up the pieces'.

Sapphire was produced by Michael Relph and directed by Basil Dearden immediately after their work on *Violent Playground*. Like that, and *Tiger Bay*, it provides us with an early view of an emerging multi-racial Britain. It benefits from a strong cast, including Bernard Miles as the head of the family, Paul Massie as the son and Earl Cameron (from *Flame in the Streets*) as Sapphire's brother. Yvonne Mitchell – a cousin of Conservative MP Keith Joseph – is particularly fine as the sister.

Like much of Rank's output, it is somewhat over concerned with being 'impartial', which means the audience is presented with various assumptions: a young woman living alone in London is likely to be promiscuous, enthusiasm for jazz is proof of dubious character, and so on. But whilst this may seem quaint today, it was innovative and challenging material at the time.

The *Daily Worker* in particular was fulsome in its praise and on its release in April 1959, *Sapphire* made a profit and won Best British Film at the 1960 BAFTAs. There was no soundtrack album, but the title theme, a nice moody piece by the Pinewood Studio Orchestra 'featuring Johnny Dankworth and his saxophone' was released as a single on Top Rank. The topicality and popularity of the film also produced a tie-in novelisation, published by Panther and written by E G Cousins.

The dangers of bigotry were also explored in *The Wind of Change*, a second feature that cost less than £20,000 to make, taking its title from a phrase in Harold Macmillan's February 1960 speech to recalcitrant Afrikaners. Co-written by Alexander Doré and John McLaren, the film concentrates on the grievances nursed by local white youths following the arrival of immigrants in the Notting Hill area.

This was certainly a fraught subject. Oswald Mosley had contested the north Kensington parliamentary seat in the October 1959 general election, and much of the housing in the area had declined into slums. The plot centres on the schism in a white family between a virulently racist son (Johnny Briggs) and a fair-minded daughter (Ann Lynn). Donald Pleasence plays their father. Viewed today its portrayal of black characters is dated and the language and attitudes are often offensive, but as directed by Vernon Sewell it made a serious argument for wider tolerance. It appeared in March 1961 and was distributed by Bryanston. Rediscovered in recent years, it has been accorded rather more critical plaudits than it received at the time.

A deeper look at white working-class attitudes toward the reality of Empire was taken by John Arden in his play *Serjeant Musgrave's Dance*. Critics then rated Arden a better writer than either Pinter or Wesker and his first play was broadcast by BBC Radio in 1956. His stage debut, *Live Like Pigs*, came two years later at the Royal Court, where he worked as a script editor. Taking place in a council estate, it featured a family of travellers, who are eventually evicted. The play didn't run, but its writing was admired and led to *Serjeant Musgrave's Dance* being staged at the same venue in October 1959.

Set in late Victorian times, it follows a group of soldiers, led by Musgrave, who desert and make their way in midwinter to a northern industrial town. They have with them a coffin containing the remains of a local soldier killed in one of the many 'little wars' that maintained peace throughout the British Empire. His death resulted in five civilians being murdered in retaliation, and their objective is to shock the populace into rejecting imperialism by telling them the story.

Lindsay Anderson directed *Serjeant Musgrave's Dance* after *The Long and the Short and the Tall* and Ian Bannen played Musgrave; Frank Finlay, Alan Dobie and Donal Donnelly were his fellow deserters. Other parts went to Stratford Johns as the Mayor and mine owner, Colin Blakely as 'a pugnacious collier' and, memorably, Freda Jackson as a widowed pub landlady with a shrewd attitude to her customers. The dialogue and acting are exceptional and the political awareness of the working class is shown as being neutralised by their uncritical patriotism and fondness for drink. Predictably, Musgrave's efforts to co-opt striking miners into an uprising fail, and the play ends on a glum note with the arrival of an army detachment to arrest him.

Like Joan Littlewood's Theatre Royal, Stratford, *Serjeant Musgrave's Dance* was an ensemble piece much influenced by Brecht. It had a great deal of music and singing, the production and arranging of which was overseen by Dudley Moore. But, despite its qualities and the nineteenth-century setting (which works well) audiences resisted the idea that British soldiers might be involved in committing atrocities abroad. The play lost money, and reviewers found the ambivalence of the plot rather baffling: it was denunciatory, but perhaps not denunciatory enough, with Arden clearly having a genuine affection for working-class culture. In short, it didn't provide a neat and simple argument.

Thus, there was no film adaptation... but it did get made more than once for TV. Granada's production in October 1961 replaced

Bannen with Patrick McGoohan. After which came a three-part
BBC Schools series in 1965 and, by the end of the decade, a West
German TV version. The Vietnam war certainly gave it added
relevance to audiences, and it remains Arden's best-known work.
The most political and acerbic of the writers to emerge post-Suez,
by 1970 he had moved to Galway in Ireland where for many
years he was a member of Sinn Féin. Unlike Alan Sillitoe, the
contemporary with whom his work has the greatest affinity, he
did not enjoy spectacular commercial success. Quite how far adrift
from popular taste his anti-imperialism was can be illustrated by
the existence, alongside *Serjeant Musgrave's Dance*, of a film like
The Queen's Guards.

This was made by Michael Powell immediately after *Peeping
Tom*, and suggests that he wanted the best of both worlds:
artistic, cutting-edge kudos from *Peeping Tom* and establishment
endorsement via an unashamedly patriotic flag-waver. The idea
for *The Queen's Guards* came from Simon Harcourt-Smith, a minor
novelist and friend of Powell's, who was inspired by watching the
Household Cavalry outside Buckingham Palace. He co-wrote a
script with Roger Milner about a family whose sons have always
served in the Guards. To the family's shame, the elder son failed
in his duties during the war, and was killed. His younger brother
seeks to redeem the family's reputation.

The project, which emphasised honour, tradition and service,
was thought suitable by the Royal Household and Powell, cast and
crew accompanied the Guards on manoeuvres to Salisbury Plain
and Libya, which still hosted British bases. The plot more or less
wrote itself. The younger brother sees some action and handles
himself well. On his return to the UK, he is allowed to command
the colour party, at the Trooping of the Colour, which the Queen
had granted Powell permission to film.

The appearance of Daniel Massey, as the younger brother, and
Robert Stephens, as a fellow officer could have lent the film a
contemporary edge, Stephens having been in *A Taste of Honey* and
both appearing in productions of *The Entertainer* (there was even
a role for Jess Conrad who sings in the film too). Instead, it seems

steeped in tradition, with the inclusion of Raymond Massey and Ursula Jeans – both veterans of Powell films – reinforcing the impression.

Essentially, the actors do their best but are hampered by the script, which remained rather vague about the events which were supposed to have happened to the family in the past. If, for instance, the younger brother was 21-22 years old in 1960, and his older sibling had died in the war, an age gap of nearly 20 years is implied between them. No background detail on this is given. Similarly, the colonial skirmish where Massey redeems their honour, is supposedly set in Kenya during the Mau Mau uprising, but on screen it takes place in a desert setting, which is not typical of that country and the Guards didn't actually serve in Kenya.

Produced by a standalone company, Imperial Films (one wonders if this was ironic) but distributed by 20th Century Fox, *The Queen's Guards* was not favourably reviewed on its release. The obloquy heaped on Powell after the critical panning of *Peeping Tom* almost definitely militated against the film but, in truth, October 1961 was very late in the day for this type of drama and after a limited cinema run it was shelved, and hardly screened on TV in the years that followed.

A similarly misjudged project, *The Hellions*, appeared a month later. One of a series of attempts to make a UK Western, it was filmed in South Africa at exactly the moment that country was declaring itself independent and imposing authoritarian minority rule on its diverse population.

Like *Serjeant Musgrave's Dance*, this was a period piece, set in a pre-1914 Transvaal. The script was based on a story by US writer Harold Swanton who had worked with some success on TV series like *Buckskin* and *Wagon Train*. The plot basically replicates *High Noon*: a gang are terrorising a small town and a solitary police sergeant (played by Richard Todd) stands up to them – eventually the citizens rally round, and the baddies are vanquished. *The Hellions* was filmed in colour and produced by the same company behind most of Anthony Newley's output. As a result, several of the cast – Lionel Jeffries, James Booth, Anne Aubrey – are familiar from appearances in these. As in Newley's films there are comedic overtones, helped by a director, Ken Annakin, who was best known for popular entertainments like *Hotel Sahara* and *Swiss Family Robinson*. Others in the cast include Colin Blakely and Marty Wilde (as gang members), Ronald Fraser and Jamie Uys, the latter huge in South African/Afrikaner cinema and credited as co-producer.

The objective seems to have been to make something akin to a John Wayne film where white settlers/frontiersmen are in the ascendancy and the local indigenous population are subservient. Larry Adler composed and arranged the music, which included a main title theme sung by Marty Wilde, who released it on the B-side of his single *Tomorrow's Clown*. Done in the style of Frankie Laine's *Ballad of High Noon*, this was very passé. The critics weren't impressed either, *The New York Times* calling the film 'wide screen drivel' but a greater criticism would be how anachronistic it was. There was hardly a black face to be seen, which for something set in Africa, was extraordinary. It may be forgotten now, but *The Hellions* received quite a PR push in the UK in 1961, which was revealing of mainstream attitudes to race, and also of attitudes to film funding. It is striking that there was money to make this and *The Queen's Guards*, but not *Serjeant Musgrave's Dance* or Albert Finney's version of *Ned Kelly*.

A much better look at colonialism, class and the realities of Empire came with *Zulu*, the source of which was an April 1958 article in *Lilliput* magazine, 'Slaughter in the Sun'. Written by John Prebble, an English writer and former Communist, it was an account of how a small British force at Rorke's Drift mission station held off an attack by a vast army of Zulu warriors during the Anglo-Zulu War in 1879. Prebble, who wrote it using the pen name John Curtis, was a published novelist, with seven to his name, one of which *White Feather* (1955) was filmed. He would subsequently adapt Jules Verne's *L'Île mystérieuse* for the cinema as *Mysterious Island* (a huge success) before writing about the misfortunes suffered by Scotland in *Culloden* (1961) and *The Highland Clearances* (1963).

Slaughter in the Sun was read by director Cy Endfield, like Joseph Losey a US exile working in the UK. He optioned it with Stanley Baker, wrote a script and eventually, three years later, secured funding from producer Joseph E Levine. Paramount agreed to distribute it in most territories and arrangements were made to film on location in South Africa, including within Zululand. It went without saying that Stanley Baker would star as Lieutenant Chard, one of two officers present at the action. Alongside him were Jack Hawkins as a Swedish missionary, Ulla Jacobsson as his daughter, with James Booth, Nigel Green, David Kernan and Patrick Magee among those playing soldiers at the mission station.

The role of the second officer (Lieutenant Bromhead) went, memorably, to Michael Caine. His film career up until that point had consisted almost entirely of uncredited bit parts, but he was becoming known on TV, appearing in plays by Bill Naughton and Johnny Speight, his fortunes lifting due to the vogue for working-class cockney characters. He auditioned whilst appearing at the Arts Theatre, London in *Next Time I'll Sing to You*, an Absurdist production by James Saunders, and was clear in later years that he landed the part because Endfield lacked the class perspective of UK directors: 'No English director would've cast me as an officer, I promise you, not one.'

Over two hours long, the film has excellently-shot battle scenes, utilising over 1,200 Zulu extras. The non-acting British defenders were played by 80 South African army soldiers, augmented by Gert van den Bergh, a South African/Afrikaner actor of some distinction, who, like Booth, can also be seen in *The Hellions*. The brutality of the hand-to-hand fighting is stressed, but never glorified, and both sides – white and African – are shown as being heroic. It concludes with the Zulu warriors withdrawing and saluting the bravery of the defenders.

Released in January 1964, it was one of the biggest box-office hits of all time in the UK. John Barry provided one of his most famous soundtracks, slotting it in between his work on the burgeoning James Bond franchise. *Zulu* attracted favourable reviews, even if some critics compared it to the guilty pleasures of reading Kipling or Rider Haggard. It was so popular with domestic audiences that it remained on general release in cinemas until 1976, after which it transferred to TV where its screenings attracted large audiences. A survey of British army personnel in the 80s recorded it as their favourite film (it is easy to see why) and it had admirers everywhere, some less likely than others (including Mark E Smith, lead singer of The Fall who claimed to be a descendant of one of Rorke's Drift's defenders, Private Hook, played in the film as a working-class hero by James Booth).

Debate continues as to how much *Zulu* was an anti-Empire film, or just racist entertainment, showing as it does the killing of thousands of spear-carrying Africans by a handful of white European soldiers. In assessing this it is best to remember that what is shown on the screen – though accurate in terms of its beginning and ending – is drama, not documentary. But it does address significant issues arising from colonialism in a way that was markedly different to how the cinema had traditionally portrayed imperial themes.

Firstly, unlike most films' depiction of black characters at the time, it portrays the Zulus as equals. They are shown as disciplined, rational and independent. Their leader, Cetshwayo was played on screen by his great-grandson, Chief Buthelezi, inspired casting which was contrary to other films of this period where black and ethnic minority figures were often played by actors of a completely different background. Secondly, class is well to the fore. The two officers bicker amongst themselves with Caine/Bromhead (a commissioned officer from a famous regiment, with illustrious forebears) looking down on Baker/Chard (a Royal Engineer). Neither are well-informed about Africa, which amazes van den Bergh playing the solitary Afrikaner. The regiment is the South Wales Borderers and a number of the Welsh infantrymen are portrayed as clear underlings in the hierarchy, while James Booth's Hook character seems to represent the disreputable, feckless working class – Nigel Green as the Colour Sergeant clearly knows his place too.

Zulu appeared when the Union Jack was being lowered across

Africa and most other parts of the British Empire. It could not have been made earlier, and although it did eventually spawn a prequel with *Zulu Dawn* (1979), other examples of this type of cinema were not produced by the UK. It repays careful viewing.

BETWEEN THE END OF THE CHATTERLEY BAN AND THE BEATLES FIRST LP

Philip Larkin wrote 'Annus Mirabilis' in 1967. It was included in his 1974 collection *High Windows*, an audio version of which appeared as an LP a year later. Written with hindsight – he was just under 40 when it was composed – it records the amazement experienced by those who grew up during the 30s, lived through the war and the drab post-1945 conformism of austerity, at the sudden, abrupt, loosening of long-standing social restrictions.

Larkin's verse considers the period between the end of the *Lady Chatterley's Lover* ban and the release of the Beatles' first LP when a more liberated attitude to sex started to spread in society: 'every life became a brilliant breaking of the bank, a quite unlosable game.' Typically, he tinges this with regret and a sense of failure, acknowledging that although life was better it was 'just too late for me'. Many others of his generation felt the same and this fine piece of pithy, poetic observation became justly famous.

Larkin was never an angry young man, but did share some attributes with them. He was provincial – born in Coventry, died in Hull – and at one point a member of 'The Movement' a poetry group in the mid-50s that included John Wain and Kingsley Amis. He had a fondness for jazz, serving as jazz critic of *The Daily Telegraph* for a decade, and in personality was not unlike Tony Hancock: lugubrious, deadpan, usually defeated but staunchly adhering to his views.

His pinpointing of *Lady Chatterley's Lover* as a turning point had significance. As a teenager his father had introduced him to Lawrence's work. Whilst most of it was available, *The Rainbow*

(1915), *Women in Love* (1920) and *Lady Chatterley's Lover* (1928)
were all banned and only accessible in expurgated form, or from
selected book shops that quietly distributed uncensored, imported
copies. Restrictions on the first two were lifted after Lawrence's
death but the latter, with its scatological Anglo-Saxon language
and detailed descriptions of sexual activity, remained inviolable, a
sacred and symbolic barrier that the population were not allowed
to breach.

In June 1959 (when Larkin was 37) the US lifted its ban
on the book and allowed a – very tame – French film version
made in 1955 to be distributed. This, and a sense that the times
were changing, persuaded veteran US producer Jerry Wald to
temporarily relocate to the UK where he made *Sons and Lovers*.
He had tried for some years, without success, to get the project
off the ground in the US, with either Montgomery Clift or James
Dean starring opposite Marilyn Monroe. Now he opted to film it
on location in Nottinghamshire, from a script by Gavin Lambert
(a friend of Karel Reisz and Lindsay Anderson) and T E B Clarke
that closely adhered to Lawrence's novel.

Wald was aware how much impact British Kitchen Sink films
were having and hired Jack Cardiff as director and Freddie Francis
as cinematographer, Francis being noted for his work on *Room at
the Top* and *Saturday Night and Sunday Morning*. At the insistence
of 20th Century Fox, who were distributing, compromises were
made in casting the leading role of Paul Morel, the artistically-
inclined son who ultimately leaves home to make his way in the
wider world. Young US actor Dean Stockwell was brought in to
play him. Otherwise, the roles were perfectly cast. Trevor Howard
and Wendy Hiller appeared as the tyrannical father and frustrated,
possessive, mother, and Heather Sears and Mary Ure as the two
women who become the objects of Paul's passion, Miriam Leivers
and Clara Dawes.

The film explores sexual frustration, infidelity and the struggle
to break class barriers. Superbly acted, particularly by Trevor
Howard, it premiered at Cannes in May 1960 and was nominated
for the Palme D'Or, losing to Federico Fellini's *La Dolce Vita*.

Enthusiastically received by critics and the public, it went on to be nominated for seven Academy Awards, winning one for Best Cinematography.

A prestige production, with music by Italian composer Mario Nascimbene, one is struck when watching it today how easy it was in the late 50s to film something set during the Edwardian era in and around Nottingham. In many respects the landscape hadn't changed very much. With its black and white industrial photography and provincial locations, it is a neglected part of the canon of works associated with Kitchen Sink cinema, particularly when one considers the acclaim with which it was received.

The success of *Sons and Lovers* occurred whilst Penguin Books were in the process of printing and distributing an unexpurgated version of *Lady Chatterley's Lover*. This had been mentioned as early as January 1960, and was confirmed that August. Larkin thought this was asking for trouble, and like many considered Lawrence a lost cause, pointing out that it was the decision to publish in paperback at only 3s 6d (17½p) that concerned the establishment, remarking in private correspondence 'the thing about pornography is that it isn't cheap' and citing the going rate for material of this type in Charing Cross Road. (He knew about such matters.)

The subsequent trial, which *Absolute Beginners* author Colin MacInnes thought farcical given that everyone who either wanted to read the book or who appreciated it as literature had already done so, was memorable for being conducted almost at the level of performance art. At one point the prosecution considered calling Rudyard Kipling as a witness, only to be reminded that he had died in 1936. It lasted until 2nd November 1960, when the jury unanimously declared Penguin not guilty of publishing obscene material. In fact, so memorable was it that a drama of the trial, based on court transcripts, was broadcast by the Canadian Broadcasting Corporation a year later as an episode of their *Quest* series. (A BBC dramatization didn't happen until 2006.)

The aftermath of the trial did not initially produce many fresh Lawrence adaptations. In 1966 ITV broadcast a series, *Stories of*

D H Lawrence, and late 1967 brought another film, *The Fox*, made in Canada. That year also saw production work start on *Women in Love* and *The Virgin and the Gipsy*, both of which had a considerable commercial and critical impact on their release in 1969 and 1970, respectively. The main beneficiaries of the verdict, and the general loosening of ties that accompanied it were other authors and producers. Post-1960 the public could explore films that looked at relationships in a far more adult fashion, including those that were transgressive or gay. Nor was this limited to sexual matters. There would be serious studies of politics and colourful escapist fantasies too, forming the path that led, eventually, to *A Hard Day's Night*.

The first such to appear was *The Greengage Summer*, released in April 1961, and based on a 1958 Rumer Godden novel of the same name. Godden was a popular writer through the 40s and 50s, with several of her works adapted for cinema, including *Black Narcissus* (1947) by Michael Powell and *The River* (1951) by Jean Renoir. In 1956 she published *An Episode of Sparrows*, filmed two years later as *Innocent Sinners*, an almost perfect portrayal of children growing up in an inner-city London full of bomb sites and dereliction. *The Greengage Summer* also involves children navigating an adult world, specifically two adolescent sisters who develop crushes on a dishonest, debonair conman.

Like the book, the film is an elegantly put together drama with a script by Howard Koch whose credits included the script for Max Ophüls's 1948 film of Stefan Zweig's *Letter from an Unknown Woman* and co-authorship of *Casablanca*. *The Greengage Summer* was directed by Lewis Gilbert, forming something of a bridge between the war heroics for which he was famous (*Reach for the Sky, Sink the Bismark!*) and his later work (*Alfie*). Importantly, it was filmed in France, in colour, which may seem like a minor point now but gave it an immensely fresh feel at the time.

The plot centres on a group of English middle-class children on holiday in France with their mother. Their father is away overseas and their mother is taken ill on arrival, so responsibility devolves to Joss the eldest daughter, aged 16 and played by Susannah York.

They end up staying in a hotel owned by two women, Madame Corbet (Claude Nollier) and Zizi (Danielle Darrieux), who are in an implied lesbian relationship. Zizi is also involved with a middle-aged Englishman, Eliot (Kenneth More), who spends his time flitting to and from Paris and keeping irregular hours. In the absence of their parents, and with them not speaking any French, he acts, by default, as a chaperone for the children. Joss is attracted to him. As is her younger sister, Hester, played by a 13-year-old Jane Asher, who also takes a liking to Paul, one of the hotel staff.

It all gets a bit complicated. Zizi is jealous of Joss. Paul is killed after falling from Joss's bedroom. Joss tells Eliot she will never love anyone else. They embrace passionately. The police are called, Eliot disappears and a remarkable denouement is played out in the hotel reception area as the police interrogate Madame Corbet, Zizi and the children. In a scene that would be at home in any French novel dealing with crimes of passion, the scale of Eliot's misdemeanours is revealed. The film ends with Eliot certain to be cornered by the police and Joss older and wiser.

Well written and played, it premiered at the Odeon Leicester Square in April 1961. Reviews were positive, the only downside being a general consensus that More was insufficiently dissolute and someone like Dirk Bogarde might have been better. The elegance of the hotel (virtually a chateaux), languorous summer setting and frisson of sexual attraction between teenage girls and older men make it hard to imagine this being made, in anything like as frank a way, pre-*Chatterley*.

An inappropriate relationship between an impressionable teenage girl and a man was also centre stage in *Term of Trial*. This began life as a 1961 novel by James Barlow, formerly a water rates inspector with Birmingham Corporation. Set in an industrial town somewhere in England, it focuses on Graham Weir, a schoolteacher who spent the war years as a conscientious objector. Because this involved a spell in prison, he is now teaching in a secondary school with unruly working-class pupils, taking an interest in one, Shirley Taylor, aged 15, who rapidly becomes infatuated with him. The book was praised and came to the attention of John and James

Woolf, the producers of *Room at the Top* and *The L-Shaped Room*. It is hard not to imagine that their interest had something to do with the ascent to worldwide notoriety of Vladimir Nabokov's *Lolita*. Published in 1955, banned (but available, like *Chatterley*, from discreet importers) Stanley Kubrick had talked about filming it from 1958, and finally went into production in 1960. With a plot about a middle-aged professor besotted by his landlady's pre-pubescent daughter, doubts about it getting a release certificate were so strong that Laurence Olivier declined the leading role which went instead to James Mason. Despite this, a few months later, with funding in place and Peter Glenville signed up to direct, he agreed to play Graham Weir in *Term of Trial*.

Glenville, the personification of the distinguished, highly cultured director, was known for his theatre work in plays by Aldous Huxley, Tennessee Williams, Terence Rattigan and Graham Greene. He had also directed Bridget Boland's *The Prisoner* filmed in 1955 with Alec Guinness and Jean Anouilh's *Beckett*, on Broadway with Olivier in 1960. The supporting roles in *Term of Trial* are played by Simone Signoret, as Weir's embittered wife, and Sarah Miles, as Taylor. There is also an interesting early appearance by Terence Stamp as an unpleasant local hooligan, speaking here with a pronounced 'northern' accent. Filmed in black and white, with Dublin standing in for the unnamed provincial location, the cinematography by Oswald Morris was excellent and the film score, by French classical composer Jean-Michel Damase, brilliant. The denouement, with Olivier on trial after being accused of indecent assault by Miles, remains powerful and the film concludes with him and Signoret reconciled.

Released in August 1962, with an X certificate, it was appreciated by domestic critics but found dull elsewhere, particularly in the US where Bosley Crowther, in the *New York Times* called it 'this British rehash of *Blackboard Jungle*, with minor *Lolita* overtones'. Olivier received a BAFTA nomination for his performance, as did Mason for his in *Lolita*. Neither won and *Term of Trial* quickly disappeared apart from occasional TV screenings after its cinema run. Its most enduring legacy would appear to be the 20 year on-off affair it instigated between Olivier and Miles, 54 and 19 respectively when filming. Looking at Glenville's (and Kubrick's) films today one is struck by the degree of licence available then to writers and filmmakers in their portrayal of sexual relationships that teetered on the edge of the perverse.

On a slightly more conventional plane, the outcome of the *Chatterley* trial also opened up the possibility of fiction and film exploring marital infidelities on a much grander scale than had previously been the case. The 60s and 70s produced many studies of middle-class couples, their affairs and open marriages, conducted in a world of nice houses, modern cars, holidays, important careers and heavy drinking. Given the social setting on display, none of this was Kitchen Sink but like its grimy working-class equivalent, novels and films of this type carried the message that this was a fearless way to live, that things had moved on from cramped pre-1960 social mores and putting all of this 'out there' was what one now did.

The Woolf brothers were alert to this too and saw the artistic potential of these scenarios early on, producing the film version of Penelope Mortimer's 1962 novel *The Pumpkin Eater*. As with *Term of Trial*, it provided a superior piece of cinema. Harold Pinter was commissioned to produce a script and Jack Clayton brought in to direct. French composer Georges Delerue – feted for his work on *Jules et Jim* and much else – did the music. The central roles were played by Anne Bancroft and Peter Finch.

Pinter made some changes. In the novel Bancroft's character is called Mrs Armitage throughout. In the film she gets a Christian name, Jo, and her marriages are reduced from 4 to 3. In the novel the family are getting ready to acquire a house in the country, a glass tower, to supplement their Georgian pile in a London square. In the film this becomes a windmill. Otherwise, the plot remains intact, providing an exploration of the psychology of marriage, desire and child-bearing from a feminine perspective.

Finch's character, Jake, is a successful writer who has branched out into screenplays. He has affairs and lies about them. Bancroft finds out the truth from a jilted husband, played by James Mason.

She has a breakdown, is referred to a psychiatrist and prescribed anti-depressants. In a rage, she attacks Jake, and has a retaliatory affair with one of her former husbands. Eventually she agrees to be sterilised. The film ends with her accepting, for the moment at least, a reconciliation, partly because Jake gets on so well with her brood of children.

None of the reviews remarked that Mortimer's story was autobiographical, though one presumes most of the critics writing them would have known this. It was drawn directly from her experience of marriage with John Mortimer, who had an affair and fathered a child with Wendy Craig, whilst Penelope was pregnant for the eighth time at the age of 42. As in the book, she agreed to have an abortion and undergo sterilisation, and for a while was reconciled to him (they eventually divorced in 1971). The extent to which *The Pumpkin Eater* was used to document her experience broke new ground. Whilst there had always been books and plays about divorces, affairs and unhappy marriages, the extent of Mortimer's candour would have been unthinkable pre-*Chatterley*. The arguing, fighting, misery, desire and deceit on display are lacerating and exhausting, but undoubtedly true to life.

Released in May 1964, it garnered mainly favourable reviews, particularly in the US. Criticism was limited to caveats about Pinter's script (his style always had detractors) and in the UK the back-handed comments of the *Monthly Film Bulletin*, who noted about Bancroft's character 'Neurotics rarely get a square, sympathetic, penetrating deal in the cinema... like many neurotics she is a fixated and evidently crashing bore, and one of the most difficult things to do is to present a bore fairly without at the same time boring your audience too.' Audiences, however, liked it and despite the *Monthly Film Bulletin*, Bancroft won Best Actress at Cannes and a BAFTA.

Pinter also did the script for *The Servant*, adapted from a 70-page 1948 novella by Robin Maugham, whose work often attracted film producers. *Line on Ginger* (1949), filmed as *The Intruder* (1953) showed a middle-class man encountering a working-class wartime colleague who has descended into a life of crime. Maugham's play *Odd Man In* (1957), adapted from a French comedy, was about the peculiar arrangements that arise when a stranger takes up residence in the home of a couple. Both echo elements of the plot in *The Servant*, which is, however, a much darker piece.

The possibility of filming it had been raised as early as 1954 by Joseph Losey. By 1958 it had been adapted for repertory performances and the rights were acquired shortly afterwards by Michael Anderson. He brought in Pinter – then in the first flush of fame – to write a script in 1961, but unable to raise money for the project sold it on to Losey a year later. The theme here is decadence, specifically the idiocy of the English class system as seen by an outsider (Losey) and conveyed by Pinter's use of economical, menacing language.

The Servant is almost exclusively set in a large Chelsea townhouse (which was actually Losey's home) and filmed in the aftermath of the shockingly cold winter of 1962-1963, resulting in Losey contracting pneumonia. We are introduced to an ineffectual and wealthy young man, Tony, who is hiring Barrett, a northerner, as his manservant. Initially they seem to get on well, and their exchanges are no different from what one would expect in a relationship of that type. Tony is supposedly connected to some kind of venture to build immense modern cities in Brazil, but does little actual work in connection with this. His girlfriend, Susan, dislikes Barrett and would like to see him sacked. Tony refuses and, in the meantime, Barrett convinces him that a maid is needed. He engineers his lover, Vera, into this role but tells Tony that Vera is his sister.

Chaos – instigated and controlled by Barrett – ensues. Vera seduces Tony. Barrett and Vera are found in bed together. Barrett says they are fiancées. Susan finds out Vera has slept with Tony and leaves, refusing to return Tony's telephone calls. Tony descends into alcoholism and Barrett fills the house with prostitutes who engage in orgies. Susan fails to convince Tony to leave. The film ends with him in a stupor, Barrett and Vera still in situ, and in control.

The Servant was filmed, edited and scored as the Profumo scandal was unfolding. Losey conjures a decadent atmosphere, possibly reflecting the sort of things that, coincidentally, went on in Chelsea – and maybe still do. We should remember that one of the battle cries of the prosecution when trying to block *Lady Chatterley's Lover* had been 'Is it a book that you would even wish your wife or your servants to read?'

Losey's cast were excellent. Dirk Bogarde as Barrett, Sarah Miles as Vera and Wendy Craig as Susan were all outstanding. The part of Tony went to James Fox, who was 24 and, notwithstanding her dalliance with Olivier, Miles's boyfriend at the time. Fox's other great role would be in *Performance*, and the elegance of the setting here as well as the atmospheric cocktail of sex, alcohol and music provided by Pinter and Losey makes for an interesting comparison with that. BAFTAs were awarded to Bogarde for Best Actor, Fox as Most Promising Newcomer and Douglas Slocombe for Best Cinematography. The quality of the script won Pinter two awards (New York Film Critics Circle and Writers Guild of Great Britain) and the Italian National Syndicate of Film Journalists voted Losey Best Foreign Director.

The film premiered at the Venice Film Festival in September 1963, reaching British cinema screens several months later. It turned a profit at the box office, but despite that no attempt was made to release a soundtrack album, which seems a bit negligent considering the talent involved. Johnny Dankworth did the score, which includes a fine jazzy-bluesy number *All Gone* sung by Cleo Laine with lyrics by Pinter. It eventually got a release in January 1964 as the B-side of a single on Fontana. Similarly, the film was also notable for an appearance by folk guitarist Davy Graham playing *Rock Me Baby*, later included on his 1965 album *Folk, Blues and Beyond*.

Taken from a short story by US writer Marc Behm, *The Party's Over*, like *The Servant*, offers moral degradation in a classy London setting. Behm, resident in Paris, had a background not unlike that of Terry Southern and had written the screenplay for *Charade*, one of the top box office films of 1963. Funding to make *The*

Party's Over came from Tricastle Films, a company put together by Jack Hawkins and Peter O'Toole after their work on *Lawrence of Arabia*. In 1953 Hawkins had starred in *The Intruder*, adapted from Robin Maugham's short story by Guy Hamilton. Now he brought in Hamilton to direct *The Party's Over*, with an idea to make something that could be marketed in the US as a film about contemporary London.

The plot concerns a young American woman who falls in with a group of Chelsea beatniks during a visit to London. They live the bohemian life to the full – meaning a lot of free love, jazz, smoking and late-night parties – and eventually her fiancé crosses the Atlantic to try and bring her back. Sadly, she ends up dead after one party too many, with one of the crowd so unaware of this that he passionately kisses her corpse and then, stricken with revulsion at his act, commits suicide. Her father arrives from the US to take her body home for burial and the leader of the beatniks attempts to apologise.

Necrophilia, either real or implied, was a step too far even in the post-*Chatterley* era and the censor promptly blocked the film. Ready for release in late 1963 it was cut (by 18 minutes), re-edited and a had a moralising voiceover added. Guy Hamilton took his name off the credits and it limped out, as a supporting feature, to little attention in April 1965. The brief notoriety that attended it does not appear to have affected the fortunes of Behm, who went on to script *Help!* – or Hamilton, who subsequently directed four of the Bond films and *Battle of Britain*. Importantly, it provided a first leading role for Oliver Reed who had previously played not dissimilar characters in *Beat Girl* and *The Rebel*. He would subsequently go on to be one of the major UK stars of the decade. Trying to gauge its worth today is hard, given the lack of a definitive directors cut. It does have good photography, from Larry Pizer, and is solidly acted, particularly by the young actresses Katherine Woodville, also in *The Wild and the Willing*, and Ann Lynn (formerly married to Anthony Newley), from *The Wind of Change*, who partners Reed at the end.

The music, a collaboration between John Barry, Tony Kinsey and Stanley Myers is fine. There was also a sequence shot in a jazz club with Spike Heatley, Dankworth's double bass player. Alas, like so many scores of this period, it never made it as far as a vinyl release. Particularly outstanding is Annie Ross's *Time Waits for No Man*, sung over the opening credits as the beatniks straggle home from another all-nighter dressed very much like extras from the mid-60s TV series *The Prisoner*.

The *Chatterley* trial, and its aftermath unfolded alongside a growing awareness that the UK's law on homosexuality needed reform. Cinematic and theatrical portrayals of the love that dare not speak its name were limited because of an ongoing threat of censorship and prosecution for obscenity, and the portrayal of gay characters was almost unreservedly negative. The publication of the Wolfenden Report in September 1957 provided a glimmer of hope that a more liberal approach might be forthcoming, and it was in this context that two separate, and worthy, films about the legal travails of Oscar Wilde were released in the UK in May 1960.

Shot in black and white, *Oscar Wilde*, with Robert Morley as Wilde, was based on a 1936 play banned by the Lord Chamberlain, performances of which were only permitted in private theatre clubs that required membership. Robert Morley was actually reprising a role he originally played 24 years earlier. The play and the film focuses primarily on Wilde's libel suit against the Marquess of Queensberry which led to his downfall.

The Trials of Oscar Wilde was directed by Ken Hughes with Peter Finch playing Wilde. This had a script by H Montgomery Hyde, formerly Ulster Unionist MP for Belfast North, and written after his deselection for advocating the decriminalisation of homosexuality. The film was in fact pulled together very quickly by producer Irving Allen, with shooting not starting until February 1960 when Finch was cast. Critics tended to prefer it to Morley's effort, and he won a BAFTA, but it was banned in the US and unable to recoup its costs.

It could be argued that the films' releases were only progressive up to a point. After all, Wilde had remained a popular figure despite his imprisonment. His books were read, his plays were performed and his witticisms widely quoted. In addition to this, films about famous criminal trials, irrespective of their content, were also popular, particularly when done retrospectively as costume dramas. The dramatic moral conclusion of both films is similar. As in life, Wilde is ruined and punished for his inclinations. By the start of the 60s, possibly excepting *Serious Charge*, a film had still not been made portraying a gay character sympathetically. This finally changed when Basil Dearden and Michael Relph began preparing *Victim* from a script by Janet Green. All three had worked on *Sapphire*, an equally pioneering work, and their intention now was to make a film that would be 'an open protest against Britain's law that being a homosexual is a criminal act'.

To do so, and still ensure a cinematic release, their plot avoided anything sensationalist or contrived, including any sexual scenes. It focussed on a successful, happily-married barrister (Melville Farr), who has had, and continues to have, homosexual urges, without ever acting on them. He is friends with a young working-class building worker (Barrett) who, it turns out, is being blackmailed about his sexuality. The blackmailers have obtained a photograph of Farr and Barrett together. After Barrett commits suicide in a police cell, Farr decides to fight those responsible, finding as he does that others are also being blackmailed.

His wife (Laura) finds out about Barrett's death, not having been previously aware of Farr's friendship with him. Laura feels betrayed by the revelation and their marriage hangs in the balance throughout the film. Farr closes in on the blackmailers with the help of the police. When they are captured, Farr agrees to give evidence in court despite the prospect that this will destroy his career and ruin his chances of becoming a QC. The film ends with Farr burning the intimate photograph of him and Barrett.

To ensure the greatest possible dramatic impact Relph and Dearden cast around for a well-known, conventional leading man to play Farr. Jack Hawkins, James Mason and Stewart Granger all declined before Dirk Bogarde accepted. Frequently voted one of the most popular actors in British films, he had just been nominated for a Golden Globe for his portrayal of Franz Liszt in *Song Without End* (1960), and women's magazines were full of articles about how he might be about to marry his co-star, Capucine. In his private life, however, he lived with his business manager and fellow actor, Anthony Forwood. Seeing this as the opportunity he had been waiting for to break away from typecasting, he accepted and gently opened the closet door by doing so.

As Farr he was dignified, determined, blameless and decent, bringing the same air of integrity he had to a variety of roles; it was a formidable performance. Sylvia Syms played Laura, Peter McEnery was Barrett and Derren Nesbitt was memorable as one of the blackmailers. The acting – though excellent – does take something of a second place to the smoky film footage of London's West End. Shot in black and white by Otto Heller, who also did *Peeping Tom*, it evokes a vanished urban landscape of which only a few elements now remain. One scene was done within *The Salisbury* (which survives today), a pub in Covent Garden, and well-known gay meeting place that Oscar Wilde frequented at one point.

After some predictable sparring with the British Board of Film Censors, who demanded cuts, *Victim* premiered at the Odeon, Leicester Square in August 1961. It was the official British entry at the Venice Film Festival a month later. Critics liked it, but praise was generally restrained by the consideration that this was a 'difficult' subject, about something that remained illegal. It was popular, made a small profit and enhanced Bogarde's reputation. In its aftermath Bogarde optioned John Osborne's *Epitaph for George Dillon*, which had played the West End and Broadway 1958-1959 with Wendy Craig and Robert Stephens, and *Covenant with Death*, a John Harris novel about the destruction of a battalion of Sheffield volunteers on the first day of the Battle of the Somme. But neither could be financed, and his next serious part took a couple of years to arrive.

Some debate still surrounds *Victim* about how significant a film it is. Its timidity and dramatic framing – Farr, a 'victim', innocently embroiled in something unpleasant because of a defect in the law – has come in for criticism. The ending, too, is less than ideal.

Farr wants to stay with his wife and destroys the photograph of the young man to whom he was attracted. At no point is the possibility of homosexuality being a positive preference entertained. But it is hard to see in the context of the time what else could have been done. If the film had been stronger and more 'upfront', let alone explicit, it would have either been banned or never made. The producers had to start somewhere, and as it stands, *Victim* is a significant achievement.

By comparison, *Two Left Feet*, from a 1960 novel *In My Solitude* by David Stuart Leslie, failed to gain much attention. A noted writer at the time, Leslie's other major work was *Two Gentlemen Sharing*, filmed in 1969. *In My Solitude* was described as 'London's teenage jungle blazing vividly to life' and charted the miseries of young adulthood, particularly the tricky business of establishing your own identity. It garnered good reviews, with *The Daily Express* stating 'Fings as they are... Fresh observation, no self-pity, no phony sociology, rough and squalid, yet redeemed often by sardonic Cockney humour. A story as convincing as it is readable.' It was quickly optioned by producer Leslie Gilliat, and filmed with Roy Ward Baker directing.

The main character, Alan, is 19, shy, and unable to find a girlfriend. The film starts with him queuing up at a West End cinema to see Pamela Green in the nudist movie *Naked as Nature Intended*. He lives in Camden, with restricted social horizons, spending much of his time in a local café where he strikes up a friendship with a new waitress, Eileen, and later with another girl, Beth. The film has a gay sub-plot involving Ronnie, 17, who clearly fancies one of Alan's friends, Brian, and is advised to decide 'which way he's going'. When Brian gets married, Ronnie ends up kissing him in a party game at a wedding reception. In another twist, Beth's father is arrested and commits suicide after being charged with sexually assaulting Angela, his other daughter.

Baker and Gilliat seemed to think there was an audience for this, and the film has a strikingly young cast, the average age just 21. Michael Crawford and Nyree Dawn Porter played Alan and

Eileen after appearing in Neil Simon's *Come Blow Your Horn* at
the Prince of Wales Theatre, directed by the man behind *Zulu*, Cy
Endfield, which has a similar plot to *In My Solitude*: a young man
learning about life and how to secure a girlfriend from his older
brother. Julia Foster, David Hemmings and Michael Craze (one of
the airmen in *Chips with Everything*) appeared as Beth, Brian and
Ronnie respectively. There was a lot of music too. Tommy Bruce
sang the main title theme, Susan Maughan contributed a song
and there was an appearance, in a jazz club scene by Bob Wallis
and his Storyville Jazzmen.

But there were mutterings about men kissing each other, not
to mention incest as an element in the plot. Set in a working-
class milieu – no barristers or respectable professionals were
involved – and without established stars, it ended up with an
X certificate, thereby excluding most of its intended audience.
Although complete by March 1963, it finally reached cinemas in
May 1965, at the same time *The Knack*, an incomparably better
film, premiered at Cannes where it won the Palme D'Or. This
also starred Michael Crawford playing a character that was a clear
variation on the one he had trialled two years earlier. Today *Two
Left Feet* is hardly remembered, but a notable admirer was Smiths
singer Morrissey, who was much taken with the sexual tension
between Ronnie and Brian.

Neither *Two Left Feet* nor its source novel concentrated on
homosexuality, treating it as just one strand in a story about
young adults searching for their identity. In comparison, the
plot of *The Leather Boys*, a 1961 novel by Eliot George, though
set in the same milieu, is explicitly gay. Eliot George was the
unsubtle pseudonym for Gillian Freeman, whose previous work
included *The Liberty Man*, about a passionate (heterosexual)
affair between a sailor and a schoolteacher that was successful
enough to be made into an ITV *Play of the Week* in 1958. She
was commissioned to write *The Leather Boys* by Anthony Blond,
one of the driving forces in the liberalisation of British life. A
publisher, whose output included *The Establishment*, a collection
of essays about the informal power structures that dominated UK

life, and *The Feathers of Death*, Simon Raven's debut novel about homosexual love in the ranks of an exclusive regiment; he was also a shareholder in *Private Eye*, and politically well connected. The son-in-law of former cabinet minister John Strachey MP, he also had political aspirations of his own, having been adopted as Labour candidate for Chester, where he narrowly failed to get elected in the 1964 general election.

Blond suggested Freeman write something about 'Romeo and Romeo in the South London suburbs' and her book describes a sexual relationship between two young working-class bikers who resort to crime so that they can raise money to move abroad. The film rights were quickly acquired by producer Raymond Stross, who brought in Sidney J Furie to direct, with Gerald Gibbs as cinematographer, both of whom had previously worked on *The Boys*.

As with *Victim*, the same practical issues arose in terms of ensuring the end result would get a release certificate. Homosexuality was illegal and explicit scenes were out of the question. Freeman's plot was modified considerably. Only one of the main male characters (Pete) is gay, and neither turns to crime to fund a new life for themselves overseas. Reggie, the one with doubts about his leanings, is married and Dot, his wife, is critical of what she sees as his excessively close friendship with Pete. In a repeat of the fumblings and uncertainties shown in *Two Left Feet*, Reggie and Dot have been married since they were 17 and 16 respectively, which made it hardly surprising that they are unsure about what they want.

They have an unsuccessful honeymoon at a holiday camp. Later, Reggie and Pete end up living at Reggie's grandmother's where they share a double bed in the spare room. Dot thinks her husband and Pete 'look like a couple of queers'. She leaves him. In the final scene, which is quite a moving piece of cinema, Pete has taken Reggie to a pub in the docks so they can join a ship as deckhands. It's also a gay bar, where Pete is well-known to the clientele. Realising this, and finally clear that Pete is gay (why has it taken him so long?), Reggie walks out, the camera following him with Pete standing silently in the background, the distance between them growing.

Toning down the plot meant increasing the character of Dot, played in the film with some vigour by Rita Tushingham. It was her third film role in quick succession, made between *A Place to Go* and *The Girl with Green Eyes*. Though something of a free spirit, she plays a very different character in it to the teenage girl she portrayed in *A Taste of Honey*. The male protagonists were Colin Campbell, from *Chips with Everything*, as Reggie, Dudley Sutton as Pete and Johnny Briggs, from *The Wind of Change*, as the young man Dot seeks solace with when her husband loses interest. Within the limitations required by the censor the acting is fine, albeit Tushingham later stated that a significant amount of the dialogue was improvised because Furie's original script 'was nothing like how the youth living in London spoke at the time'.

Visually, the film captures the monotonous desolation of suburbs like Merton and Wandsworth, as well as featuring the Ace Cafe, on the North Circular Road, a famous gathering point for bikers ('ton-up boys' or slightly later, 'rockers') the footage of which makes the film popular with motorcycle enthusiasts. Furie and Gibbs also include a memorable sequence of a trip to Edinburgh and back (a 'burn up'), partly filmed at night with little dialogue and no music. The score, once again unreleased, was by jazz pianist Bill McGuffie, who did a lot of film work including *The Boys*, which was presumably why he was brought in here, and *The Comedy Man*.

Released in February 1964, *The Leather Boys* was generally reviewed favourably but failed to make much of an impact with the public. Tushingham would shortly go on to partner Michael Crawford in Richard Lester's successful film of *The Knack*. It seemed that stardom beckoned for Dudley Sutton, who was Sloane in the original 1964 production of Joe Orton's *Entertaining Mr Sloane* at the New Arts Theatre as well as appearing on both sides of the Atlantic in *The Hostage*. But he was passed over for the role in the 1970 film of *Sloane*, losing out to Peter McEnery (nearly a decade after playing Barrett in *Victim*); though Sutton was always busy as an actor, major roles eluded him. Meanwhile, Gillian Freeman continued to be an under-appreciated novelist, whose later film work *Girl on a Motorcycle* (1968, with Marianne Faithfull) and *I Want What I Want* (1972, an early transvestite/trans-gender drama) remain interesting.

Again, Morrisey was a strong admirer of this example of Kitchen Sink, and he used sections of *The Leather Boys* in the promotional video for The Smiths' 1987 hit *Girlfriend in a Coma*. This seems to have kick-started a latter-day reassessment. Although not listed in the 1989 edition of the *Time Out Film Guide* (the bible of the serious filmgoer in those days), a battered old print was found in a distribution library and *The Leather Boys* was screened at the Scala, Kings Cross in April 1990 (with *Last Exit to Brooklyn*), leading eventually to fresh screenings. It takes its place today alongside *Victim* as a pioneering artefact, deserving respect for having been made in difficult times.

Unlike homosexuality, lesbianism was not illegal, though a censorious attitude prevailed toward women who were attracted to other women. Portrayals of the subject on stage or in film were almost never sympathetic, and, in comparison with the US and Europe, the UK only produced a modest body of published fiction on the subject. A rare exception to this came with the release, in October 1963, of the film *The World Ten Times Over*.

The company responsible for it, Cyclops Productions, was run by Michael Luke and Wolf Rilla, both interesting, if somewhat marginal, figures in the UK film industry at that time. Luke was a well-connected socialite, not unlike Anthony Blond and with similarly louche, liberal tendencies. He was a familiar figure on the Soho scene during the 40s, particularly the Gargoyle Club at 69 Dean Street, and something of a dandy. By the early 50s he was in Rome, where he worked on a couple of films and had a relationship with Irish actress Constance Smith, formerly Mrs Bryan Forbes, returning to London when this finished. Rilla was a German-Jewish émigré. Originally a BBC employee, he moved into film, mainly directing crime dramas and wrote the script for *The World Ten Times Over*. Funding was provided by Associated British.

The film concerns two young women, Billa and Ginnie, who work as hostesses in a dubious Soho club. They share a flat and fend off advances from predatory men. Ginnie gets involved with a married man (Bob) causing jealousy, and Billa has a father so wrapped up in himself that he is hardly able to talk to her when he arrives in London. The club scenes are brilliantly authentic, and the emotional gravity of the film is strengthened by its depiction of the male characters, shown almost without exception as unpleasant, boring and self-centred. Eventually the men are banished and the women remain together.

Sylvia Syms and June Ritchie played Billa and Ginnie, with Edward Judd as Bob and William Hartnell as Billa's father. Like *The Leather Boys* and *Victim*, the film was toned down to ensure a release certificate. A precursor of *The Killing of Sister George*, in which the lesbian relationship is considerably more overt, it got a predictably modest reception. Where it does succeed is in accidentally giving us a contemporary view of the world frequented by Mandy Rice-Davies and Christine Keeler, the two young nightclub hostesses who became embroiled in the Profumo affair.

Publicity for the film steered clear from this, but comparisons were made with *West 11*, another Associated British production to which this was seen as a (sort of) companion piece. Retitled *Pussycat Alley* in the US (where there was a genre of lesbian pulp fiction), it faded quickly from circulation, wasn't shown on TV after 1974 and only finally recognised as a pioneering work after a 2009 DVD re-issue. Its main title theme, by Edwin Astley, was considered memorable enough to merit release as a single, on Oriole, in November 1963.

If sexuality between consenting adults was one area the UK kept under wraps pre-*Chatterley*, another was politics, depictions of which, pre-1960, tended to be satirical, comical or childishly simple – a typical example being 1959's *The Mouse That Roared*. The gritty political landscape of the time, in the shape of party politics and trade union membership, with moral challenges involving naked ambition and corruption, for example, was seemingly foreign to filmmakers. A truthful approach was overdue and arrived in 1960 and 1961 with *The Angry Silence* and *No Love for Johnnie*.

The first of these was a drama by Guy Green and Bryan Forbes about industrial relations, from a script by actor Michael Craig (who co-starred), Forbes and Craig's brother Richard Gregson. Something like a grimly realistic version of *I'm All Right Jack*, *The Angry Silence* marked the point at which Forbes abandoned dramas about wartime heroism for a run of socially-aware films.

The film was produced at a time when it was not unusual for significant disputes to be caused by local shop stewards. Moreover, allegations were occasionally made about these being influenced by external players, particularly those from the political left. Set in a factory in a provincial town (and filmed in Ipswich), *The Angry Silence* focuses on a local campaign to establish a closed shop, led by an ostensibly fatherly shop steward guided by an outside activist. During an unofficial strike one of the workers, Tom, with two children and a wife, Anna, pregnant with a third, carries on working, and matters rapidly get out of control after he is 'sent to Coventry'. He is feted by national newspapers, but deeply resented by some of his colleagues, who ominously decide to take matters into their own hands.

After Kenneth More rejected the role for *Sink the Bismarck!*, Richard Attenborough, long adept at playing put-upon little men, was cast as Tom with Pier Angeli as Anna. Angeli is excellent as the distraught wife and Alfred Burke turned in a fine performance as Travers, the sinister outsider; Michael Craig appears as a womanising lodger in Tom's house. This was a British Lion production dating from when the studio was owned by the government, having been effectively nationalised in 1954 to protect loans made to it by the National Film Finance Corporation. But made at a time when the Conservatives had been in government for nearly a decade, *The Angry Silence* highlights the conflict between the right to strike and the right of the individual to work, represented by Attenborough's character. When released in March 1960, its message was strongly endorsed by *The Daily Mail*.

Despite the *Mail* endorsement, the film was made when the idea of unions having too much power had yet to take hold with the public and the anti-union message implicit in *The Angry Silence* caused it to be banned by many working men's clubs. These clubs (along with women's institutes and youth clubs and more) were an important factor in film distribution, with distributors manufacturing 16 mm copies for their screeenings, alongside the 35 mm copies for mainstream cinema chains. As a result, *The Angry Silence* performed poorly in terms of receipts and took many years to show a profit.

No Love for Johnnie is probably unique in being a film based on a novel by an MP, Wilfred Fienburgh, who represented Islington North whilst having a separate career as a significant figure at Granada TV. Fienburgh died in a car crash in February 1958 with his book appearing posthumously to great success. The film rights were sold, initially with the hope that Jack Clayton would direct something akin to a political version of *Room at the Top*. Neither Clayton nor suggested producer, David Deutsch, proved to be available and the project passed to Betty Box and Ralph Thomas who arranged a distribution deal via Rank.

Fienburgh's story centres on Johnnie Byrne, a Labour MP for a seat in Yorkshire. Considered too left-wing to be given a government job, he joins a group of party rebels, vocal in their criticism of current policy. Byrne indulges in the parliament rituals of late-night votes, late-night drinking, and extended conspiratorial meetings. Being away from home much of the time means he has chaotic personal life. His wife leaves him, a single woman living in the flat upstairs makes overtures but he gets involved with a model considerably younger than himself.

News of this affair gets back to his constituency and a vote of no confidence is passed, but deselection can be averted provided he changes his ways. He attempts a reconciliation with his wife, but changes his mind when the Prime Minister calls, offering him a post as a junior minister. It is revealed that Byrne's earlier non-promotion wasn't due to his being too left-wing; it was because his wife had Communist Party connections. Byrne accepts promotion and the film ends with him on the front benches in the House of Commons, with his feet up, a happy career politician, bantering with the opposition.

Partly filmed in Halifax, Peter Finch appeared as Byrne, Stanley Holloway as Fred Andrews, an amiable northern MP and Billie Whitelaw as the woman upstairs. *No Love for Johnnie* was released with an X certificate – presumably because of Byrne's bed-hopping – in February 1961 and proved popular with politicians: director Thomas remarking that 'half the cabinet came to the premiere'. Critics were positive and Peter Finch's performance was a BAFTA-winning one (his third), but the film didn't really attract the wider public, who seem to have decided that they could do without politics on a night out at the cinema. It has remained a seldom-seen forerunner in the sparsely-populated political film genre and is missing from key film reference works – nevertheless, it is still worth watching as a portrait of political cynicism and a still-relevant illustration of how power operates within a party-political system.

Moving to the outer reaches of what might be classed as political, between *Victim* and *The Servant*, Dirk Bogarde appeared in *The Mind Benders*, virtually the only UK drama made about sensory deprivation. Inspiration may have come from the success of Richard Condon's 1959 novel *The Manchurian Candidate*, and its 1961 film adaptation starring Laurence Harvey and Frank Sinatra. Cold War paranoia informs the James Kennaway script of *The Mind Benders*, with the Soviet Union, rather than China being the enemy.

The film opens with an Oxford professor committing suicide. It turns out that he was working in a research laboratory studying sensory deprivation and was suspected of passing secrets to the Russians. His colleague, Dr Longman, disagrees and thinks his experiments caused his death. Longman offers to test his theory by repeating the experiments himself. Having done so, Longman undergoes a massive change in his personality, that he struggles to reverse.

At this point the spy plot recedes into the background and the film flits between genres, one of which is an exercise in experimental stylism with high-quality photography, particularly in the immersion tank scenes with peculiar music. There are also elements of a weird marriage drama being played out, Longman's character getting involved with another woman but returning to help his wife give birth to their fifth child. (A connection being made here between the scientist in the dark immersion tank, and the baby in the mother's womb.) Some of this is conveyed by the use of a faux-documentary format including a voiceover, making it even more unclear what type of film *The Mind Benders* was trying to be.

The photography, by Denys Coop, who had worked on both *A Kind of Loving* and *This Sporting Life*, was excellent, as was the music, by Georges Auric. A French modern classical composer, Auric had been associated with Erik Satie and Jean Cocteau in the 20s before moving into film scores where his work included *Bonjour Tristesse.* In keeping with the then rudimentary approach to such matters no attempt was made to release his music for *The Mind Benders*. The acting is exceptional. Dirk Bogarde played Dr Longman, with Mary Ure as his wife, Michael Bryant as a research colleague and Wendy Craig as the other woman. John Clements, a considerable force in UK theatre in the 40s and 50s, gave a typically dependable performance as Major Hall, the military intelligence officer tasked with ferreting out how the Soviet Union is acquiring secrets.

It's a film with two disparate parts: half old-fashioned thriller (including a scene where a character commits suicide by leaping from a steam-hauled train) and half psychological drama, *perhaps* a decade ahead of its time. Sensory deprivation – 'brainwashing' – had been tested by the KGB, the Chinese and the CIA (notoriously, via the MK Ultra programme) from the 40s. Despite *The Manchurian Candidate* and *The Mind Benders*, it was still a niche 'interest' up until its fullest exploration on film in 1980, Ken Russell's *Altered States*. Russell's film was relatively successful but *The Mind Benders*, which appeared with an X certificate in February 1963, was a commercial failure.

Getting away from a *Dixon of Dock Green* approach to criminology, and setting stories in an exciting wider world was a notable feature of several TV drama series. Though neither Kitchen Sink nor mining a thick seam of social realism, these represented a growing demand for escapism which ultimately reached its zenith in the swinging sixties when fanciful plots about spies, secret agents and globetrotting playboys became commonplace.

Prior to the advent of The Beatles, three such series dominated UK TV, the first of which was *Danger Man*, first screened by ITV in September 1960. A Cold War spy drama, its hero John Drake (played by Patrick McGoohan) was, initially, an Irish-American, working for NATO for whom he did 'messy jobs' to protect 'world peace'. Designed for export, and made in 25-minute episodes, it failed, pre-Bond, to interest US networks and was dropped in 1962. Post-Bond it was a different matter. Two further series were commissioned, with 45-minute episodes, and Drake became a secret agent employed by the UK government 'to undertake missions involving national and global security'.

Running until 1966, and in black and white throughout, it proved popular and was noted for its continually evolving theme music. The first series had a guitar and saxophone heavy instrumental written by Edwin Astley, which appeared as a Parlophone single by Red Price in June 1961. From Liverpool, Price had played in the Ted Heath Band in the mid-50s, became a regular on Jack Good's *Oh Boy!* and later backed Frankie Vaughan and Billy Fury and his recording is a brilliant evocation of that vanished time. The second, *High Wire*, was performed by Astley and featured tinny harpsichord-style keyboards. It appeared as a single on RCA in November 1965. Finally, once US audiences had bitten, there came *Secret Agent Man* by Johnny Rivers, which reached No 3 in the US charts in April 1966. There might have been more, but a 1968 attempt at a colour series was abandoned after two episodes when McGoohan walked out, not wanting to be typecast.

The Avengers, on ABC TV, appeared in January 1961 and was originally relatively conventional in its plot lines. Ian Hendry and Patrick Macnee appeared as a GP, Dr Keel, and an Eton-educated secret agent, Steed, both attired in trench coats as they solved crimes that dumbfounded the authorities. Johnny Dankworth's title theme was released as a single on Columbia, and like Price's early version for *Danger Man*, was a nice jazzy piece conjuring up images of smoky clubs and foggy streets. A year later Hendry quit and was replaced by Honor Blackman as Dr Gale, an anthropologist. At which point the story lines and imagery began shifting somewhat.

Steed gradually became a Savile Row dandy, complete with bowler hat, rolled umbrella, mews house and vintage sports car. Gale adopted leather outfits, including thigh-high boots, and frequently displayed her judo skills. (Hence the February 1964 novelty single *Kinky Boots* released on Decca by Macnee and Blackman. The height of camp, it failed at the time but reached No 5 in the charts when re-issued in 1990.) Blackman, who memorably played Pussy Galore in *Goldfinger*, was replaced by Diana Rigg, as Emma Peel, who like Steed has some sort of espionage role. The leather gear and martial arts were retained, but Peel was also a style icon, wearing a lot of fashionable Pop Art and Op Art clothing.

The series was sold to the US and shifted to filming in colour with plots that became increasingly parodic and fanciful. As with *Danger Man*, the title theme changed too. Laurie Johnson's 1965 version on Pye, all sweeping strings punctuated with brass interludes, is the one everyone remembers. Rigg quit in late 1967, but with personnel changes, and Steed/Macnee the only constant, it survived as late as 1977.

Finally, in October 1962 ITV – none of these pioneering series appeared on the BBC – began screening *The Saint*, adapted from Leslie Charteris's detective novels, featuring Simon Templar. The first of these had appeared in 1928, but its longevity proved no handicap. Templar is an independently wealthy do-gooder fighting all manner of criminals and organisations that the police (who find him irritating) cannot bring to justice.

Roger Moore starred as Templar, and like Steed has a London mews house, wears Savile Row suits and drives a fancy sports car, in this case a stylish, modern Volvo. There were no regular co-stars, and the series, shot on 35 mm film, was exceptionally popular, being sold to 60 countries including the US. Each episode ran for 50 minutes (the length of a supporting feature) with some made by well-known film directors, including Leslie Norman, Roy Ward Baker and Jeremy Summers. Like *The Avengers*, after a few years it shifted to colour and had a title theme that went through several iterations. Performed by Edwin Astley, its basic melody was composed by Charteris and the earliest version consisted of a simple riff augmented by a walking bass line, some brass and backing vocals. Astley, keeping the same tune, put out a very cool jazzy re-recording in 1965 and then reworked it on a regular basis.

The series ended in 1969 when Moore quit to film *Crossplot*. But episodes were repeated for years afterwards, most recently on ITV4 and Astley's theme music was memorably sampled by Orbital in 1997, their version reaching No 3 in the UK charts. Nobody would maintain that *The Saint* is great drama, but its louche settings and effortless modernity would have been unimaginable in the 50s. Charteris was Anglo-Chinese, born in Singapore, and Templar is his idea of a perfect English gentleman. The creators of *Danger Man* and *The Avengers*, Ralph Smart and Sydney Newman respectively, were Australian and Canadian, which makes one think that all three series represent a re-imagining, by outsiders, of UK social mores during a time when these were changing.

Similarly, *The Running Man*, filmed in 1962, is set partly abroad in locations far removed from traditional UK thrillers. Filmed in colour, it plays like an extended feature length episode of these series, with high production values, and is an early precursor of the international 'caper' films that proliferated a few years later. Its source was *The Ballad of the Running Man*, a 1961 novel by crime writer Shelley Smith, the pen name of Nancey Bodington.

About insurance fraud, it follows a married couple, Mr and Mrs Buchanan. Mr Buchanan comes up with the idea of changing his identity, taking out a life insurance policy when he does so, allowing time to pass, staging his death via illness (or accident) and leaving his wife to collect the pay-out. After a decent interval they move to another town and repeat the process. Initially the insurance company is easy to convince, until one day one of their investigators accidentally encounters Mrs Buchanan on holiday under a different name.

The methodical way that the couple pursue their fraud, constantly increasing their income, is resonant of *Nothing But the Best*. It also seems to reflect the avarice of big football pools winners, exemplified by Viv Nicholson who had just become a national figure, famous for her 'spend, spend, spend' lifestyle. Curiously, though, like Nicholson, the Buchanans (who are, after all, criminals) do draw some sympathy from the audience as characters.

Shelley Smith was a bankable author, who had worked in US TV and written the screenplay for *Tiger Bay*. Her novel was quickly optioned and Carol Reed, of *Third Man* fame, was confirmed as director and producer. With three BAFTAs and two Academy Award nominations to Reed's name as well as a track record of making profitable films, raising finance was not an issue and Columbia agreed to distribute. John Mortimer was brought in to adapt the book and the result, as might be expected, provides civilised entertainment.

On screen Laurence Harvey and Lee Remick play the couple and Alan Bates, who managed to appear in both this and *Nothing But the Best*, is the insurance man. It was filmed, in colour, in Spain for ten weeks, with the remainder of the footage being completed at Ardmore Studios in Ireland. The ease with which the action unfolds in clearly warm, shimmering, settings, and the smooth delineation of the plot make for a very entertaining film. The novelty, for UK audiences at that time, of seeing a film shot in such locations would have been quite notable.

On its release in May 1963 critics were somewhat divided. Some thought it lightweight compared to Reed's darker and more literary work, such as *The Third Man* and *Odd Man Out*. Others considered it better than Hitchcock. Despite its qualities, it remains somewhat overlooked today. To watch it now, with its lengthy sequences in Malaga, Algeciras and Gibraltar, is to realise what a long way Harvey and Bates had travelled from Halifax and Morecambe in *Room at the Top* and *The Entertainer* respectively.

It was also a long way from Liverpool where *Violent Playground* and *These Dangerous Years* had kicked off the Kitchen Sink as a cinema phenomenon. Music played a role in both, and the idea of making a film about a band on the road had connections there too. In his 1965 autobiography *Owning Up*, Liverpool-born jazz and blues singer George Melly describes Ealing Studios' attempt to do a feature about a jazz band touring the dance halls and clubs of the UK. It would have been produced by Michael Relph and directed by Michael Truman from a script by James Kennaway and seems to have been a follow-on project from *Violent Playground*. Around 1957-1958 they followed Mick Mulligan's Magnolia Jazz Band – fronted by the ebullient Melly – from gig to gig, noting their picaresque adventures. Sadly, Ealing Studios folded before it could be put into production.

The idea finally reached maturity late in 1963, with *A Hard Day's Night*. A snapshot of 36 hours in the life of The Beatles, and a terrific debut for them, it was not the first time they were offered a part in a film. Had they passed their Decca audition in early 1962, it is likely they would have been one of many acts included in *Just for Fun*, which was made that summer. Instead, in June that year they signed to Parlophone, an EMI subsidiary label whose main pop acts were Adam Faith, Mike Sarne and Shane Fenton, but much of whose output consisted of comedy/novelty records by Bernard Cribbins, Spike Milligan, The Temperance Seven, The Alberts and Michael Bentine. Many of these were produced by George Martin, who was assigned similar duties with The Beatles. When *Love Me Do*, their debut single, appeared in October to above average sales (it eventually peaked at No 17 in the UK charts) it was suggested they appear in *The Yellow Teddy Bears*.

Most bands would have done it, and had managers who assumed this a natural career progression. Not so The Beatles, whose manager Brian Epstein had studied at RADA in the late 50s and still harboured ambitions to act. He turned it down out of hand, considering it too low budget and not the sort of material he wished his artistes to be involved with. He was right. Based on tabloid press stories about adolescent girls wearing a teddy bear badge to show they were no longer virgins, it was a cheap road-to-ruin drama directed by Robert Hartford-Davis. The cast included two minor pop stars of the type The Beatles were just about to consign to oblivion – Iain Gregory and Doug Sheldon. *The Yellow Teddy Bears* concludes with one of the girls heading off to London with a lorry driver, whilst back at school a socially-conscious biology teacher gives her pupils a lecture about the facts of life.

Largely forgotten today, though regarded in some quarters as a cult film, *The Yellow Teddy Bears* was a minor sensation at the time. It appeared in July 1963 when The Beatles had already had two further substantial hits, including their first No 1, *From Me to You*. At this point, its producers, Michael Klinger and Tony Tenser, asked them to do a slot in their next film *Saturday Night Out*, which Hartford-Davis also directed. Equally low budget, though it did have a cast led by Heather Sears and Bernard Lee, this was a melodrama about merchant seamen on leave in London after their ship docks. The usual explanation for Epstein turning this down is that the producers wouldn't pay the band's travelling costs from Liverpool. It's hard to know if this is accurate, or if it's a garbled version of why they declined *The Yellow Teddy Bears*, as by mid-1963 The Beatles, with a No 1 hit, would have been mainly based in London anyway and finally moved there in July of that year. Whatever the case, they would surely have wanted a more substantial film production to debut in.

Instead, fellow Liverpool band The Searchers were featured, playing a couple of numbers in a pub scene including the title theme, which subsequently appeared as the B-side of their hit *Needles and Pins*. Despite this, few remember the film now. By the time it was released The Beatles had released two more No 1 hits, *She Loves You* and *I Want to Hold Your Hand*. The scale of their ascent was unprecedented, easily eclipsing any of their UK predecessors. Nor was it just them. Two other Epstein acts, Gerry and the Pacemakers and Billy J Kramer and the Dakotas, had also emerged from Liverpool, racking up four No 1 hits between them. The Searchers were almost as successful and The Fourmost, The Merseybeats and The Swinging Blue Jeans only slightly less so. Suddenly the airwaves were full of guitar bands and scouse accents.

The cognoscenti sensed a phenomenon occurring, and in the autumn of 1963, Daniel Farson visited Liverpool to make *Beat City*, an ATV documentary. The year closed with Merseyside groups having achieved 19 Top 30 hits, eight of which had reached No 1. This occurrence was so striking that ATV commissioned *Around the Beatles*, a Jack Good-produced special, allowing the group to choose their own guest stars.

At this point, sensing correctly that he could insist on certain standards, Epstein agreed a three-film deal for the band with Walter Shenson of United Artists, which gave the studio the right to release their material on film soundtracks, separately from their existing contract with EMI. Shenson matched them with director Richard Lester, who had just made the Cold War satire *Mouse on the Moon*, for their debut film. With a budget of £200,000, it would be shot in black and white and built around their music. In terms of co-stars, Norman Rossington, Albert Finney's friend in *Saturday Night and Sunday Morning*, was cast as the band's manager. Shenson speculated about having Margaret Rutherford (who was in *Mouse on the Moon*) as a foil to the group, but settled on Wilfrid Brambell, from *Steptoe and Son*. The band, impressed by *No Trams to Lime Street*, asked that Alun Owen do the screenplay, and it became his second feature film credit after *The Criminal*.

Eventually named *A Hard Day's Night*, on paper there really wasn't much of a plot. The group, manager, managers assistant (John Junkin) and McCartney's grandfather (Brambell) get the train down to London, pursued by armadas of screaming girls. Once there they rehearse for a TV show (at the Scala Theatre in Fitzrovia) and sneak out to a casino (Les Ambassadeurs, Mayfair, also frequented by the likes of Lord Lucan). Kenneth Haigh, the original Jimmy Porter, has an uncredited but significant part as the owner of a fashion house, trying to get George Harrison to be his latest model. After various misadventures the concert goes ahead and the band depart on a helicopter for their next gig, in Wolverhampton. The end credits, a set of fashion magazine photos of the band members by Robert Freeman, effectively combine style with simplicity.

A *Hard Day's Night* began shooting March 1964, for a July release, so spontaneity was the name of the game with much of the footage being shot cinéma vérité style. The cutting and rhythm of the film owed much to contemporary French and Czech cinema, with Lester using the same speeded-up action segments he had in *The Running Jumping & Standing Still Film*. The Beatles perform 12 numbers, with a further two interpreted by the George Martin Orchestra. Owen's script was fast-moving and witty, but the songs were, and still are, sensational, far superior to the material performed on screen by Elvis Presley or Cliff Richard.

This was a film about four young working-class men with unashamed regional accents who defer to no one. They dress as they wish, speak as they wish and on occasion mock their elders. It was an attack on the privilege-based society that still existed in the UK, and critics adored it. There was scarcely a bad review. Between its inception and the commencement of filming, The Beatles finally broke into the US charts. By the time the film was released they had achieved 11 US Top 30 hits (one a reissue of something they recorded in Hamburg with Pete Best) of which 4 had reached No 1. A *Hard Day's Night* ended up a massive international hit. It was the 10th biggest film in the US in 1964 and was nominated for two Academy Awards, Best Screenplay (Alun Owen) and Best Score (George Martin).

The welcome given to A *Hard Day's Night* by American critics and audiences may have been assisted by the runaway success of the Albert Finney comedy *Tom Jones*, which regularly topped the US box-office listings in the months prior to July 1964. Directed by A *Taste of Honey* director Tony Richardson (and with a screenplay by John Osborne no less), *Tom Jones*, based on a period novel, was a fast-paced, irreverent comedy that could easily have been directed by Richard Lester. Both productions represented the exuberance of British youth culture, clear signifiers of the British Invasion that was to come.

It only remains to record that United Artists got their soundtrack album. A *Hard Day's Night*, a US-only release with a different selection of music to the UK studio album, entered the charts on 18th July 1964, remained there for 51 weeks – an entire year – and reached No 1, a position it held for 14 weeks.

The film and album made so much money for the studio that it was really just a question of how many more productions they, and their rivals, would make in the UK, particularly London.

THE NORTH IS FINISHED

The triumph of The Beatles was not just about their music. Because of *A Hard Day's Night*, every US film company worth its salt arrived in London, hoping to replicate its success with similarly-themed productions. European directors arrived too. And thus, was born 'swinging London' with its frenetic plots, pop music and 'with-it' settings. In 1962, 98 feature films were produced in the UK, falling to 85 a year later and 79 in 1964. This slow decline suggests that if Epstein had never met the band (or failed to get them a deal) the number of feature films made in the UK would have carried on dropping away through the 60s, precipitating the crisis in production funding some years before it eventually occurred in 1971-1972. Now, with London, and not the north, briefly anchored as the centre of the cinematic universe the numbers increased: to 86 within a year as the cycle kicked off with *The Knack* (June 1965) which won the Palme D'Or at Cannes and *Help!* (July 1965). Both were directed by Richard Lester, who became, and to a certain extent, remains, synonymous with the era which lasted through to 1970 when 89 productions were recorded.

But there are no neat divides in history. Mixed in amongst the many memorable works of that time were outliers that owed much to the preceding era, or were even a continuation of it. John Schlesinger's *Darling* (July 1965) with Dirk Bogarde, Laurence Harvey and Julie Christie, would have been unthinkable without *The Servant* (or *Nothing But the Best*) as predecessors. Powered by a Frederic Raphael script and Johnny Dankworth music, *Darling* won 3 Academy Awards and 4 BAFTAs. Similarly, where does one place one of the big hits of 1966, *Georgy Girl*? Filmed in unfashionable black and white and adapted from a Margaret Forster novel, it wasn't typical of the post-Beatles fare, and with Alan Bates, Lynn Redgrave, James Mason and Charlotte Rampling, seemed more akin to an up-tempo version of *The L-Shaped Room*.

One undeniably Kitchen Sink writer who took a long time to reach public prominence was Bill Naughton. From Bolton, he wrote extensively for theatre and TV from 1956, scoring an early success with *My Flesh, My Blood*. Originally filmed for BBC TV *Playhouse* in 1958 with Andrée Melly, Marjorie Rhodes and Wilfred Lawson, it was repeated as a BBC *Sunday Night Play* in 1960 with Tom Bell and finally reached the big screen as *Spring and Port Wine* in 1970 with James Mason, Susan George and Rodney Bewes. His other work included *Honeymoon Postponed*, written for TV in 1961 and filmed as *The Family Way* with a Paul McCartney soundtrack in 1966, and a radio play *Alfie Elkins and his Little Life*, broadcast on the BBC Third Programme in January 1962 with Bill Owen. Shorn to just *Alfie* it opened at the Mermaid Theatre, London in June 1963 with John Neville and Glenda Jackson before being filmed in 1966 with Michael Caine.

Another person who didn't really fit this new colourful era was David Mercer, a former artist from Wakefield who wrote seven TV plays between 1961 and 1963, one of which, *Morgan: A Suitable Case for Treatment* was filmed in 1966 by Karel Reisz with David Warner, Vanessa Redgrave and Robert Stephens with music from Johnny Dankworth. Like *Darling*, *Georgy Girl* and *Alfie*, it was successful with critics and audiences alike and Warner's deranged character Morgan brought to a logical conclusion the stream of angry young men that had been initiated by John Osborne's Jimmy Porter.

Thereafter, and increasingly apart from what the remainder of UK cinema was offering, came *Charlie Bubbles* (1967) with Albert Finney from an excellent Shelagh Delaney script; the anti-militarism of John McGrath's *The Bofors Gun* (1968) with David Warner and Nicol Williamson; Lindsay Anderson's acerbic anti-establishment parable *If...* (1968) and the grim, still in black and white, juvenile delinquency drama of *Bronco Bullfrog* (1969), improvised by a largely unknown cast. In a final cinematic twist, with the north now seen as being in decay (both morally and in terms of its physical environment), dramas like *The Reckoning* (1969) and *Get Carter* (1971) appeared in which Nicol Williamson and Michael Caine respectively played successful men, gone south, but now returning home to 'sort out' family problems in Liverpool and Tyneside.

The collapse of UK film production that finally occurred when the US and European money men quit London after the break-up of The Beatles was severe. Productions declined to 48 by 1976, 29 by 1982 and then, excluding animations and co-productions, to a mere 24 in 1986 as state funding evaporated.

But, if cinema was no longer a place where one was likely to see contemporary films set in the north, or indeed set anywhere, drama of this type was still, for the moment, broadcast frequently on TV. Interestingly, ITV provided a great deal of this, and had done so from its inception in 1955. Together with both BBC channels, several series were running at any one time, the peak year being 1973 when viewers could choose from *Play for Today* (BBC 1, weekly), *Play of the Month* (BBC 1, monthly), *Comedy Playhouse* (BBC 1, weekly), *Thirty Minute Theatre* (BBC 2, weekly), *Armchair Theatre* (ITV, weekly), *Playhouse* (ITV, weekly) and *Sunday Night Theatre* (ITV, weekly). To which could be added two specific regional variations: *Late Night Theatre* (a mixture of Granada, Southern, Westward and Scottish TV, weekly) and *Second City Firsts* (BBC 2, from Birmingham, weekly). Collectively these produced something like 200 original, standalone works of drama per annum, the bulk of which tackled contemporary themes and situations with many of them set outside London.

From this peak the numbers reduced, spectacularly so post-1983. ITV withdrew early, and the final example of this type of programming came to an end when BBC *Screen Two* broadcast Stephen Poliakoff's *The Tribe* starring Joely Richardson on 21st June 1998. To those managing the UK's terrestrial TV channels in the late twentieth and early twenty-first century it mattered little that many of these programmes had won awards and went on to be screened as feature films abroad. Nor was their overall quality a decisive factor. Instead, it was simply taken as axiomatic that presenting drama in this way was now a thing of the past. This was a striking choice, and ignored the fact that many gifted writers, directors and actors had gone on to achieve great things after emerging from *Play for Today* and its fellow series. None more so than Mike Leigh and Ken Loach.

From Salford, Mike Leigh had initially been involved in theatre. In 1965 he staged the original version of Huddersfield dramatist David Halliwell's *Little Malcolm and his Struggle Against the Eunuchs*, a ferociously absurd caricature of revolutionary socialist students, the main protagonist of which is another candidate for the ultimate ending point of Jimmy Porter. After directing a touring Royal Shakespeare Company production of *The Knack*, he worked in both TV and film from the early 70s, with his work in the former medium including the unforgettable *Abigail's Party* (1977). To date his films have been nominated for 7 Academy Awards, 15 BAFTAs (winning 5), 5 Palme D'Or's (winning 1) and 3 Golden Lions (winning 1).

He is run a close second by Ken Loach who, among a similar galaxy of honours, has won the Palme D'Or twice, and the Jury Prize three times at Cannes, the latter a record. Like Leigh he began his career as an actor, moving into TV in 1964 when he directed some episodes of *Z-Cars*. He made his name with the BBC *Wednesday Play*, *Up the Junction* (1965) and *Cathy Come Home* (1966) both featuring Carol White, who also starred in his first full-length film, *Poor Cow* (1967). Between them Loach and Leigh directed 23 TV plays at a time when the flame of social realism still burned brightly in the UK.

Through the 70s and 80s the public would also have been viewing TV screenings of most of the original Kitchen Sink films. These could also be seen at selected independent cinemas, usually as part of a double or triple bill, often put together as an 'all-nighter'. A key venue, The Scala at Kings Cross, regularly showed *Peeping Tom* and *The Servant* (but not *Victim*) with Tony Hancock's

The Rebel another frequent option, as were *Expresso Bongo*, *Beat Girl* and *A Hard Day's Night*. Access to some of this material was a bit random, dependant on whether prints were still held by distributors and whether the copyright holders had already sold them to TV. Tracking down printed copies of the various novels and plays at the core of the genre was similarly hit and miss. Some remained available in new editions, others had to be hunted down in charity shops and jumble sales, and purchased for a few pence. Most could be found.

Thus, the generation that had been born post-1956 grew up absorbing Kitchen Sink in two distinct ways: via its contemporary equivalents on TV and through a personal accumulation of the original works backed up with occasional screenings of the original films whenever available. By the late 70s a surprising amount of this had leeched into popular music. Sometimes this seemed like a continuum from an earlier era, a case in point being Mark E Smith. Leader of Manchester band The Fall (originating from 1976, when he was 19), his onstage persona resembled many of the characters seen in *Play for Today*: a latter-day saloon bar Porter-Seaton autodidact, declaiming slabs of prose, catchphrases and lyrics.

Somewhat more retrospectively, a few years later Dan Treacy, leader of Television Personalities was writing material like *Geoffrey Ingram* (the character played by Murray Melvin in *A Taste of Honey*), *This Angry Silence* and *Look Back in Anger*. All appeared on the band's 1981 LP *And Don't the Kids Just Love It*, with Treacy attracted to Kitchen Sink cinema because of 'the stark reality being portrayed'. Later he would be equally drawn to swinging sixties imagery and psychedelia and as such was very on-trend with the mood of the time as exemplified, from 1980, by *The Face* magazine. This revived interest in a phenomenal array of cultural artefacts from the UK's recent past, including the 50s street photography of Roger Mayne and cool, modern jazz from the bebop era. Somewhat excessively curated, it provided its readers with a ready supply of striking images and interesting sounds for which the term iconic is an understatement.

No one however was as diligent, or obsessive, about the period as Steven Patrick Morrissey. Born in Manchester in 1959, Morrissey... intelligent, disaffected, usually retiring, was a music obsessive who had sung briefly for punk band The Nosebleeds and worked intermittently as a music journalist, before shooting to fame as lead singer and lyricist of The Smiths between 1983 and 1987. None of their releases were without a carefully selected image, borrowed lyrics or sampled dialogue, among which could be found Shelagh Delaney, A Taste of Honey, Terence Stamp, Viv Nicholson, Pat Phoenix, Yootha Joyce, The L-Shaped Room, Saturday Night and Sunday Morning, The Leather Boys, Billy Fury and Billy Liar. His level of interest in Kitchen Sink seemed to amount to an obsession, and his knowledge was remarkable especially given the difficulty he would have experienced in hunting down much of this material.

By the late 80s the cumulative success of The Smiths (who were awarded a dozen gold or platinum selling discs) and The Face (which sold 100,000 copies per issue) had produced a reappraisal of the Kitchen Sink/angry young man period. Most of the classic films were released on video and were the subject of screenings in independent repertory cinema. There were even some additions to the genre, notably from Terence Davies whose Distant Voices Still Lives (1988) and The Long Day Closes (1992) were immaculate recreations of 40s and 50s Liverpool, the latter nominated for the Palme D'Or at Cannes.

The genre seemed to have something worth saying for many people. Boff Whalley from the band Chumbawamba, who were active from the early 80s onwards, commented when contacted for this book, 'I'd say we were reasonably influenced by that era of drama, cinema and literature. I loved Sillitoe's Loneliness of course and we used a quote from the book/film on a single release in the 1990s... We also sampled a small section of dialogue from Jo when talking to Geoffrey Ingram in A Taste of Honey. We were always quite attached to those films and books by dint of their "northernness" also it felt like there was a line that threaded between those films and the Lindsay Anderson films (and obviously as a political band we loved If...), especially O Lucky Man with the band. Theatre-wise

I was influenced a lot by John McGrath's *A Good Night Out* which tied in with the Liverpool poets, the Beats, a lot of it very northern and down to earth... And I almost forgot the ubiquitous *Kes* image that we had as a record sleeve!'

Born in Burnley 1961 (and like Colin Smith, a keen runner) it seems reasonable to suppose that, like Morrissey and Treacy he would have become aware of the Kitchen Sink genre during the 70s. The band, an anarchist collective-cum-punk ensemble based in Leeds, used a key still from Ken Loach's *Kes* on the cover of their 1993 single *Timebomb* and went on to achieve significant commercial success between 1994 and 1998, most notably with their 1997 release *Tubthumping* which won any number of platinum discs.

More recently there have been revivals of *Look Back in Anger* in 1999 and 2005, in which Porter was played by Michael Sheen and David Tennant respectively. These together with Davies's 2008 look at Liverpool, *Of Time and the City*, mean that a traditional view of 'the North' is still available for new generations to access as contemporary, albeit slightly retro, entertainment. The same holds true for the 2011 BBC TV remake of *Room at the Top* with Maxine Peake in the role played by Simone Signoret in the 1958 film. Peake seems to have an affinity for this era, her appearance in *Funny Cow* (2017) set in the working men's clubs of the 60s being also notable.

The notion that there ought to be more of this – in a country with a population of nearly 70 million – leads us to the post-Brexit UK debate about 'levelling up', which in many ways is a sharpening of an argument that has beset the country for the best part of fifty years. When considering the period of the angry young men, the Kitchen Sink and its variations, looking at how much money was invested – then – by the state in higher education and public broadcasting is unavoidable. How many young people today can study acting, writing (or anything creative) without incurring significant levels of personal debt? Excluding detective series, thriller series and soaps, how much original contemporary drama is broadcast now on TV?

Which is not to say that spending on the arts was always better in an imagined past. In *British Economic Policy since the War* (1958) Andrew Shonfield, after comparing the UK with the small German state of Hesse concludes 'For West Germany as a whole, the expenditure of public money on the arts per head of the population works out at about nine times as much as the corresponding figure in this country.' By 2000 the US National Endowment for the Arts noted this had evened up (slightly) with the UK spending $26 per capita on arts activities (compared with $85 (Germany) $57 (France) and $46 (Netherlands)) only to drop away markedly post-2010. A 2022 EU study on cultural services, broadcasting and publishing services, stated that budgets typically varied between 2.25 per cent and 0.5 per cent of government spending, with an average of around 1 per cent. The UK estimate for 2015 was 0.4 per cent.

The position regarding education is similar. An OECD report in 2018 gives overall UK spending on education at 3.9 per cent of GDP compared with Denmark (7.6 per cent) Belgium (6.5 per cent) Germany (4.8 per cent) Spain (4.2 per cent). Another study, published on the website Statista in 2020 indicated that publicly-funded higher education spending in the UK was equal to 0.5 per cent of GDP. This compared with Belgium (1.4 per cent) Denmark (1.6 per cent) France (1.2 per cent) Ireland (0.6 per cent) and the Netherlands (1.2 per cent). Even the US was 0.9 per cent. With additional funding equal to 1.5 per cent of GDP being raised 'privately' (i.e. by UK students themselves and/or their parents) what was striking was how little the British government was committed to furthering the education of the population of its own country. We should be clear that this is only in comparison with most European nations, as what the UK has opted to do since the end of the 70s is replicate the policies of the US, Australia, Canada and Chile where the private sector and various sponsors are firmly in charge.

Anyone interested in trying to return to the world of the Kitchen Sink – a time of immense social mobility – rather than just looking at it through an agreeably retro lens, should be clear about the political and economic changes that have occurred since its heyday. Indeed, for a non-nostalgic view, put over with some force, the views of Ken Loach are of interest.

I was fortunate to speak with him in 2024 and he quickly pointed out that terminology is critical and that whilst we may use Kitchen Sink as a shorthand description of a particular era we should also be aware that it is very much a middle-class view of the working class, reducing everything to an image of a woman at a kitchen sink. As he pointed out: 'Italian and some eastern European directors had long featured stories set among the working class. People like Lindsay Anderson were aware of the Neo-Realists, De Sica, Wajda. Much of what appeared was an acknowledgement of what was happening in European cinema.' As for the authors of the original works, 'most of the Angry Young Men were not angry. Osborne was cross, not angry. They all moved to the right. None of them had serious political views. Stan Barstow was the one I liked, the one I respected. David Storey too.'

His own involvement in directing came about in the early 60s when after National Service, a law degree at Oxford and some acting experience, he applied to the BBC Directors Course. His feature film debut, *Poor Cow*, was originally the first part of a two-picture deal, the second instalment of which was to have been an adaptation of David Storey's *Flight into Camden*. This appears to have been the second time such a project was attempted, and like the first (with Glenda Jackson circa 1964) it came to grief when his producer Joseph Janni 'said to me "the north is finished as a subject" and it never happened. That exchange summed up to me the triviality of their approach'.

Janni, who had previously produced *A Kind of Loving*, *Billy Liar* and *Darling*, clearly considered the game was up for social realism and decamped to Switzerland. There, his assumptions proved false. He made *In Search of Gregory*, which flopped, and then came back to the UK for *Sunday Bloody Sunday* and *Made*, two of the better films of the early 70s. By that point Loach had proved him wrong. After a couple of TV plays set in Liverpool, *The Golden Vision* (1968) and *The Big Flame* (1969) he had a stroke of luck when Tony Richardson persuaded United Artists, who had distributed Woodfall productions, to put money into *Kes*, an adaptation of Barry Hines 1968 novel *A Kestrel for a Knave*. Filmed in the mining villages of south Yorkshire, and first released in London in 1969 (before nationwide release in 1970), it was a big hit, critically and commercially, as well as containing a critique of how the education system failed to engage with adolescent working-class children that couldn't conform to its structures. It was proof, if any were needed, that 'the north' was still alive as a subject whatever the money men might say.

In its wake he made David Mercer's *In Two Minds* (1971), an acclaimed drama about schizophrenia, declined an offer to go to the US ('...it was a serious offer, but it didn't interest me...') and kept working away at TV plays and whatever else came his way. Looking back at that time in 2024, he saw it as a period when 'The arts expanded. People were more confident. The benefits of education for working-class people were clear. There was a genuine interest in stories and writers from that background, and a feeling that they had to be told. But it was transient because there was no political structure to enable it to sustain.' The latter point is open to interpretation in a number of different ways, but seems apposite when considered alongside the paucity of funding in the UK, as noted above, and particularly in relation to neighbouring countries, since 1980. Had there been *better* political structures, either devolved, or just genuinely more representative, the funding might not have been reduced.

He was also modest about how he was able to grasp the opportunities presented to him, noting 'I've been very lucky. For people starting now it is much more difficult. The dominance of US cinema makes it very hard. TV is also much harder. We were given a brief to do contemporary fiction on prime time. There was *no* micro-management. We were lucky in the mid-60s. Hugh Greene was more liberal. But political appointments at the BBC gradually squeezed things out.' The reference to Sir Hugh Greene, younger brother of novelist Graham, and his period as Director-General of the BBC (1960-1969) is a reminder that his tenure saw the commissioning of programmes like *That Was The Week That Was*, *Z-Cars* and *The Wednesday Play*, with Loach clearly benefitting from the existence of the latter two. Greene remains famous for having reputedly said in private, 'We are going to use this organisation to change the way the rest of the country thinks. We want them to see stuff they don't like. We don't really care if they complain.' He also maintained that morality campaigner Mary Whitehouse's insistence on 'family values' reminded him of Nazi Germany (where he worked as a journalist, until expelled in 1939).

Whether Greene said what is attributed to him, or even if one feels it was unfair for him to pursue policies at odds with 'mainstream' values, it only reflected his approach to a minority of the material broadcast by the BBC. But it was an important and vital component. There can be no denying the quality of what was produced during his tenure, and for some time afterwards. Without this as a structure people like Loach, Mike Leigh and many others would not have thrived and never become the world-famous figures they are today. Anyone seeking to reboot the arts in Britain should note that as well as increasing funding, and ensuring that its supply cannot be arbitrarily terminated by a single political party, cinema, drama and TV should be allowed and encouraged to explore contemporary society, as thoroughly as possible. As part of this the voices of those who are not usually heard should, once again, be to the fore. As Loach says 'the key thing is working-class stories are important'.

Before going forwards, sometimes we need to go back.

APPENDIX

COMMERCIALLY RELEASED MUSIC RELATING TO FILM, THEATRE AND TV PRODUCTIONS 1955-1965

45s

Frankie Vaughan *These Dangerous Years* (Philips: August 1957)

Ian Carmichael *Lucky Jim (How I Envy Him)* (HMV: October 1957)

Johnny Luck *Play Rough* (Fontana: February 1958)

Jim Dale *Tread Softly Stranger* (Parlophone: April 1958)

Anthony Newley *I've Waited So Long* (Decca: April 1959)

The Pinewood Studio Orchestra Conducted by Philip Green Featuring Johnny Dankworth and his Saxophone *Sapphire* (Top Rank: April 1959)

The Pinewood Studio Orchestra Conducted by Philip Green *Tiger Bay* (Top Rank: April 1959)

Anthony Newley *Idle on Parade* (Decca: May 1959)

Cliff Richard and The Drifters *Livin' Doll* (Columbia: July 1959)

Al Saxon *I'm All Right Jack* (Fontana: July 1959)

Cliff Richard and The Shadows *A Voice in the Wilderness* (Columbia: January 1960)

Philip Green and The Pinewood Studio Orchestra *League of Gentlemen March* (Top Rank: April 1960)

John Barry and His Orchestra *Never Let Go* (Columbia: June 1960)

Adam Faith *Johnny Comes Marching Home* b/w *Made You* (Parlophone: June 1960)

Cleo Laine *Thieving Boy* b/w *Let's Slip Away* (Fontana: October 1960)

Max Harris With His Group *Gurney Slade* (Fontana: November 1960)

Michael Cox and The Dave Lee Group *Linda* (HMV: January 1961)

Reg Owen and his Orchestra *Payroll* (Palette: March 1961)

Jess Conrad *Why Am I Living?* (Decca: April 1961)

The Shadows *The Frightened City* (Columbia: May 1961)

The Red Price Combo *Theme from Danger Man* (Parlophone: June 1961)

The Planets *Jungle Street* (HMV: July 1961)

Johnny Dankworth And His Orchestra *Avengers Theme* (Columbia: September 1961)

The Corona Kids *The Big Ship Sails on the Alley-Alley-O* (Philips: October 1961)

Adam Faith *The Time Has Come* (Parlophone: October 1961)

Marty Wilde *The Hellions* (Philips: October 1961)

Joe Brown and The Bruvvers *What a Crazy World We're Living In* (Piccadilly: November 1961)

Ron Grainer and his Group *Old Ned* (Pye: January 1962)

Johnny Keating *Theme From Z-Cars (Johnny Todd)* (Piccadilly: February 1962)

Joe Brown and The Bruvvers *A Lay-Abouts Lament* (Piccadilly: April 1962)

Pat Phoenix *Coronation Street Monologue* (HMV: June 1962)

The Eagles *Bristol Express* (Pye: June 1962)

Valerie Mountain *Some People* (Pye: June 1962)

Ron Grainer and The London Wind Symphony *Johnny's Tune* (Fontana: July 1962)

Adam Faith *Mix Me a Person* (Parlophone: August 1962)

Carol Deene *Some People* (HMV: August 1962)

The Mike Cotton Jazzmen *Zulu Warrior* (Columbia: October 1962)

Harry H Corbett *Junk Shop* (Pye: October 1962)

Ian McShane *Harry Brown* (Columbia: November 1962)

Johnny Pearson *Theme from The L-Shaped Room* (Parlophone: January 1963)

Millicent Martin with David Frost *That Was The Week That Was* (Parlophone: February 1963)

Barbara Windsor *Sparrows Can't Sing* (HMV: March 1963)

Tommy Bruce *Two Left Feet* (Columbia: April 1963)

Harry H Corbett *Like the Big Guys Do* (Pye: August 1963)

Iain Gregory *Yellow Teddy Bear* (Columbia: August 1963)

Tom Courtenay *Mrs Brown You've Got a Lovely Daughter* (Decca: August 1963)

Joe Brown and The Bruvvers *Sally Ann* (Piccadilly: September 1963)

Wilfrid Brambell *Secondhand* (Pye: September 1963)

Wilfrid Brambell and Harry H Corbett *Steptoe and Son at Buckingham Palace* (Pye: November 1963)

Edwin Astley and his Orchestra *Theme from The World Ten Times Over* (Oriole: November 1963)

Harry H Corbett *Things We Never Had* (Pye: November 1963)

Cleo Laine *All Gone* (Fontana: January 1964)

The Searchers *Saturday Night Out* (Pye: January 1964)

Frankie Vaughan *Alley Alley Oh* (Philips: February 1964)

Millicent Martin *Nothing But the Best* (Parlophone: April 1964)

Mike Sarne *A Place to Go* (Parlophone: April 1964)

Edwin Astley *Danger Man* b/w *The Saint* (RCA: November 1965)

The Laurie Johnson Orchestra *Theme from The TV Series The Avengers* (Pye: December 1965)

EPs

Cliff Richard and The Drifters *Serious Charge* (Columbia: May 1959)

Anthony Newley *Sings Four Songs from Idle on Parade* (Decca: June 1959)

Cliff Richard and The Shadows *Expresso Bongo* (Columbia: January 1960)

Johnny Dankworth and his Orchestra *Soundtrack Music from The Criminal* (Columbia: October 1960)

Tony Hancock *Little Pieces of Hancock* (Pye: 1961)

Adam Faith and John Barry *Music from the Film Beat Girl* (Columbia: February 1962)

Tony Hancock *More Little Pieces of Hancock* (Pye: 1962)

Valerie Mountain and The Eagles *Some People* (Pye: July 1962)

Johnny Keating and the Z-Men *Z-Cars* (Piccadilly: September 1962)

The Shadows *The Boys* (Columbia: September 1962)

The Mike Cotton Jazzmen *The Wild and the Willing* (Columbia: October 1962)

Steptoe and Son *The Facts of Life* (Pye: August 1963)

Tom Courtenay *Sings Mrs Brown You've Got a Lovely Daughter and other songs from the ATV Production The Lads* (Decca: August 1963)

Tony Hancock *The Publicity Photograph* (Pye: August 1963)

Steptoe and Son *The Wages of Sin* (Pye: November 1963)

Heinz *Live it Up* (Decca: December 1963)

Freddie and the Dreamers *Songs from The Film What A Crazy World* (Columbia: January 1964)

LPs

David Heneker, Monty Norman, Julian More, Paul Scofield *Expresso Bongo (A Musical Play)* (Pye Nixa: May 1958)

Frank Norman and Lionel Bart *Fings Ain't What They Used T'Be* (Decca: February 1960)

Tony Hancock *This is Hancock* (Pye: March 1960)

Frank Norman and Lionel Bart with Alfie Bass, Adam Faith, Harry Fowler, Joan Heal, Sidney James, Alfred Marks, Marion Ryan, Tony Tanner, the Williams Singers, John Barry, Tony Osborne *Fings Ain't What They Used T'Be* (HMV: March 1960)

Tony Hancock *Pieces of Hancock* (Pye: September 1960)

John Barry, Adam Faith and Shirley Anne Field *Music from the Film Beat Girl* (Columbia: December 1960)

Anthony Newley with Anna Quayle *Stop the World – I Want to Get Off* (Decca: August 1961)

Various Artists *It's Trad, Dad!* (Columbia: February 1962)

Tony Hancock *The Blood Donor, The Radio Ham* (Pye: February 1962)

Various Artists *Music from The Soundtrack All Night Long* (Fontana: February 1962)

Wilfrid Brambell and Harry H Corbett *Steptoe and Son* (Pye: February 1963)

David Frost With Millicent Martin, Lance Percival, Roy Kinnear, William Rushton, Kenneth Cope and David Kernan *That Was The Week That Was* (Parlophone: February 1963)

Various Artists *Just for Fun* (Decca: April 1963)

Joe Brown and the Bruvvers, Susan Maughan, Harry H Corbett, Marty Wilde *What A Crazy World* (Piccadilly: January 1964)

Wilfrid Brambell and Harry H Corbett *More Junk!* (Pye: January 1964)

Frankie Vaughan, The Springfields *It's All Over Town* (Philips: February 1964)

INDEX

OLDCASTLE BOOKS

POSSIBLY THE UK'S SMALLEST INDEPENDENT PUBLISHING GROUP

Oldcastle Books is an independent publishing company formed in 1985 dedicated to providing an eclectic range of titles with a nod to the popular culture of the day.

Imprints include our lists about the film industry, KAMERA BOOKS & CREATIVE ESSENTIALS. We have dabbled in the classics, with PULP! THE CLASSICS, taken a punt on gambling books with HIGH STAKES, provided in-depth overviews with POCKET ESSENTIALS and covered a wide range in the eponymous OLDCASTLE BOOKS list. Most recently we have welcomed two new sister imprints with THE CRIME & MYSTERY CLUB and VERVE, home to great, original, page-turning fiction.

oldcastlebooks.com

| OLDCASTLE BOOKS	| CREATIVE ESSENTIALS	| THE CRIME & MYSTERY CLUB
| POCKET ESSENTIALS	| PULP! THE CLASSICS	| VERVE BOOKS
| KAMERA BOOKS	| HIGHSTAKES PUBLISHING	